GW00836718

BLOODY ALBUERA
The 1811 Campaign in the Peninsula

'Oh, Albuera, glorious field of grief!
As o'er thy plain the pilgrim prick'd his steed,
Who could forsee thee, in a space so brief
A scene where mingling foes should boast and bleed!'

Byron, Childe Harold's Pilgrimage

First published in 2000 by
The Crowood Press Ltd
Ramsbury, Marlborough
Wiltshire SN8 2HR

© Ian Fletcher 2000
Colour plates © Gerry Embleton & The Crowood Press Ltd 2000

Edited by Martin Windrow
Design by Tony Stocks / Compendium
Printed and bound in Great Britain
by the Alden Group, Oxford

All rights reserved. No part of this publication may be reproduced or
transmitted in any form or by any means, electronic or mechanical,
including photocopy, recording, or in any information storage and
retrieval system, without prior permission in writing from
the publishers.

British Library Cataloguing-in-Publication Data
A CIP catalogue record for this book
is available from the British Library

ISBN 1 86126 372 4

BLOODY ALBUERA
The 1811 Campaign in the Peninsula

Ian Fletcher

Colour plates by

Gerry Embleton

The Crowood Press

CONTENTS

CHAPTER ONE

The Spanish Ulcer

On 14 June 1808 Lieutenant-General the Honourable Sir Arthur Wellesley was appointed by His Majesty King George III to command 'a detachment of his army, to be employed upon a particular service'[1]. Whatever that 'particular service' was, it was certainly a mystery to the vast majority of the 9,000 officers and men of the British Army who had mustered at Cork in southern Ireland in the summer of 1808. They had very little idea of their final destination, but there were rumours that the force was bound for South America, in order to rekindle British aspirations on that continent which had been so shamefully doused following the disastrous attack on Buenos Aires the previous summer. There was some grain of truth in this; the force had indeed been assembled in Ireland for that very purpose. However, events elsewhere in Europe were dictating the destination of Wellesley's command, and by the middle of July the expedition had set sail for the Iberian Peninsula.

The seeds of the Peninsular War, as it is known in Britain, were effectively sown on 18 October 1807 when 25,000 French troops of the Army of the Gironde, under General Andoche Junot, crossed the Bidassoa river and entered Spain - then ostensibly France's ally - on the pretext of marching to Lisbon. There Junot intended to seize the Portuguese Prince Regent John VI, who had stoutly refused, despite threats which his country was ill-placed to defy, to implement Napoleon's so-called 'Continental System'. This was the Europe-wide policy by which Napoleon hoped to starve Britain into impotence, and to reduce her pernicious influence over some elements among his sullen vassal states, by denying her all trade and other maritime contacts through European ports.

There was simply no credible strategic reason for him to invade the Iberian Peninsula other than to enforce this blockade (which was in any case an unrealistic ambition, given Britain's naval supremacy). True, he had harboured a bitter resentment since a Portuguese naval squadron had interfered with his Egyptian campaign in 1798; but in 1807 Portugal's military and political position was so weak that Napoleon could surely have attained any realistic goal by diplomatic threats falling short of the choice which he gave her - between utter ruin, and invasion.

Spain had been France's uneasy but malleable ally against Britain since 1796, and Napoleon had long since proved that he could bribe or threaten the ineffectual King Charles IV and his venal minister Godoy into dancing to almost any tune he cared to play. Spain was, as Napoleon himself famously remarked, a place where large armies starved and small ones disappeared; and yet in October 1807 his armies crossed the Bidassoa and began the long trek to Lisbon. It was the first step on a campaign that was eventually to last until 1814, cost the lives of tens of thousands of French troops, and consume vast quantities of valuable resources.

Sir Arthur Wellesley, later 1st Duke of Wellington (1769-1852). Save for a period when he returned home to face the inquiry into the Convention of Cintra, Wellesley commanded the British expeditionary army, and later the Anglo-Portuguese field army, from 1808 until the close of the Peninsular War in 1814. The dominant figure of the war, he transformed his command from an object of French indifference - or even derision - into one of the finest armies Britain has ever put into the field, universally admired for its spirit and professional excellence.

His military commitment to the Peninsula would become, again in his own words, a running sore, his 'Spanish ulcer.'

The easy pace of Junot's march along the traditional 'invasion' route between Ciudad Rodrigo and Almeida was evidently too slow for his Imperial Majesty, and Junot was ordered to march further to the south, along the valley of the Tagus via Alcantara and Castello Branco. This was a more direct route on paper, but on the ground it presented much greater difficulties. The countryside was and still is a bleak wilderness, bare of the sort of provisions that were to be found elsewhere; and as the weather slowly turned against him Junot could only watch as his men, short of supplies and half-starving, strove stubbornly to keep up as he forced the pace towards Lisbon. His efforts were in vain; when his bedraggled army entered the Portuguese capital on 30 November they found that their prey had escaped

Spanish troops of the Marques de la Romana's division, which was sent by the French to the Baltic in 1807, before war broke out in Spain, to form part of a multi-national corps under Bernadotte. After the national uprising they mutinied and managed to reach the coast, whence they were shipped home by the Royal Navy. Many were sketched in Hamburg by Suhr: these are a pioneer, a grenadier and a fusilier of the Zamora regiment in marching kit. The checked trousers were not 'regulation issue' but are typical of the sort of campaign expedients adopted by all armies in the field.

their grasp by just three days. The prince regent and some 15,000 of his supporters had sailed for the safety of distant Brazil, where he would continue to provide a focus for loyalty at home.

Nevertheless, Junot set about disbanding the Portuguese Army and taking a firm grip on the capital and the country at large. He was assisted to some extent by a pro-French faction, though its credibility among the population soon suffered from the cruelties inflicted by the French occupiers under the leadership of such hated figures as the one-armed General Maurice Loison – 'Maneta'.

Meanwhile, Napoleon's manipulation of the mutually hostile parties among the Spanish leadership brought its due

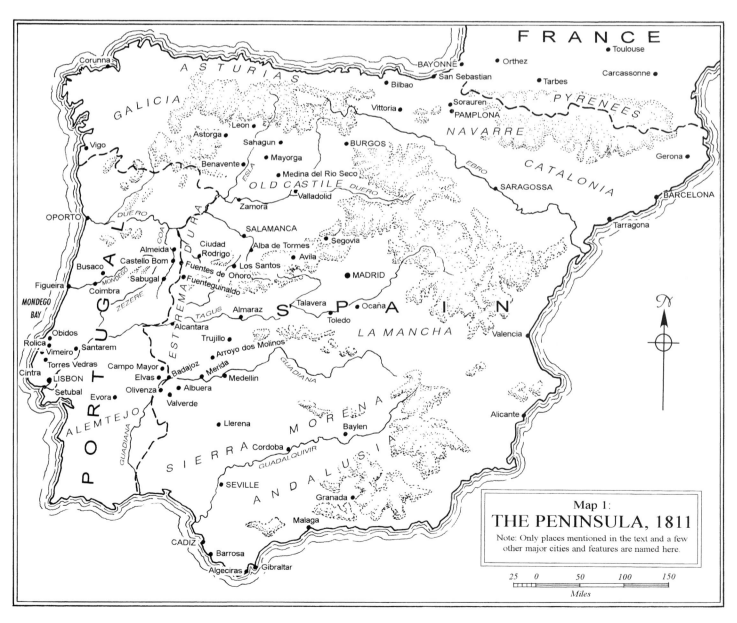

Map 1:

THE PENINSULA, 1811

Note: Only places mentioned in the text and a few other major cities and features are named here.

The battlefield of Vimeiro, as seen looking south from the position held by Anstruther's brigade (2/9th, 2/43rd, 2/52nd, 2/97th) on the slopes just in front of the village. French attacks by the brigades of Charlot, Foy and Thomieres came straight on towards and to the left of the camera. The French tirailleurs were held off by British riflemen, who also sniped the enemy artillery crews and prevented them bringing guns forward; the undulating ground frustrated the French cavalry; and carefully placed British lines beat off the French attack columns by superior firepower. The first major British engagement of the war, Vimeiro raised Wellington's reputation - in the words of the French general Maximilien Foy - to equal that of Marlborough. By this apparently wild exaggeration he probably meant that Wellington was the first British general since Marlborough who seemed to have an effortless answer to French tactics. By the time the Penisnsular War was over it would be no exaggeration at all.

harvest. The self-interested conspiracies which divided King Charles IV, his son Ferdinand, and the power-hungry minister Manuel Godoy ripened to the point when both king and prince sought the assistance of Napoleon. The French emperor callously imprisoned them both; and his troops, more of whom had begun moving into Spain in January 1808, were perfectly placed to take possession of many of the major Spanish fortresses such as Pamplona, San Sebastian, Figueras and Barcelona. However, the passage of these long French columns through the Pyrenees to occupy their country was immediately and hotly resented by the Spanish people.

Risings occurred in the Asturias as early as March 1808, completely discrediting the puppet Godoy. The infamous crushing of the 'Dos de Mayo' uprising in Madrid provided the catalyst for scores of other attacks on the French throughout Spain, and for the formation of regional *juntas*. Open warfare now broke out, culminating in July in two major battles. Medina del Rio Seco was a crushing victory for the French; but, more significantly, at Baylen on 19 July General Castaños's scrambled-together Spanish army defeated and captured the whole of a French force of some 20,000 men under General Dupont. Even as Castaños and his men were taking stock of the French Imperial Eagles captured in this inspirational victory, Wellesley and his 9,000 redcoats were sailing across the Bay of Biscay bound for northern Spain. The British government had decided that intervention by its army in that country was likely to prove of greater benefit to Britain than another harebrained attack on a distant Spanish colony in South America. The British Army's campaign in the Peninsula was about to begin.

Wellesley began to land his force at Figueiras, at the mouth of the Mondego river, on 1 August. The first fatalities were suffered on this day, but not through enemy action. Despite the small boat skills of the Royal Navy seamen ferrying the troops from the transport ships to the beach they were no match for the great Atlantic breakers that came crashing in, sending boats tumbling in the surf and drowning men and horses. Finally the force got itself ashore, dried off and organised, and Wellesley could plan his advance south towards Lisbon. Four days later he was joined by a further 5,000 troops under Brent Spencer, who had sailed up

from Cadiz. With 14,000 British troops now under his command, almost all of whom were infantry, Wellesley began his march south towards the Portuguese capital. On 15 August they made first contact with the French. The skirmish, close to a mill at Brilos near Obidos, was insignificant, involving as it did a few men of the 95th Rifles. For Lieutenant Ralph Bunbury, on the other hand, this brush with the French was far more than that, for it was here that he achieved the dubious honour of becoming the first British officer to be killed in the Peninsular War.

Two days after Bunbury's demise came the first real action of the expedition. Fought on 17 August, the battle of Roliça was itself little more than a skirmish by later standards. Indeed, when we consider the multitude of small affairs which were fought later in the war – engagements which were, nevertheless, much larger and fiercer than Roliça, and yet were never recognised by their award as formal battle honours – we may wonder why 'Roliça' was ordered emblazoned on drums and Colours. The reason was presumably that after the previous year's poor showing by the British Army in South America and Egypt, Wellesley's success at Roliça came as a tonic to the mood of the nation and a relief to the government. The 14,000 British troops certainly outnumbered the French, under General Delaborde, by about three or four to one, but they still had to shift the French from a couple of good positions. The first, on some rising ground to the north of Roliça, was turned very easily when Wellesley sent two columns under Trant and Ferguson around Delaborde's flanks. The French commander waited before skilfully withdrawing his men to a much stronger position atop a rocky ridge south of the village of Columbeira. This proved to be a more difficult proposition. Nevertheless, it was carried successfully by Wellesley's infantry in a frontal attack on the ridge, fighting their way up the gulleys and across the broken ground beneath the feature before finally driving Delaborde's men off it. The attack was only marred by the misadventures of Colonel Lake of the 29th Regiment, who mistook the heavy skirmishing at the foot of the ridge for the main attack, and so led his men up one of the gulleys instead of waiting for the main assault to begin. It was a mistake which cost him his life; fortunately, the error did not prove crucial to the overall attack. Delaborde was driven from the position with some loss, and while he and his men beat a retreat south in the direction of Lisbon and French reinforcements, Wellesley's men congratulated themselves on a good start to their campaign.

Vimeiro

Four days later Wellesley achieved an even greater success with a victory over the French at Vimeiro. Here, for the first time, were demonstrated some of the tactics that were eventually to sweep the French from the Peninsula. As the French columns ascended the hill in front of the village of Vimeiro they encountered a heavy skirmishing line, which consisted largely of green-clad soldiers of the 95th Rifles. Each man was armed with the beautiful Baker rifle, a weapon which, although slow to load, could find its mark from a range well in excess of that of the normal smooth-bore musket carried by the men in the long red lines which lay in wait behind the riflemen. The French, accustomed to brushing aside enemy skirmishing lines elsewhere in Europe, had great difficulty in pushing back the 95th, who began to take a toll not only of the French skirmishers but

also of the main columns themselves. And while the 95th and the other British skirmishers fired away at the French, the guns of the Royal Artillery also played on them with roundshot and with air-bursting 'spherical case' - later to become known as 'shrapnel' - a new weapon which, like the Baker rifle, was destined to play a major role on battlefields across Portugal and Spain.

Inevitably, the galled French columns began to push back Wellesley's skirmishers and approach the main British infantry line which had been watching, silently, as the fight unfolded below them. In later battles the British infantry would not be visible to the French, as Wellesley developed his tactic of keeping his men hidden on a reverse slope. At Vimeiro, however, they appear to have been positioned at the top of the hill behind which lay the village, while the supernumeraries - cavalry, ammunition wagons, etc. - lay out of sight.

As the French approached Wellesley's infantry they were met by what appeared to be a long red wall tipped with black (the shakos of the British infantry had yet to become distorted and discoloured by the rigours of campaign life). The noisy approach of the French soon quietened, as if they

The wounded Piper Clark of the 71st (Glasgow Highlanders) playing on at Vimeiro, 21 August 1808. At this date the 71st were still a kilted regiment; they adopted tartan pantaloons later that year, and light infantry dress in 1809.

The 1st Foot Guards embark at Ramsgate in September 1808, bound for the Peninsula. This painting by Loutherborg features several interesting aspects of uniform, including three different types of legwear - white trousers, white breeches with knee-length gaiters, and dark blue trousers - all worn by different men of the same battalion.

The cavalry action at Benavente, 29 December 1808, where the British 10th and 18th Hussars and 3rd Light Dragoons KGL successfully charged the elite Chasseurs à cheval *of the French Imperial Guard, inflicting about 60 dead and wounded and 76 captured, including their commander, General Charles Lefebvre-Desnouettes. This was just one of a series of fine actions fought by the British cavalry in the Peninsula. This particular fight took place under the watching eyes of the Emperor Napoleon himself, who witnessed Paget's fine charge from a hill overlooking the Esla river, on the far bank of which the action was fought.*

were wary of what they were about to receive. The long, two-deep British line overlapped the French column by a considerable distance on each side, every musket having a clear field of fire. Against this, the French could bring to bear only those muskets in the front rank or on the flanks of their close-packed column. It was a simple mathematical equation, the sum being simply an overwhelming superiority of firepower enjoyed by the line over the column; yet it was an equation which the French would never quite master during the coming six years. One of the British officers watching the French approach was Captain John Patterson of the 50th Regiment (the 'Dirty Half-Hundred,' so called because of their black facings). 'Not good looking, but devilishly steady,' was how Lord Hill described them. Patterson later wrote:

'When the latter [the French], in a compact mass, arrived sufficiently up the hill, now bristled with bayonets, the black cuffs poured in a well directed volley upon the dense array. Then, cheering loudly, and led on by its gallant chief,

the whole regiment rushed forward to the charge, penetrated the formidable columns, and carried all before it. The confusion into which the panic-struck Frenchmen were thrown it would be difficult to express. No longer able to withstand the British steel, Laborde and his invincibles made a headlong retreat, and never looked behind them till they reached the forest and vineyards in the rear'[2].

The outcome of the clash between the British and French in front of Vimeiro probably came as no great surprise to Wellesley, who watched, satisfied, as a succession of French attacks were driven off by a combination of a heavy skirmishing line, the two-deep infantry line, and artillery which, instead of playing upon enemy batteries, concentrated their fire upon the infantry. The only blemish on an otherwise very successful day was the mishap to the 20th Light Dragoons who, while pursuing the beaten French, charged too far and were themselves badly mauled by French reserves, losing their colonel in the process. With barely 240 cavalry Wellesley could ill-afford to lose any of these precious soldiers, who would be needed to provide all-important patrols and security for his army during the coming campaign.

Vimeiro was a remarkable victory for Wellesley, his second in five days. It was the more remarkable in that he had fought it in the knowledge that he had been superseded as commander of the British army in Portugal - on grounds of simple seniority - by Sir Harry Burrard, who had arrived the day before. Burrard in turn was superseded by Sir Hew Dalrymple, who himself knew that the impending arrival of Sir John Moore, bringing with him further reinforcements, would alter the command yet again.

As it was, all three British officers - Wellesley, Burrard and Dalrymple - found themselves back in England by October as a result of the Convention of Cintra. This notorious agreement was, in effect, an armistice which had been negotiated between the British and French with very advantageous terms to the latter, allowing Junot's men to sail back to France rather than face incarceration in British prisons. This arrangement certainly had its advantages for both sides; after all, the major fortresses of Portugal, all of which had been garrisoned by French troops, were, at the stroke of a pen, delivered back into the hands of the Portuguese without the loss of a single life. However, the manner in which the negotiations took place - with little regard to Portuguese interests - resulted in an inquiry into the Convention and the recall of the British generals. The main issue was the way in which the French were allowed to sail back to France not only with their arms and equipment, but with all of their accumulated plunder. It was an unsavoury end to a campaign which had got off to such a promising start.

Corunna

With Sir John Moore now in sole command, the British army looked east towards Spain, and an advance against Napoleon himself. It was to result in the ill-fated Corunna campaign, one of the most harrowing in the history of the British Army. Moore advanced into Spain with the intention of drawing Napoleon away from Madrid, thus giving the defenders time to organise themselves. Unbeknown to Moore, events were developing at such a rapid pace that no sooner had he made one decision than information was received which forced him to change his plans. Indeed, one of the features of the Corunna campaign was the marked lack of reliable intelligence gleaned by either side. Consequently both Moore on one side, and Napoleon and Soult on the other, were completely ignorant of each other's whereabouts at various times, the result being a series of plans which, once issued, had to be hastily modified soon afterwards. Eventually both sides grasped the reality of the situation, with the result that Moore, denied the anticipated Spanish support and faced with an advance by Napoleon leading a far greater number of troops, was forced to retreat

to the waiting ships of the Royal Navy at Corunna. The winter retreat through the Galician mountains was a terrible experience for both British and French, although morale was naturally far higher within Napoleon's army and consequently their progress was far less traumatic. The British retreat was not without its high points, however: Moore's cavalry, under the skilled hand of Henry, Lord Paget, won significant victories at Sahagun, Mayorga and Benavente. Napoleon himself gave up the pursuit at Astorga

The body of Sir John Moore is lowered into its grave in Corunna on the morning of 16 January 1809. Henry Hardinge, later to play such a key role at Albuera, was standing beside Moore when a roundshot struck him, mangling his shoulder and chest. Hardinge tried to remove the general's sword which had become embedded in the terrible wound: 'It is as well as it is', said Moore, 'I had rather it should go out of the field with me.' The words of Charles Wolfe's famous poem, 'The Burial of Sir John Moore', adorn the walls of the San Carlos garden where Moore lies today. After the battle Marshal Soult had a memorial erected to his dead adversary.

An incident during the retreat to Corunna: Sergeant Newman of the 43rd rallies a mixed bunch of British troops and leads them in a spirited rearguard action outside Betanzos.

and handed over command to Marshal Soult (the 'Duke of Damnation', as he became known to the suffering British troops).

The retreat came to a climax on 16 January 1809 when the British turned to face their French tormentors in sight of the harbour of Corunna itself. The battle of Corunna, essentially a British victory, allowed the army to embark in relative safety and sail home to England. Sadly, Moore was not with them. At the height of the battle a French round-shot smashed into his shoulder, mortally wounding him, and while the army sailed away he was left 'alone with his glory' in a shallow grave on the town's ramparts.

Barely three months after the ignominious flight of Moore's army from Spain, Sir Arthur Wellesley was back in Portugal. Acquitted of all charges relating to the Convention of Cintra, he had been asked by the Castlereagh government for an appreciation of the chances of liberating 'Britain's oldest ally'. His clear-sighted memorandum was approved, and on 22 April he arrived in the Tagus to join those British troops which had remained in Portugal throughout the Corunna campaign; reinforcements soon brought the total up to some 30,000 men. Wellesley's plan of campaign involved a march north to Oporto, where Marshal Soult was idling away his time awaiting an attack from the mouth of

the Douro river to the west. It was Wellesley's intention to march north and expel Soult from Portugal, and then to head back south to deal with any possible incursions into the country which the two nearest French commanders in Spain, Victor and Lapisse, might make in his absence. As Jac Weller wrote, 'Seldom had a general conceived so detailed a plan in so short a time'[3].

Oporto and Talavera

The plan worked well. At Oporto on 12 May, Wellesley's troops crossed the Douro in one of the most daring operations of the entire war. A bridgehead was established on the northern bank, and even as more British troops crossed the river Soult's army was streaming away from the city in retreat, abandoning its artillery and baggage train. A week later the second French invasion of Portugal was at an end.

With Soult expelled, Wellesley returned south to consider his next move, which was a junction with the Spanish army of General Cuesta, a 73-year-old relic of a previous age of warfare who travelled around in a coach. As Moore had discovered to his cost, the transport and supplies promised by the Spaniards to Wellesley simply did not materialise. Co-operation between the two commanders was difficult at best; nevertheless, they managed to bring their

A contemporary painting of Wellesley's army crossing the Douro at Oporto, 12 May 1809. This was one of the most daring operations of the war, carried out beneath the very noses of Soult's men, whose slack guarding of vessels tied up on the north bank enabled the British to ferry themselves across in wine barges.

respective armies to Talavera where, on 27-28 July 1809, the second great battle of the war was fought. It was a desperate struggle beneath a blazing summer sun. As at Vimeiro, Wellesley watched as his lines of infantry beat off successive attacks by French columns, whose formations had been badly disrupted by the broken nature of the ground. Only an over-zealous pursuit by the Brigade of Guards threatened to deprive him of his fourth triumph of the war, but this was avoided when the 48th Regiment was thrust into the gap to bring yet another large French attack to a halt. This hard-fought battle ultimately resulted in victory for the Allies, although the Spanish troops played very little part in the fighting. Even a second mishap to his cavalry, on this occasion the 23rd Light Dragoons, could not spoil Wellesley's day.

Two months afterwards Wellesley was created Viscount Wellington of Talavera in recognition of his victory; but despite this welcome advancement the overall aftermath of the battle brought few other rewards. When French forces took Plasencia British communications with Portugal were severed, and Wellesley was forced to cross to the south of the Tagus and put that river between himself and the French on the north bank. Even then any loitering on the south bank might have proved dangerous once French troops crossed the Tagus. In the event, Soult marched north again and Wellington, as we can now call him, marched his army to Badajoz where, in the first week of September, they halted. They did not have a particularly enjoyable stay in the town, where many of the people harboured pro-French sympathies, and it came as something of a relief when most of Wellington's men marched north to Almeida, although Hill's 2nd Division, along with a Portuguese division, remained to control the corridor between Portugal and Spain in which Badajoz lay. The British army would return to Badajoz in the future, under circumstances which would prove unforgettable.

Drawing the lines

With an apparent stalemate on his hands, Wellington took himself off to Lisbon with his chief engineer, Sir Richard Fletcher, and other select members of his staff. During the lull between the battle of Vimeiro and the Convention of Cintra, Sir Arthur had made use of his time by riding around the Lisbon peninsula, making observations on possible defensive measures to be taken should the Portuguese capital ever again be threatened by the French. These observations later came to fruition as the celebrated Lines of Torres Vedras. After exploring the ground again in October 1809, Wellington issued his memorandum on the construction of the Lines and work began soon afterwards. Claims as to who actually devised the Lines of Torres Vedras have been discussed at length over the years, and range from Wellington, to Fletcher, and to Major Neves Costa, an officer of the experienced and respected Portuguese Royal Corps of Engineers whose name appears on the monument to the Lines above Alhandra. In fact it was obviously a joint project, with British and Portuguese engineers working in harmony. It must have been fairly obvious to even a modest military intellect that the hills to the north of Lisbon made a wonderful natural barrier which, if exploited by a defensive force, could be transformed into an impenetrable one. And so it proved. Fletcher received his orders on 20 October 1809 and work began on three lines of defensive fortifications, stretching from the Atlantic in the west to the Tagus in the east[4].

The construction of the Lines involved a massive sacrifice by the Portuguese people, who saw their livelihoods virtually destroyed by Wellington's 'scorched earth' policy. But it was all necessary if the French were to be defeated. Financially it was a cheap investment by today's standards, ultimately costing around £100,000 – and, more importantly, it was a secret one. Many of the journals kept by British officers and men mention the construction of forts and redoubts on the hillsides, but few had any inkling of either their extent or of the way in which they were linked together. The test of their strength would come a year later.

Meanwhile, as tens of thousands of Portuguese labourers toiled away at the Lines under the guidance of the engineers, Wellington's troops stood on the Portuguese border at Almeida, waiting for the expected third invasion by Marshal Masséna, now in command of the Army of Portugal. With the coming of 1810 Wellington entered his most anxious year of the war. This was due not only to the impending invasion but also to the unhelpful atmosphere created by the so-called 'croakers', British officers who held out few grounds for optimism and who advocated an abandonment of the Peninsula. These were not only junior officers, but included such senior figures as Robert 'Black Bob' Craufurd and Charles Stewart. It was 'coffee-house talk', but Wellington could well do without it; it would not take long for the despondency to be transmitted to politicians at home, many of whom would have not the slightest hesitation in ordering the army's recall if they could. The situation was not helped by the field army's long inactivity; a full 14 months passed between the battles of Talavera and Busaco, the next major action, fought on 27 September 1810.

Nevertheless, it was during this period that the 3,500-strong Light Division, under Craufurd, established itself as probably Wellington's finest formation. 'The Division', as the men called it, patrolled 400 square miles – a front 40 miles long and ten miles deep – along the Coa and Agueda rivers, without the French ever piercing its chain of outposts. There were certainly alarms and close calls, none more so than the desperate battle on the Coa on 24 July; but by the end of the summer the riflemen and light infantry of the Light Division could reflect on a job well done.

A contemporary view of Oporto looking east, showing the crossing point of Sherbrooke's men on 12 May. Wellesley watched the whole operation from the Observatory on the right. The Bishop's Seminary is shown more accurately than in the previous picture, high up on the left hand hillside. It was seized by the 1/3rd (Buffs), and held against French attacks by General Edward Paget, brother of the famous cavalry commander, with able support from British artillery still on the south bank.

Despite the efforts of the Light Division and, more important, of its tenacious governor Herrasti, Ciudad Rodrigo, the Spanish fortress which controlled the northern corridor between Portugal and Spain, fell to Marshal Ney's 6th Corps on 10 July 1810. Masséna was then free to push his troops forward to begin besieging Almeida, Ciudad Rodrigo's Portuguese counterpart. This fortress, which Wellington hoped would hold out for some time, fell – somewhat fortuitously for the French – on 25 August. This was on account of a massive explosion the previous day in the fortress's powder magazine, which killed hundreds of Portuguese troops and rendered the place indefensible. This was a great stroke of good fortune for the French, and would oblige Wellington to retreat into Portugal without the luxury of the extra two weeks or so which he had hoped a prolonged defence of Almeida would buy him. As it turned out the fall of Almeida did not cause Wellington any undue problems. One of his unpublished letters, written in August 1810, clearly states that he always intended to retreat to the Lines of Torres Vedras and that he would fight a delaying action during his retreat[5]. That action came on 27 September 1810, at Busaco.

Busaco and Torres Vedras
The battle of Busaco is often the centre of a dispute between pro-French and pro-British historical factions, both of whom claim victory for their respective sides. The French claim is based on the fact that after the battle Masséna discovered a road to the north of Wellington's blocking posi-

An impression of the Foot Guards in action against a formidable column of French infantry at the battle of Talavera, 27-28 July 1809. Talavera was one of the bloodiest actions of the war, and was certainly the costliest of the set-piece battles at which Wellington himself commanded. The victory earned Wellesley his title of Viscount Wellington.

The spectacular gorge of the Agueda river as seen from the bridge at Barba del Puerco. The first crossing point north of Cindad Rodrigo, this strategically important bridge was the scene of a sharp fight between riflemen of the 95th and grenadiers from Ferey's division on 19 March 1811.

tion and thus turned his left flank, forcing him to continue his retreat. This is, however, a flawed claim which in the light of Wellington's cited letter becomes all the more so. Furthermore, there is the small matter of the hundreds of French casualties suffered in the course of a series of brave but foolhardy attacks on Wellington's strong position atop the ridge of Busaco. These attacks ended in bloody failure owing to the superiority of the command, leadership and behaviour of the British and Portuguese infantry. Wellington gave Masséna a bloody nose at Busaco, but his victory was never intended to be anything more than that. As we have seen, he had long been planning a much larger and nastier surprise for Napoleon's 'darling child of victory'.

When the vanguard of Masséna's army arrived in front of Sobral they were confronted by a range of hills bristling with some 154 forts and redoubts, the majority of which were armed with artillery totalling well over 500 cannon and mortars, and linked by a system of signal masts manned by the Royal Navy. The hillsides had been scarped to make them steeper and more difficult to climb, while the passes between them were blocked with felled trees; small rivers and streams were dammed, and roads broken. The civilian population had been herded within the Lines along with their herds, flocks, and everything useful that could possibly be carried. At a huge human cost, everything possible had been done both to retard the advance of the French and to deprive them of much-needed supplies during their stay in

The infamous bridge over the Coa river, the scene of Robert Craufurd's failure on 24 July 1810. Craufurd quickly lost control of events when attacked by elements of Ney's 6th Corps, and the fight devolved into a typical 'soldier's battle'. Fortunately the Light Division was blessed with fine regimental officers who managed a successful if hair-raising retreat to the near side of the bridge before forming up in the hills behind the camera. Scores of French troops were shot down on this bridge as they tried in vain to cross it.

front of the Lines.

The forts comprising the Lines were manned not by Wellington's regulars, but by garrisons of British seamen, Portuguese militia and volunteers; his main field army was kept in reserve, ready to advance on any point that might come under French attack. But the attacks never came; in fact the Lines were tested only once, at Sobral on 14 October, and with little success. Thereafter Masséna, after making an extensive reconnaissance, decided that the Lines were far too strong to attempt an all-out assault, and instead simply sat down and waited. But for what? It is true that reinforcements were sent to him, but it was not more hungry mouths that he needed. What he really wished for was a key to unlock the Lines. In the meantime, he just sat there, watching his army stripping the land bare of any meagre winter provisions they could find. Inside the Lines Wellington's army settled down comfortably enough in their winter hutments, amply supplied through Lisbon by the ships of the Royal Navy.

Today we regard the Lines as being one of the most successful innovations in our military history. They certainly proved a major war-winning asset for Wellington. And yet, curiously, some Royal Engineer officers, writing reports at the time, expressed grave doubts as to the ability of the Lines to withstand a French assault. Furthermore, they feared the Portuguese would run at the first shot. Fortunately, the situation never arose[6]. The Lines of Torres Vedras proved to be a cornerstone of Wellington's victory in the Peninsula, for not only were they a formidable barrier but they served as a kind of safety net for future operations. No matter what mishaps might occur to Wellington and his army, he knew that he would always have the security of the Lines waiting for him should he ever again be forced to retreat deep into Portugal in the future.

Masséna, meanwhile, continued to watch and wait. He could do little else. He could not launch frontal assaults without risking immense loss; nor could he outflank the Lines, for the Atlantic lay to the west while the Tagus, to the east, was patrolled by scores of British gunboats. On the surface it might appear that a stalemate had been reached; but at his headquarters in the tiny village of Pero Negro Wellington rested easy. He knew that it would be only a matter of time before starvation began to fight his campaign for him, after which a French retreat would not be long in coming.

CHAPTER TWO

Wellington's Army:
'The Moral Power of Steadiness'

On 21 November 1813, eleven days after his crushing victory over Marshal Soult at the battle of the Nivelle, Wellington was moved to say of his army, 'it is probably the most complete machine for its numbers now existing in Europe'[1]. Given the condition of the British Army at the outset of the war in August 1808, and given his mercilessly exacting standards, this was quite a compliment.

His field command - which by November 1813 had become a truly Allied army - had indeed come a long way. The British Army which entered the war had been regarded with some disdain by the mighty and hitherto undefeated army of Napoleon Bonaparte. The recent memory of the disasters at El Hamet and Buenos Aires in 1807 weighed heavily on the minds of Britain's military leaders. Seven long years had passed since Sir Ralph Abercrombie had achieved his famous victory in Egypt, and Sir John Stuart's victory at Maida in Italy in July 1806 was regarded as being relatively insignificant. Wellington's own past victories in India were too distant to offer much cause for celebration. Victory on mainland Europe was what the people of Britain wanted, but this seemed a distant prospect when Sir Arthur Wellesley's men emerged literally from the Portuguese surf in the August of 1808. And yet, during the next six years, he would transform his army from a small, relatively untried force, apparently cast ashore in one of those ill-considered and probably foredoomed landing expeditions with which the public were growing sadly familiar, into one of the finest armies Britain has ever possessed.

The infantry

At the heart of Wellington's army were his red-jacketed British infantry, who were responsible for winning the majority of his battles in the Peninsula. The basic manoeuvre unit was the battalion, identified as the 1st, 2nd etc. battalion of a numbered Regiment of Foot, most of which had territorial designations (e.g. 2nd Battalion, 66th or Berkshire Regiment - abbreviated here as 2/66th). Most regiments had two, occasionally three battalions, but each of these was a separate tactical unit. Normally one battalion served abroad while the other remained in Britain as the depot battalion, recruiting and forwarding replacements for the battalion on service.

Each battalion was organised into ten companies: eight 'centre' or 'battalion' companies; and two 'flank' companies - the grenadier and light infantry companies, which in theory contained respectively the strongest and most aggressive, and the quickest and most agile, of the rank and file. On paper, each company had a strength of three officers and about 100 men, giving the battalions an establishment of about one thousand. In reality, however, this was far from the case. Sickness and battle casualties often reduced the battalions to skeleton strength, leading Wellington to combine some weakened units into what he called Provisional Battalions. He recognised the value of experienced campaigners over fresh, green troops who were often prone to sickness, and he fought hard to keep the Provisional Battalions rather than sending units back to Britain to recruit up to strength as was the normal practice. In this he was relatively successful, although many veteran battalions inevitably did return home during his campaigns. The aver-

A field officer - major or above, wearing two epaulettes - of the 28th Regiment (North Gloucestershire) in the typical uniform of a British infantry officer in 1811. The long-tailed coat and bicorn hat had yet to be replaced by the jacket and shako. The 2/28th served in Abercrombie's brigade at Albuera; their regimental facings were yellow. Note the shirt ruffle beneath the black stock at this officer's throat; the hussar-style 'Hessian' boots with braided tops; and the watch fob hanging from the breeches pocket — all features typically seen in Regency officers' portraits.

Rowlandson's caricature of British soldiers on the march, published in 1811; the nearest knapsack is marked 'Old Buffs'. Note the dandy officer, right, being carried on the shoulders of one of the women. (One of the most attractive anecdotes of the campaign describes Wellington's rage at seeing officers making their men carry them thus, and his bellowed order that they be dropped immediately. As hard as campaign life was for the women and children who followed the drum, it appears to have been preferable to having to remain behind in England once their husbands were sent overseas. Only six women per company were allowed to travel with their regiments and draw rations, though once in the Peninsula many more unofficially added themselves to the marching army's 'tail'. We should not forget that this is a cartoon; even so, there are some interesting details. The close-fitting white 'mosquito' trousers, shaped to fit over the shoes and buttoned up the outside calf, were issued in tropical stations; whether they were commonly worn in the Peninsula is uncertain, although see page 57.

age strength of an infantry battalion was between 500 and 600 men, with only the Foot Guards battalions and a few others maintaining a strength of anything approaching a thousand.

Each battalion was commanded by a lieutenant-colonel, with a staff consisting of two majors, one adjutant, one surgeon, two assistant surgeons, one quartermaster, one sergeant-major, one staff sergeant paymaster, one sergeant armourer, one drum major, one corporal pioneer and ten pioneers. Each company was commanded by a captain, with two subalterns (lieutenants or ensigns), two sergeants, three corporals and a drummer, and a varying number of privates. The reality on campaign could be rather different from this 'paper' establishment; majors often commanded battalions, and it was not unknown for a captain to be the senior officer, particularly after a severe action.

The officers of the regiment came generally from the professional classes, the landed country gentry and other families with means. When a man was commissioned as an officer in King George's army he had to possess sufficient funds to be able to live well, to pay his mess bills, to buy his kit and uniform and, often, to employ a servant or servants to look after his baggage. John Mills of the Coldstream Guards was only an ensign but had a 'stud and retinue' consisting of 'a horse, Docktail, who was taken from the French at Salamonde - a great favourite. Two mare mules, Bess and Jenny. Both are very quiet. A small he mule, Turpin; a rogue, he carries William. Mare mules carry the baggage and I ride Docktail. My servants consist of William, a private servant, Duckworth, a soldier servant who looks after the animals, Joseph, a Portuguese boy under him'[2]. A campaign could be an expensive business.

Above all the British officer had to be a gentleman, for without this elusive but instantly recognisable quality it would be almost impossible for him to persuade men to follow him into battle. Lieutenant-General John Whitelocke, of Buenos Aires notoriety, was known for his attempts to court favour with his men by using the language of the barracks; however, this only served to alienate them further. An officer without respect was an ineffectual one.

It is a myth that the majority of British officers came from the aristocratic families of England, although judging from comments made by John Kincaid of the 95th, himself a proven officer, this was regrettable. 'With regard to officers,' he wrote, 'I think I mentioned before that in war we had but a slender sprinkling of the aristocracy among us ... I have often lamented however that a greater number had not been induced to try their fortunes on the tented field, for I have ever found that their presence and example tended to correct many existing evils ... They were not better officers, nor were they better or braver men than the soldiers of fortune, with which they were mingled; but there was a degree of refinement in all their actions, even in mischief, which commanded the respect of the soldiers, while those who had

British infantry drilling under the watchful eyes of two officers. The men, wearing white fatigue jackets with facing-colour collars, cuffs and shoulder straps, are being put through their paces by two sergeants in red coatees. The officers also had to undergo such drilling before they themselves could assume command of any unit.

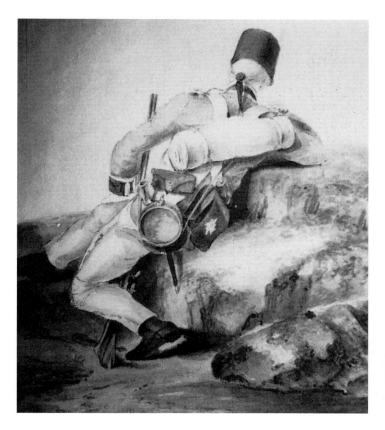

Front and rear views of a private of the 3rd Foot Guards in 1807, immediately prior to the Peninsular War. The uniform and equipment would have been much the same; but the infamous 'queue' - the greasing, powdering, and tying back of the hair - was abolished from August 1808, much to the relief of the men. There are several interesting points in these well-observed drawings, attributed to J.Atkinson. The Guardsman wears his tightly rolled greatcoat strapped at a slant to the back of his crossbelts in 'guard-mounting order'; he has a canteen, but no haversack. Attached to the bayonet crossbelt just above the hilt is the rarely-seen 'magazine', an extra pouch for 24 cartridges which was ordered in 1798 when the main pouch held only 36 rounds; it was abolished in 1808 when the 60-round pouch was introduced. The white trousers, buttoned up the whole length of the outside leg, are not the 'mosquito' type, but finish above the ankle, over black gaiters.

been framed in rougher moulds, and left unpolished, were sometimes obliged to have recourse to harsh measures to enforce it'[3].

The Foot Guards, in particular, certainly had their fair share of 'Gentlemen's Sons', but even in those battalions the majority were not from aristocratic families but from the lesser landed or professional classes. Whatever his background, however, the British officer could be relied upon to do his duty in the field. They were not expected to be highy educated students of their profession; they were not expected to share all their men's discomforts on campaign if they could avoid them; but they were expected to show complete disregard for their own safety, and to lead from the front. In this they rarely disappointed.

The men themselves came from a variety of backgrounds and volunteered for all kinds of reasons - and it is important to remember that, unlike the crews of Royal Navy warships, all soldiers were volunteers. Many fell victim to the tales of glory and bounty whipped up by the recruiting sergeants who, on a balmy summer's evening in England, would have little trouble in inducing a gullible local, primed with ale, to take the King's Shilling and enlist. Others, influenced by the public mood of their day, simply thought it their duty to fight the French and keep them from Old England's shores. Some joined the army to escape from cruel employers or to find a refuge from unfortunate circumstances at home. Others enlisted simply to escape poverty, to join an army which they believed would pay them, feed them, clothe them and generally look after them.

Wellington's men are usually portrayed as brutes, and much attention has been given to the sort of disgraceful scenes that followed the stormings of Ciudad Rodrigo, Badajoz and San Sebastian and the victory at Vittoria. It would appear that control was lost most often following successful stormings when, in the dead of night and the

confusion of scattered battalions with few surviving officers, the men were free to loot and pillage as they saw fit - something which they anyway considered as their unarguable right following such an ordeal. Wellington himself did them few favours when, a few days after Vittoria, he referred to his men as 'the scum of the earth, enlisted for drink' - an outburst which, with the passing of another 18 years, he would temper with 'it is only wonderful that we should be able to make so much out of them afterwards'[4]. They certainly displayed their darker nature on several occasions between 1808 and 1814; but, when called upon to fight, they rarely let their commander, their regiment and their country down. By today's squeamish standards they may well have been brutes; but the last thing Britain needed when the time came to storm the breaches of Badajoz, for example, was a bunch of Regency dandies.

Every regiment in the army had a core of bad characters who were usually the catalyst for the sort of disorders mentioned above. Others, easily led, simply followed their example, but were usually brought to their senses pretty speedily, either by the hanging or flogging of the ringleaders or by stern but effective leadership from regimental officers. It remains evident that under normal circumstances the behaviour of British soldiers in the Peninsula towards the civilian population was a good deal more restrained than that of the French, and that whenever possible Wellington enforced an iron discipline in this regard. Soldiers were hanged not only for murder and rape but also for looting.

Judging from a census conducted in May 1809, of the 57th (West Middlesex) Regiment - the 'Diehards' of Albuera fame - the present writer would suggest that it would come as a great surprise if we could see a Peninsula regiment on parade today. Of the 852 men only two stood 6 feet tall, while no fewer than 443 measured 5 feet 5 inches - noticeably short by today's standards [5]. Like most 20th century soldiers they were also young, their average age

The 71st Highlanders on the march (to judge from the heavy horses, while still in Britain), complete with baggage train, women and children. Wellington must have had this sort of thing in mind when he described his army on the march as resembling a moving country fair. Note the man in the ferns at bottom right, who has dropped out of the column with a bottle. The 71st are shown here still in kilts, but already wearing the bonnet blocked into shako shape – see commentary to Plate A1 on page 65.

being in the early twenties; another random sample of an infantry company of the period shows a spread of ages between 15 and 35, roughly 48 per cent being under 25 and 33 per cent being over 30 years old. What we have to envisage, standing there in the firing line at Talavera, Busaco and Albuera, is a long line of very short young men.

They were also very fit men, once they had become accustomed to the rigours of campaign life and to the endless marching back and forth across the Peninsula. In fact it is estimated that Wellington's men marched an average of 6,000 miles during the war. If tempted to regard this as an exaggeration, consider a single march by the 1st Foot Guards, for example, who walked more than 400 miles from Seville to join the main army near Salamanca during a number of weeks in the summer of 1812. Prior to this Wellington's army had marched from Oporto to Talavera, back to Badajoz, north to Ciudad Rodrigo, and then, in the autumn of 1810, to Lisbon to take up positions inside the Lines of Torres Vedras. The 1811 campaign which is our subject in this book was just as wide-ranging. After Salamanca would come another retreat from Burgos into Portugal, the advance to Vittoria, the march across the Pyrenees, and finally the advance to Toulouse. These were just some of the main advances and retreats; in between there were endless marches and counter-marches, all of which accumulated many miles and made very fit men of those of Wellington's soldiers who survived them.

When these men enlisted in the British Army they acquired a new family – the regiment into which they enlisted. British military history is full of stirring deeds and backs-to-the-wall fights in which soldiers emerged victorious from seemingly impossible positions. It is also full of tales of devotion to duty and self-sacrifice, where regiments

perish, fighting to the last despite hopeless odds. It was regimental pride and fierce loyalty to their comrades that inspired such deeds. A number of memoirs from the ranks also reveal, beyond argument, that the rank and file held strong opinions about their individual officers; they willingly followed into murderous danger those they considered brave and fair-minded, but responded with 'gallows humour' to the unregretted deaths of the nervous or tyrannical.

As we shall see, it was just such loyalty to their 'military family' and their regard for its honour that inspired officers like Matthew Latham and Ensigns Vance and Furnace to endure horrors and to make the ultimate sacrifice in order to preserve the symbol and embodiment of their regimental spirit: the regimental Colours. The shout of 'Save the Colours!' rings out from many pages of British military history. To lose the Colours was seen as an almost unforgivable disgrace, and the fights that raged around them on battlefield after battlefield were often savagely intense – as were those which broke out around the prized Imperial eagle standards carried into battle by Napoleon's regiments. The capture of an enemy's Colour or Eagle was a great achievement and often brought promotion for those concerned. Each British infantry battalion in the field carried two

Colours, a King's and a Regimental Colour. These flags were 6 feet 6 inches wide by 6 feet deep, and were mounted on a wooden staff 9 feet 10 inches long, tipped with a spearhead and a metal ferrule. It was the most junior officers - 'ensigns' - who carried them; and it was a proud moment indeed for a young man, perhaps still in his teens, to go into his first battle carrying a Colour. It was also often a test of sheer strength if it was windy, for a flapping Colour was large enough to become seriously unwieldy. The Colour bearers were usually protected by a guard of several sergeants carrying their pikes of rank, and placed between the 4th and 5th Companies when the battalion was in line formation. (After 1813 the senior rank of 'colour sergeant' was introduced, one per company, but this was a mark of seniority rather than necessarily of actual function in battle.)

Unlike their French counterparts, British infantry battalions were not known for their manoeuvrability - a weakness which was not lost upon some of their officers. 'For three hundred and sixty days in the year, a Frenchman is a better soldier than an Englishman,' wrote John Mills of the Coldstream. 'Their movements compared with ours are as mail coaches to dung carts. In all weathers and at all times they are accustomed to march, when our men would fall sick by hundreds ... Another peculiar excellence of the French troops is their steadiness in manoeuvring under fire.' But then Mills delivered the sting. 'But at fighting we beat them, and they know it'[6]. Given the British infantry's record in the Peninsula it is hard to argue against such a verdict.

Infantry tactics and weapons

The drill of the British Army of the early 19th century was based upon Sir David Dundas's *Rules and Regulations for the Formations, Field Exercise, and Movements of His Majesty's Forces*, which had appeared in 1792. The men drilled in ordinary step, which was 70 paces, of 30 inches length, per minute. Quick step was 108 paces per minute, and was used mainly when deploying from column into line and vice versa. The quickest step, used mainly for wheeling or making up time, was 120 paces per minute, each of 20 inches.

The favoured fighting method of Wellington's infantry was the two-deep line, which was used to great effect at such battles as Vimeiro, Talavera, Salamanca and, indeed, Albuera. However, the line was not the only tactical formation adopted. Whenever ground allowed and conditions were favourable the line was indeed used, but quite often we find examples of British infantry moving in column. At both Vittoria and the Nivelle both column and line were employed. Wellington's regimental commanders were confident enough to adopt whichever formation was practical on the day and appear not to have been handicapped by strict adherence to one particular formation.

The subject of column versus line is dealt with in several works and space precludes any lengthy discussion here. The superior firepower of the two-deep line over the column has been well documented, but it was not just the simple mathematics which defeated the French time after time. It was the combination of a heavy screen of skirmishers, judicious use of artillery and, of course, the occupation of a reverse slope wherever possible, which combined with superiority of linear firepower to deliver the decisive advantage on the battlefield.

One of the vital but sometimes unremarked advantages of the reverse slope position was that it denied enemy commanders sight of Wellington's deployments and thus of the opportunity to choose their attack formations accordingly. It must sometimes have been for this reason that French infantry were taken under withering fire while still in column. Their commanders - who were, after all, battle-proven veterans - had intended to deploy them from column into appropriate formations, including line, when the British battle line was revealed, but the volleys came too soon. However, the classically lethal combination of reverse slope, skirmish line, linear formation and direct artillery support was in fact used on far fewer occasions than popular myth would have us believe. Of Wellington's major victories in the Peninsula, only three - Vimeiro, Talavera and Busaco - involved the two-deep line in a defensive mode defeating an attacking French column. His other victories - Roliça, Oporto, Fuentes de Oñoro, Salamanca, Vittoria,

Light dragoons gathering intelligence in the Peninsula, depicted wearing the pre-1812 uniform of this branch: leather 'Tarleton' helmets with bearskin crests, and dark blue jackets lavishly corded on the breast. Historians dwell too much on the British cavalry's handful of notorious mishaps, and frequently overlook the mass of successful but unglamorous routine work carried out by the light horse throughout the war.

Sketch of British cavalry types in 1811 by Luard, who served in the Peninsula with the 4th Dragoons. To the left of the lemonade seller is a light dragoon in Tarleton helmet and laced jacket, and 'the Wellington trowser and boot, which were afterwards issued to all the cavalry'. At right are 'two of the old heavies ... one belonging to the third dragoon guards, the other to the fourth dragoons ... The heavies at that time wore plush breeches and a boot to the knee; the breeches never looked clean, and the boots were always dirty. The cocked hat, from being exposed to weather, and carelessly thrown down in camp, had acquired all sorts of curious shapes.'

masse in order to ensure that a high proportion of balls actually found their mark. This fact is sometimes under-emphasised in reports of the results of modern experimental firing with individual replica muskets. Commanders and soldiers of the Napoleonic period were intimately familiar with the musket's shortcomings, and employed it in battle in such a way as to minimise their effect.

Although the musket proved a reliable weapon in the Peninsula, it was often the psychological effect of the 17 inches of steel fitted to its muzzle that finally drove the French from successive battlefields. Contemporary accounts show that actual bayonet-fighting was an unusual occurrence in the Peninsula (as it has been in most wars throughout modern history). In some specific types of action - e.g. the storming of breaches, or the street fighting at Fuentes de Oñoro - the nature of the encounter certainly leant itself to the use of the bayonet. Generally, however, it was the firepower of Wellington's line followed by a bayonet charge at the decisive moment that was the battle-winning tactic - although the charge rarely involved pushing the bayonet 'home to the muzzle'. The French simply did not want to stand and lock horns with the British infantry, and it was only those trapped at the front of their columns by the pressure of those behind who had no choice but to stand and face them.

In addition to the standard issue 'Brown Bess' musket, Wellington's army made great use of the Baker rifle, which was issued to the battalions of the 95th and the 5/60th Rifles. (A large minority of each Portuguese Cazador battalion were also armed with the rifle, as were selected men within units of the King's German Legion.) The Baker had a rifled barrel just over 30 inches long, of .625 inch calibre.

the Nivelle, and Orthes - were fought either as offensive battles or, as in the case of Fuentes de Oñoro, involved street fighting. Ciudad Rodrigo, Badajoz, San Sebastian and Toulouse were all assaults on towns. The battle of Salamanca saw the two-deep line in action, as did Vittoria, but on both occasions Wellington was firmly on the offensive.

These tactics required a trained infantryman capable of firing, reloading and firing again, according to the commands of his officer, while under fire himself. Wellington's infantry engaged in live ammunition fire while drilling, which was certainly more beneficial than firing blanks. Through extensive practice the British infantryman in the Peninsula was capable of firing three rounds per minute, which was itself quite a feat with a flintlock muzzle-loader. The musket in question was the .75 inch calibre 'India pattern', weighing in at around 10lbs, or 11lbs with a fixed bayonet. The India pattern - so named when the hard-pressed British government decided to requisition large stocks of muskets originally destined for the East India Company's troops - had a smooth-bored barrel 39 inches in length; its accuracy beyond a range of about 50 yards was therefore extremely questionable. Contemporary tactical doctrine recognised the fact that it needed to be fired *en*

It was slow to load but made up for this with its accuracy, and the 'reassuring clang' of the rifle is mentioned by several Peninsula diarists. A trained rifleman was capable of hitting a target 200 yards away, and sometimes even further – as Tom Plunkett demonstrated with his famous shot at Cacabelos during the retreat to Corunna, when he put an aimed bullet through the forehead of the French General Colbert.

Although its long effective range was famous, and was employed to great effect on some occasions – for example, to silence enemy artillery – the Baker was mainly used over shorter distances, being well suited for its main employment as a skirmishing weapon. It was equally effective when whole battalions of the 95th were deployed in close order like line infantry, for example at Tarbes in March 1814.

The cavalry

Wellington's much-maligned cavalry – the British regiments, not the excellent units of the King's German Legion – emerged from the Peninsular War with a reputation for 'galloping at everything', as he himself put it. This reputation was not entirely deserved, and is largely based on a few very high profile misadventures, such as Vimeiro, Talavera and Maguilla. However, for each of these failures the record can show an even greater number of successes: Sahagun, Benavente, Mayorga, Usagre, Salamanca, Fuentes de Oñoro, Villagarcia, Morales de Toro, Carpio – the list is extensive. Even Campo Mayor would have ended in success had the cavalry involved been supported, as we shall see in a subsequent chapter. The fact remains that flawed analysis by historians such as Oman – particularly his treatment of Campo Mayor – plus Wellington's own outbursts, have left the

British cavalry with a stained reputation which is not deserved.

Cavalry regiments were organised in either four or five squadrons, each of two troops; one squadron remained to form the home depot when the others were posted overseas. The basic tactical unit was the troop. The establishment of a troop (in 1800) was three officers and 90 rank and file, but in the Peninsula the actual strength was more often about 50, and regiments on service were lucky if they could put many more than 400 sabres into the field. The regimental staff broadly resembled that of an infantry battalion, with the obvious addition of veterinaries and farriers. Troop trumpeters took the place of the infantry company's drummers; and it is not believed that cavalry standards or guidons were carried on campaign.

The cavalry in the Peninsula suffered through not having a single consistent commander. Lord Paget had commanded the cavalry with considerable success during the

'Troops Bivouacked near the village of Villa Velho on the evening of the 19th of May 1811.' This wonderful picture was painted by Major Thomas St Clair, three days after the battle of Albuera. This British officer-artist, who served throughout the campaign with Portuguese troops, is one of the most important pictorial sources of the Peninsular War. The wealth of detail is obvious and evokes the spirit of the day magnificently. All St Clair's works repay careful study with a magnifying glass. Here we see a ridge tent rigged on stands of arms, and a bell tent; men in forage caps, stable jackets and shirtsleeves about their camp chores - grooming horses, milking goats and butchering sheep; and infantrymen unloading pack mules, with some difficulty in one case. Almost hidden in the crease between these pages is a long row of stands of muskets with a pair of Colours crossed at the near end.

A troop of the Royal Horse Artillery in action in the Peninsula. They wore uniforms very similar to those of the light dragoons pre-1812. Although never present in great strength, these 'flying' gunners proved extremely reliable and valuable in the field and emerged with great credit, although Wellington was not always quick to acknowledge their efforts.

Corunna campaign but, after scandalously eloping with Wellington's sister-in-law, was unable to regain his place until the Waterloo campaign in 1815. In his absence the cavalry was led mainly by Stapleton Cotton, a good, reliable commander who adhered to Wellington's principles but who possessed none of Paget's dash and flair.

The cavalry in Portugal and Spain were constantly handicapped by the difficulties of obtaining enough mounts of sufficient quality; of feeding them, and keeping them up to condition; and of replacing them when, almost inevitably, they eventually foundered and died under the harsh conditions of Peninsular campaigning. Good horses were not available locally in the numbers required, and although English and Irish remounts could be shipped out thanks to the Royal Navy's control of the seas, this was a lengthy and uncertain undertaking. This was one reason why the cavalry also suffered through being understrength for most of the war. For example, when the British army took its first tentative steps into Portugal in August 1808 it could count just 240 cavalry among its 16,000-man strength. By the time of the Vittoria campaign this had risen to 5,913 - although by then, ironically, they were on the eve of entering the Pyrenees, and terrain where the majority of the cavalry simply could not operate.

This was a problem the cavalry faced throughout the war. Only the wide open expanses of Estremadura and Andalusia were really suitable for the large scale deployment of cavalry, which is why so many creditable cavalry actions occurred in that region - which includes Albuera. Elsewhere the cavalry found it almost impossible to operate to their full potential. Portugal is too rugged, as is the border country between Ciudad Rodrigo and Almeida - the home of the army for so many months during the war. The less said about the Pyrenees and much of southern France the better. Apart from the south, the only other region suitable for a wider use of cavalry was between Ciudad Rodrigo and Burgos, and this was an area traversed very briefly during the Salamanca campaign and the retreat from Burgos only.

Wellington's cavalry fell into two categories, heavy and light. The former were the dragoons and dragoon guards. To these men fell the shock of the charge, a tactic that was best demonstrated at Salamanca and by the King's German

Legion at Garcia Hernandez. This was not to say that they could not manoeuvre or skirmish, however; indeed, the 'heavies' could scrap with the best of them on their day. The retreat from Quatre Bras during the Waterloo campaign saw them skirmishing and withdrawing in fine style, much like the light cavalry. These latter - the light dragoons and hussars - were used for outpost work, escorts, patrols, screening and intelligence-gathering as well as in a fighting role on the battlefield.

Much of the focus of attention has fallen on the alleged failures of the cavalry in pitched battles, and their performance in some of these other vital roles is often overlooked. The task of intelligence-gathering has usually been associated with the so-called 'exploring officers' such as Grant, Cocks and Waters. But apart from these famous men there were scores of anonymous cavalry officers - and NCOs - who would spend long periods behind enemy lines, gathering intelligence and sketching for the Quartermaster General's Department. This vital contribution should not be forgotten.

Like the infantry, the cavalry had undergone wholesale changes towards the end of the 18th century. Cavalry drill was poor, to say the least, with the colonel of each regiment seemingly drilling his men as he saw fit. It was not until 1796 that a common drill for cavalry regiments was applied throughout the Army following publication of *Instructions and Regulations for the Formations and Movements of the Cavalry*, of which each cavalry officer was to obtain a copy[7]. The implementation of the drill laid out within the manual took some time to achieve, and it could be argued that many officers were still incapable of rudimentary manoeuvres even in the Peninsula. However, it was a step in the right direction. A further leap forward came the same year with the publication of John Gaspard Le Marchant's *Rules and Regulations for the Sword Drill of the Cavalry*, coinciding as it did with the introduction of the 1796 pattern light and heavy cavalry swords - the light cavalry sabre being designed by Le Marchant himself.

The two manuals admittedly had their flaws. For example, in the *Instructions and Regulations* very little attention was paid to skirmishing and outpost duties, the majority of the manual being devoted to movements on the battlefield, particularly the charge. Le Marchant's manual, on the other hand, appears to have been written with light cavalry only in mind, with the illustrations featuring the 1788 light cavalry sabre. However, it did address all aspects of sword drill and, in particular, included the famous 'six cuts', which involved standing four feet from a wall and practising cuts at a simulated enemy 'head'.

All in all, the British cavalry regiments serving in the Peninsula, with relatively little experience of campaigning, found themselves negotiating a very steep learning curve. They would emerge as a far more effective force than is generally credited, although some failings still surfaced during the Waterloo campaign in 1815 - here again, many of them revealed by regiments with little experience which had seen no Peninsula service.

The artillery
Wellington's infantry and cavalry were supported on the battlefield by the Royal Artillery and Royal Horse Artillery. Administratively and for purposes of individual career advancement this corps came under the auspices of the Board of Ordnance rather than Horse Guards, setting its officers rather apart from those of the other arms. There was often some conflict between the Board and Horse Guards as to the appointments of officers, their duties, and so on. Although this arrangement, which had evolved from dim historical beginnings, might appear somewhat ludicrous, in practical terms it did not hamper Wellington's operations drastically. The artillery officers knew themselves to be the most professionally educated in the Army; they tended to be touchy about their standing, and sometimes complained of what they felt to be Wellington's less than textbook deployments, but it was not until much later than 1811 that this developed into real ill-feeling.

Wellington's use of artillery on the battlefield mainly involved his gunners firing upon attacking enemy columns, as it was these that he perceived to be the threat. It was rarely his policy to engage in counter-battery fire with the French, although Vittoria was one exception. In fact Vittoria marked a watershed for the British artillery in the Peninsula, there being some 74 Allied guns present - far more than Wellington had ever been able to call upon in previous battles.

It was the number of guns at Wellington's disposal at any one time which largely dictated his handling of artillery. He was usually too short of guns to employ classic massed tactics, and unable to await events before moving them around the field to meet threats as they developed. Hence the companies - composed of six pieces - were usually split up into twos and threes; it was only when he had appreciable numbers, as at Vittoria and Waterloo, that he was able to mass them together in the traditional Napoleonic manner.

Both Royal Artillery and Royal Horse Artillery were organised into horse-drawn 'companies' or 'brigades'; these different terms were used under different circumstances, but both referred to the same tactical unit consisting of six pieces, usually five guns and a howitzer. (Modern writers often use the term 'battery', but in Napoleonic times this referred to the emplacement, not the men, horses and guns.) The guns were direct fire weapons firing on a fairly flat trajectory at targets in the line of sight; the howitzer gave the capability for indirect fire, 'lobbing' projectiles at a high angle to fall behind obstacles. During the early part of the war British guns were 6-pounders, although these were later replaced by heavier 9-pounders.

The guns fired a variety of ammunition, the commonest of which was simple roundshot - a solid iron ball weighing either 6lbs or 9lbs, which was capable of ripping huge gaps through ranks of men with horrific results. 'Common shell' was simply a hollow ball filled with gunpowder; a fuse inserted in it was ignited when the gun was fired. If the fuse was cut to the correct length beforehand the ball would fall amongst the enemy and explode, pieces of the shell being distributed amongst unlucky recipients. One of the most effective (and exclusively British) inventions of the period was the 'spherical case' shell, later to become known as 'shrapnel' after its inventor Henry Shrapnel. This was a hollow sphere filled with both a bursting charge and many musket balls, which was designed to explode in the air above enemy troops. Again, depending upon the correct cutting of the time fuse, this was capable of inflicting severe casualties (although early experience prompted the substitution of heavier balls for the filling, after some dismissive comments about prisoners 'picking duckshot' out of their heads and shoulders).

For direct fire a similar effect was achieved with 'grape', 'canister' or 'case' shot. Strictly speaking 'grape' was a naval munition, but the term was often used by soldiers; it consisted of large balls arranged like a bunch of grapes and confined in a canvas bag. Canister or case shot was a cylindrical tin filled with balls - of varying size and number - which ruptured when fired and sent the balls spreading in a cone from the muzzle, like a shotgun blast; employed at close range, these were devastating against formations of troops. A combined load of a roundshot and a canister were often used together for maximum point-blank effect.

As well as these conventional forms of artillery, there was also the notorious Royal Horse Artillery Rocket Troop armed with the Congreve rocket system. These were, in effect, huge fireworks - simply rockets mounted upon sticks, fired from iron troughs. The rockets ranged from small 6-pounders mounted on 8 foot sticks, right up to massive 42-pounders fired on sticks 17 feet long. The rockets were not widely employed in the Peninsula, although good use was made of them during the crossing of the Adour in February 1814. They were infamous for their uncontrollable aim, having a tendency to shoot up into the air or even to trail back the way they had come, and frequently proved more dangerous to the firer than the fired at.

The really heavy guns were the 18- and 24-pounders which were necessary for the successful prosecution of the great sieges (although before his capture of Ciudad Rodrigo in January 1812 Wellington was handicapped by the lack of a proper siege train). These monsters were capable of firing a huge iron ball at the rate of one shot per minute, assuming the massive smoke cloud cleared in time for the gunners to see their target after each firing. An inspection of the walls of both Ciudad Rodrigo and Badajoz today testifies to their power and effectiveness; the walls of Badajoz were in places over 40 feet thick, and bringing them down required both enormously powerful ordnance and great skill. Both were clearly available to Wellington. At Ciudad Rodrigo he had four 18-pounders and 34 24-pounders for his batteries. As for the skill of the gunners, if one stands in their firing positions today the target area presents itself as being very small indeed. The fact that the gunners had to find the foot of the walls in order to bring the whole tumbling down bears testament to their skill; it was certainly not a 'hit and hope' affair.

The infantry, cavalry and artillery were the main elements of Wellington's army on the battlefield. There was also a small but very professional corps of Royal Engineers, all officers, who supervised the construction of redoubts, forts and other field works and supervised siege operations. The destruction or repair of bridges also came under their remit, although the Staff Corps also took a hand in these matters. The Royal Engineers made a great contribution to the war effort in the Peninsula, but as they played little part in the Albuera campaign this book is no place to go too deeply into either their work or organisation; the essentials are touched upon in Chapter Eleven in connection with the first siege of Badajoz.

There were, in addition, several other departments which dealt with the day-to-day administration, organisation and running of the army. These were responsible for such matters as the movement and quartering of the troops, the issuing of orders, intelligence, cartography, medical and hospital matters, the supply of arms, equipment, stores and supplies, and, last but not least, all things spiritual. Again, space precludes any lengthy study here of these departments[8].

Portuguese and Spanish troops

Thus far we have looked at the British elements of Wellington's army. It should not be forgotten, however, that by this stage of the war Wellington's command was not a British but an Allied army. As early as 1808 Portuguese units were serving under him, although they did not really begin to make their mark until towards the end of 1810.

The disbanded Portuguese Army had been reorganised from early 1809, at the request of the Portuguese Council of the Regency, by a British military mission led by the Anglo-Irish general William Carr Beresford, who was given overall command and the Portuguese rank of marshal. Beresford spoke the language and had a genuine respect for the qualities of the Portuguese soldier; he also had the advantage of Portugal's long-established and sophisticated system of regional recruitment. This successful collaboration produced an infantry organised in much the same way as its British counterpart, in ten-company Portuguese battalions officered by a mixture of Portuguese and British. These had a larger establishment than British battalions, however, with an official strength of 1,552 all ranks. The light infantry or Cazadores battalions were five companies strong, totalling 628 all ranks at full strength; about 200 men in each unit had Baker rifles, the remainder the standard India Pattern musket. (The Loyal Lusitanian Legion, a light corps which fought at Albuera but was soon afterwards disbanded to form new Cazadore units, had about 120 riflemen in its ranks.)

Three-battalion brigades, often of two line battalions and one of Cazadores, were occasionally incorporated into British divisions; usually, however, they were simply designated as independent brigades and, more often than not, were commanded by British officers, of whom Denis Pack was probably the most famous. Pack's 1st Portuguese Brigade (1st and 16th Infantry and 4th Cazadores) fought in several major actions during the war and gained a tremendous reputation; indeed, the whole line and light infantry arm came to enjoy the warm respect of the British alongside whom they fought.

The same could not be said of Portuguese cavalry regiments, who were liable to run when faced by superior enemy numbers. They were much weaker than their British counterparts, and were seriously handicapped throughout the war by a chronic shortage of suitable mounts. While they enjoyed several creditable moments in the Peninsula, they could never be totally relied upon.

At Albuera in May 1811 Beresford's command was truly an Allied army, with a combination of British, Portuguese and Spanish troops in almost equal proportions. Of 35,284 Allied troops at Albuera, 10,449 were British, 10,201 Portuguese, and 14,634 Spanish. As we shall see, however, the respective casualty figures bear testimony to the burden shouldered by the British troops, although Zayas's Spanish battalions certainly suffered their fair share of losses.

Significant Spanish forces really only came under Wellington's direct command in 1813, during the Vittoria campaign. Until then their regional armies – varying considerably in equipment, training and leadership – had acted independently under their own generals. Operating under enormous disadvantages in a ruined country largely occupied by the enemy, they suffered countless defeats at the hands of the French. Although regularly trounced, however, they were never totally defeated, and would always put some sort of army back in the field again within a short time. It must be remembered that until 1812 it was Spanish armies which bore the brunt of the war inside Spain, albeit with huge financial and material support from Britain. Their spirit and endurance ensured that the French could never ignore them and bring their overwhelming numerical superiority to bear against Wellington – if they had, his situation would have been untenable. The Spanish armies in the various regions, and – perhaps predominantly – the relentless guerrillas who infested the nominally French-occupied areas, never allowed the French respite to concentrate on the Anglo-Portuguese field army. Their contribution to the final Allied victory should never be underestimated.

CHAPTER THREE

The French Armies: 'Coming On in the Old Style'

There is little doubt that – perhaps second only to his decision to invade Russia – Napoleon's invasion of the Iberian Peninsula was one of the greatest mistakes he ever made. Unlike Austria, Russia and Prussia, neither Spain nor Portugal possessed an army that was capable of even considering an attack upon France, let alone carrying it out. It is therefore ironic that they were to be so instrumental in his first downfall.

When Napoleon chose to march into Spain he committed his troops to a war not only against the armies of the two Iberian nations but also against the peoples themselves. Their national characters were very different, but they shared an instinctive patriotism which prompted a spontaneous and sacrificial fury against the invaders – a phenomenon which Napoleon had not yet encountered among his colder-blooded northern vassals. The guerrilla war which the Spanish people waged would be as costly and even more savage than the conventional campaigns; only in Calabria, in southern Italy, was a more violent guerrilla campaign prosecuted against the French.

Wellington himself later said that he could not have achieved victory in the Peninsula without the guerrillas. Their value as gatherers of intelligence was obviously high, but they also had a direct effect upon the French ability to mount operations. The French forces in Spain - the Armies of the North, Centre, South, Aragon, Catalonia and Portugal - were armies of occupation in a country which remained unpacified much beyond musket range of any French garrison. The guerrillas assembled in large bands; their claims for their strength were sometimes exaggerated, but can to some extent be compared against British lists of weapons supplied, and French intelligence reports. Chiefs such as Espoz y Mina in Navarre, Don Julian Sanchez and El Cura in Old Castile, and El Empecinado in Guadalajara each led several thousand men – adequately armed, and a proportion of them mounted – and thus presented a lethal threat to the necessarily dispersed French.

Military movement often proved very difficult for the French, particularly in the mountainous regions where the guerrillas operated with ease. Tens of thousands of French troops were employed against them, and this had significant consequences for their conventional operations. For example, prior to the battle of Vittoria in June 1813 General Foy's division was engaged in hunting down guerrillas around Bilbao, and was thus prevented from taking part in the great battle, where its presence might have been decisive.

Apart from the demands of specific counter-guerrilla operations the whole war took place against a background of 'low intensity' threats which had a huge cumulative effect. Each occupation of a major town or city required that a strong garrison be left behind when the field army moved on - otherwise the population would simply rise up and the guerrillas move in, often with dire consequences for the French. Lines of communication also had to be guarded by building and manning blockhouses and providing relays of mounted escorts. Even single couriers carrying despatches between Spain and Paris had to be protected by hundreds of cavalry; essential wagon convoys of food, ammunition and other logistic necessities were likewise in constant danger of ambush (so, horribly, were convoys of French wounded after major battles).

A measure of the drain upon French resources which the war in the Peninsula represented can be gauged from the

'Campagne en Espagne, 1809', *after Lapeyre: French infantry are holed up in a building under fire from the enemy. French commentators, resting on the absence of Napoleon himself except for a brief period in 1808, often treat the war in Spain as a sideshow, but the campaign lasted longer than any other in the Napoleonic Wars. The inescapable fact remains that the emperor made a tremendous effort to win this war, sending more than 300,000 troops and several of his best marshals to the Peninsula, but to no avail. Spain was, as Napoleon famously remarked, a country where large armies starved and small ones got swallowed up.*

French infantry in the firing line, a typical scene in the Peninsula. This dramatic treatment, after Maffet, emphasises several characteristic features. Note the military finery - the French army decked out its soldiers' uniforms in splendid plumes, cords and epaulettes, down to the level of the two flank companies in each infantry battalion. It also formally rewarded individuals for gallantry half a century before this became the practice in the British Army; note the decoration worn by this senior NCO, who also sports long service chevrons on his sleeve.

fact that at its height there were around 350,000 French troops in Spain. Wellington's Anglo-Portuguese army rarely got above the 50,000 mark, save for the campaigns in 1813, and on the face of it should have been easy prey for Napoleon's marshals. In 1811 the regular Spanish armies were reckoned to total about 90,000 men, although only parts of this total strength were in the field at any one time. Although it is impossible to number the guerrillas with any certainty, it is estimated that in 1810-11 there were 25,000 active in northern Spain alone, tying down some 50,000 French troops. It was against this background that the French armies in the Peninsula had to wage their war.

★   ★   ★

As Wellington's army was an alliance of British, Portuguese and Spanish troops, so the French armies were comprised of similarly diverse contingents. As well as the French there were Germans from a number of states, Poles, Swiss, renegade Spaniards, and even some Irish, not to mention over 50,000 Italians. The effectiveness of these foreign contingents was naturally variable. In defence, sheer self-preservation prompted most troops to fight well; but the stubbornness of, for instance, the Hesse-Darmstadt garrison at Badajoz went far beyond the necessary minimum effort. Some other German and Swiss contingents certainly lived up to their historic martial traditions. Even in prolonged and costly assault operations, few troops could have surpassed the courage and stamina of the Polish Vistula Legion at Saragossa. The bulk of Napoleon's armies were Frenchmen, however; and they served their emperor well.

The French soldier in the Peninsula was not that different from his British counterpart in background, the main difference being that while the British were volunteers the French were usually conscripts. Their army had been built twenty years beforehand on a foundation of Republican patriotism, the regiments being a mixture of untrained volunteers and conscripts swept up by the *levée en masse* formed around an armature of ex-regulars from the old royal regiments. By 1811 there would have been few left in the ranks who had worn the white coat of the Bourbons. There would still have been a number of volunteers, who had enlisted for more or less the same reasons as their British equivalents; but the great majority were conscripts. There were ways to avoid the draft; but in general, when an able-bodied, unmarried Frenchman who was not the sole support of aged parents or orphaned siblings reached his twentieth year, he was liable for conscription - in wartime, for an unlimited period. It might be argued that the draft brought into the ranks a wider social mix than the self-selecting British volunteer system, but in practice this seems to have made little military difference.

The fervour of the Revolutionary army had to some extent been transformed into enthusiasm for the cult of the Emperor Napoleon. All soldiers take heart from belonging to a winning army, and under Napoleon the habit of victory was strong. Beyond this basic level of patriotism and pride, battlefield morale owes little to political abstractions; men fight well or badly out of their feelings for their immediate comrades and their regimental officers, modified by physical conditions and circumstances. British and French alike cheered their generals when they had won a victory, and cursed and muttered when they were driven into retreat. They complained of the same arbitrary tyrannies inflicted by their sergeants, died of the same wounds and illnesses, and suffered the consequences of much the same logistic failures.

Discipline on the battlefield was certainly the equal of that in Wellington's army, although foreign observers were struck by the amount of straggling that was tolerated on the march (probably unavoidably, given that once a campaigning army were inside enemy territory the men were badly fed, badly supplied and badly paid). At least one memoir suggests that discipline could be more arbitrary than in the British service, varying in an unsettling way between laxity and harshness; and others, that a greater familiarity of manner between officers and rankers sometimes survived from the Revolutionary tradition. The troops were urged to maintain the honour of their regiments, and we read of unofficial soldiers' courts dealing with those who absented themselves from the battlefield. In the opinion of the veteran Marshal Bugeaud, who served in the Peninsula as a junior officer, the French army reached its peak of professional excellence in 1805-06; its expansion in numbers from about 1807 led to some dilution in quality, with rather too many middle-aged and very young soldiers.

There was no very dramatic difference between the regimental officers of the two armies. Many French officers had been appointed from the ranks during the Revolutionary Wars, and Napoleon certainly aimed to promote for talent alone, recognising in the salary scales the fact that most officers lacked private means. A few shining examplars achieved meteoric progress through the ranks; but with the return of a certain professional stability under the Consulate and early Empire the social mix became reasonably broad. Officers' letters show that regional and political connections were still important in securing commissions, advancement and desirable postings. A large number of men from the traditional officer class - the petty landed gentry, and even a few genuine aristocrats - threw in their lot with the new regime; it was still, after all, the army of France, and following Napoleon's star offered the hope of glittering rewards for the brave, energetic and lucky. However, the proportion of officers from the provincial middle classes outnumbered both aristocrats and former private soldiers (who were usually disqualified by illiteracy).

An analysis of the army in 1805 reveals one interesting difference which would presumably still have applied to a greater or lesser extent in 1811: the apparently greater age of many junior officers than most of their British counter-

parts (although impoverished talent could still languish for years in the subaltern ranks of the British army, too). Supposedly, the average age for both colonels and captains was 39 years, for lieutenants 37, and for *sous-lieutenants*, 32 years; this does seem to suggest that many subalterns were promoted NCOs with years of service behind them.

The British and French soldier in fact had a healthy respect for one another, and memoirs prove that fraternisation was rife. Most ordinary soldiers, while instinctively patriotic, could come to feel that they had more in common with each other than either had with civilians or their rulers. On the battlefield they would do their best to rip each other apart; but once the strife was over it was not unusual for piquets to be seen engaging in conversation. In southern France, in particular, fraternisation was so common that it was not unknown for French troops to leave their muskets with the British piquets as a sort of 'deposit' as they went off to buy, at the request of their enemy, some local produce - usually brandy. Private Wheeler of the 51st recalled having struck up a warm friendship with a French soldier when wounded of both sides were being transported together. Even officers used to exchange flasks and civil-

French infantry campaign uniforms and equipment items are displayed on mannequins at the Musée de l'Empéri, Salon de Provence. The shako is protected by an oilskin cover, but the pompon - and the epaulettes - still identify this voltigeur's company. The epaulettes have been shifted from his blue uniform coat to this grey-brown greatcoat, worn with loose white trousers on the march. Apart from his crossbelts and pack he has slung on a fife case and a personally acquired water bottle; and something is tied to his sabre scabbard - possibly a parade plume, wrapped and tied here to stop it getting broken?

The British army's logistics often broke down; but French troops were even less well supplied when in the field, relying on foraging and looting when in enemy or occupied country. This not only often condemned them to hunger; it made them ever more hated by the local population, while at the same time obliging them to disperse as they stripped the nearby countryside, thus inviting guerrilla attack. (Courtesy the late M.Raoul Brunon)

French infantry under fire from British Royal Horse Artillery in the Peninsula. Note that the men on the right and in the centre wear striped 'ticking' trousers, often depicted from the Revolutionary Wars onwards.

The French armies in the Peninsula never gave up despite years of hard fighting during which they gained few successes against Wellington. Even after their crushing defeat at Vittoria on 21 June 1813 clearly doomed their last footholds in Spain they recovered remarkably quickly, and fought well in the Pyrenees and in the south of France.

ities when they encountered one another in no man's land between battles. After all, before 1814 neither was invading the other's homeland; and they lived in a happier age, before ideologies preached unthinking mass hatred.

The same could not be said of the relationship between the French and Spanish, however. The invaders were hated by the large majority of the Spanish and Portuguese peoples, and it was a foolish French sentry who did not keep his wits about him whilst on guard duty. Every rock, bush and dark alley was a hiding place for covert killers who would slit his throat and disappear into the night as silently as they had come. The fate of French wounded or stragglers who fell into the hands of the guerrillas or vengeful peasants was often medieval in its cruelty. The French returned this hatred in a spiral of merciless violence. Reprisals for guerrilla activity were always brutal and often horrific. Wanton, unprovoked attacks on villages were equally appalling, particularly during Masséna's retreat from Portugal in 1811.

The impact of the hatred towards the French was felt in many ways. For example, when Wellington said he always knew what was going on 'on the other side of the hill' he meant that he had the advantage of receiving a huge amount of intelligence from the local people, while his officers were relatively free to go as they pleased among a friendly population. When maps were needed British officers were able to scout the land, sketching the terrain and providing important intelligence for the Quartermaster General's Department, whose job it was to make and distribute maps. The French enjoyed none of these advantages. When it came to sketching terrain they could really only map the ground which they occupied, since no small party dared risk straying too far from their own camps. There are in existence 'itinerary maps' which were issued by senior French officers to officers of detachments, showing basic routes between two given points. The officers would then have to literally 'fill in the blanks' along the way; in this way they were able to build up a knowledge of the country, but it took an enormous amount of time and resources.

The infantry

The backbone of the French armies in the Peninsula was, naturally, the infantry, whose organisation had undergone many changes since the days of the Revolution. At the beginning of the Peninsular War French infantry regiments still consisted of two or three battalions, each of nine companies. A decree of February 1808 reduced the battalion establishment to six companies: one of light infantry or *voltigeurs*, one of *grenadiers*, and the remaining four being 'centre' or *fusilier* companies. (The nominal difference between regiments of Light and Line infantry was not tactically significant by this date. The Light battalion had one voltigeur company, one of *carabiniers* corresponding to Line *grenadiers*, and four companies of *chasseurs*.) The company establishment was officially three officers, a sergeant major, four sergeants, a corporal quartermaster, eight corporals, and 121 rankers, giving a supposed company strength of 140 and a battalion about 850 all ranks – although, as in the British army, these figures were rarely if ever achieved. Each regiment was to have one depot battalion and four 'war' battalions; on paper regimental strength was 3,970[1] but the average strength of, for example, the regiments in Werlé's brigade at Albuera was 1,873[2].

The most noticeable difference between British and French orders of battle is that battalions of a French regiment served together, while those of a British regiment almost never did. There was thus a command staff at regimental level, consisting of a colonel commanding, a major, four *chefs de bataillon*, five adjutants and five assistants, a quartermaster/paymaster and a payment officer, a surgeon major with five assistants, ten sergeant majors, a drum major, a corporal drummer, eight bandsmen, and four master craftsmen.

The staff was completed by a lieutenant Eagle bearer and senior NCO second and third bearers, selected with the emperor's personal approval from battle-proven, long-service veterans whose path to promotion was otherwise blocked – in the case of the rankers, usually by illiteracy. The Eagle standard – by 1811, only one per regiment, carried on service by the senior battalion – was a deliberate element of the emperor's cult of personality; each was presented by his own hand, and the flag bore the inscription 'From the Emperor of the French to the ??th Regiment ...". They were regarded in the same light as a British battalion's Colours, and many epics of courage were recorded in their defence (although the more irreverent rankers referred to the Eagle as 'the cuckoo').

Two or three regiments made up a brigade, and two brigades a division, although formations were frequently dependent upon the numbers available at any given time and place. For example, at Albuera, Werlé's brigade consisted of three regiments each of three battalions (nine in all); Girard's division had four regiments, one with three battalions and the remainder with two (nine in all); and Gazan's division had two three-battalion regiments and two of two battalions (ten in all).

The need to train the massive numbers of recruits during the Revolutionary Wars of the 1790s led to the adoption of the attack in column, a system that yielded great results in Napoleon's early campaigns. French tactics became more refined and sophisticated during the early years of the 19th century, the most typical 'general purpose' formation – for everything from a battalion to a division – being the so-called *ordre mixte* in which a line provided a base of fire, flanked by deeper columns for the assault. However, the column - preceded by a strong screen of skirmishers to prepare its way - remained the mainstay of French battlefield tactics. Napoleon himself employed a variety of strategic techniques which won him countless victories, but on the battlefield it was his tactical use of the column which invariably triumphed over the Austrians, Prussians and Russians. Against the British line, however, it was rarely if ever successful. Only at Sorauren did the French actually break through, and even then their success was brief. This has proved a most contentious issue among historians ever since, and although space precludes any detailed analysis, it will not go amiss to quote here the famous passage from Bugeaud in which he recalls the experience of attacking a British line with a column:

'The English generally occupied well-chosen defensive positions having a certain command, and they showed only a portion of their forces. The usual artillery action first took place. Soon, in great haste, without studying the position, without taking time to examine if there were means to make a flank attack, we marched straight on, taking the bull by the horns. About 1,000 yards from the English line the men became excited, spoke to one another and hurried their march; the column began to be a little confused. The English remained quite silent with ordered arms, and from their steadiness appeared to be a long red wall. This steadiness invariably produced an effect on the young soldiers.

'Very soon we got nearer, shouting *Vive l'Empereur! En avant! À la baionnette!* Shakos were raised on the muzzles of the muskets; the column began to double march, the ranks got into confusion, the agitation produced a tumult; shots were fired as we advanced. The English line remained silent, still and immovable, with ordered arms, even when we were only 300 yards distant, and it appeared to ignore the storm about to break. The contrast was striking; in our inmost thoughts each felt that the enemy was a long time in firing, and this fire, reserved for so long, would be very unpleasant when it did come. Our ardour cooled. The moral power of steadiness, which nothing shakes (even if it be only appearance), over disorder which stupifies itself with noise, over-

came our minds.

'At this moment of intense excitement, the English wall shouldered arms; an indescribable feeling rooted many of our men to the spot; they opened a wavering fire. The enemy's steady, concentrated volleys swept our ranks; decimated, we staggered, seeking to recover our equilibrium; then three deafening cheers broke the silence of our opponents. At the third they were on us, pushing our disorganised flight. But to our astonishment they did not pursue their advantage beyond about a hundred yards, but returned quietly to their position to await a second attack, which when reinforcements arrived we rarely failed to deliver - under the same conditions, and too often with the same lack of success and with fresh losses'[3].

These columns were preceded by a screen of *tirailleurs*, skirmishers and light troops, whose job it was to annoy and 'soften up' the enemy position for the attack by the main assaulting columns; they were also to protect the columns from enemy light troops. Since Wellington's battle line was seldom exposed to their fire, they usually failed in the first objective. The second was often denied them when the British sent forward a strong skirmishing line of their own - not only riflemen of the 5/60th and 95th, but also the light infantry companies of line battalions, and sometimes whole light infantry battalions. These encounters between skirmishers in the ground between the armies could involve prolonged fighting between large numbers of men.

The trick for the leaders of attacking units was, of course, to know exactly when to deploy from column into line; but owing to Wellington's clever use of terrain this was not always possible. And so it was that French columns, on reaching what they thought was the British position, would begin to deploy, only for a long red line to appear as if from the earth itself and pour in volley after volley before charging out of the smoke and sending them flying at bayonet point, as described by Bugeaud. It was something that the French never quite got to grips with, despite long experience. Officers like General Foy, for example, were present at the very first battle of the war in 1808 and were still there in 1814 and, indeed, at Waterloo the following year. They had seen countless French attacks fall victim to the firepower of Wellington's line, and yet they appear not to have attempted to change their tactics. It is true that strategically French officers varied their movements, but on the battlefield they stuck rigidly to the old scheme of things. Hence it is no surprise that at Waterloo Wellington was moved to remark that the French 'came on in the old style.'

It would have been interesting indeed to have been a 'fly on the wall' of French headquarters after the first few failed attacks, to listen to the post mortems - surely there must have been such discussions? Clearly, they bore little tactical fruit. Bugeaud again: 'I served in the Peninsula for seven years. Sometimes I defeated the English in isolated encounters, and in surprise attacks which, as the senior officer present, I was able to prepare and direct myself. But during that long war, to my sorrow, I saw only a few actions in which the English did not get the better of us. The reason was obvious. We nearly always attacked without taking any account of our own experience - that the methods which nearly always succeeded against the Spanish nearly always failed against the English'[3].

Hence, when Foy sent his men forward to attack Hill at the battle of St Pierre on 13 December 1813, he sent them

The regulation uniform of a French infantry grenadier before 1812; the artist has given him the shako plate of the 21e de Ligne, which fought at Saragossa in 1808-09. The blue coat has white lapels and red collar, cuffs and piping; grenadier company status is marked by red epaulettes and shako tuft and a sabre; he probably carries a grenadier's parade bearskin in the cover on top of his knapsack. White breeches are confined by high black cloth gaiters. The more usual appearance of infantry on campaign is illustrated on page 29 and Plate F.

forward in the same fashion as he had done at Vimeiro on 21 August 1808. It is interesting to note that when the French did employ linear tactics, such as for Clausel's counter-attack at Salamanca and – in the form of a very broad *ordre mixte* – for Soult's attack with his 5th Corps at Albuera, they came very close to achieving victory.

The cavalry

The French cavalry in the Peninsula suffered from many of the same problems that beset Wellington's mounted units. The terrain was often difficult, forage was not easy to procure, and good horseflesh was in short supply. Very large numbers of horses died through sickness and lack of care on campaign; Spain did not offer a plentiful supply of local remounts, the Royal Navy ruled the sea-lanes, and bringing large numbers of horses overland from France was difficult and time-consuming. Although the French cavalry were present in great numbers their varied and dispersed missions frequently meant that they could not muster in decisive strength on the battlefield. We have already seen how regiments of cavalry were needed to escort despatches and convoys. Similar peripheral but necessary tasks included the gathering of forage, patrolling, screening, rearguard and outpost work and, of course, operations against guerrillas. Much of their work was typical of the cavalry of all combatant nations, but being an invading army in a hostile country meant that the numbers deployed for any detached duties had to be far greater for their own protection.

The mainstay of the French cavalry were the dragoons, who were present in large numbers; of the 30 regiments in this branch only five did not serve in Spain. In the French army the dragoon's dual function as a 'mounted infantry-man' survived to a greater extent than in the British service, where there was no meaningful distinction between 'light dragoons' and any other light cavalry. French dragoons were armed with muskets as well as sabres, which allowed them to adapt to different tactical circumstances far easier than other types of cavalry. Of about 12 regiments of French cavalry at Albuera six were dragoons. Other types of cavalry included chasseurs, lancers and hussars – all essentially light horse. The heavy cuirassiers, and regiments of the Imperial Guard, were rarely seen in Spain.

The record of the French cavalry in the Peninsula was not particularly outstanding against Wellington's army, although it achieved great things against the Spanish armies. We shall see how devastating cavalry could be when hurled against unformed infantry when we come to the field of Albuera; but that attack by the 1st Lancers of the Vistula was exceptional – nowhere else in the Peninsula did the French cavalry really cause any great damage to Wellington's men. Much of the reason for this can be traced to the engagement at Campo Mayor on 25 March 1811 (see Chapter Seven). This was a pivotal action in which two and a half squadrons of the 13th Light Dragoons routed the French 26th Dragoons. From this point on, French cavalry would be very wary of engaging British cavalry in stand-up fights. Even the notorious action at Maguilla, in June 1812, began with Slade's British dragoons scattering the French dragoons before his wild gallop ended in his own defeat. Indeed, the history of the Peninsular War is rich with instances of British success against French cavalry, for which due credit is rarely given.

Other arms

The strong French artillery was organised into companies of six to eight guns, usually 8-pounders, and either 6in or 5½in howitzers (an over-hasty attempt to introduce a 6-pounder field gun after 1803 was not a success). The heaviest field pieces were 12-pounders. Foot artillery companies were to have six guns and two howitzers, horse batteries four guns and two howitzers, the higher proportion of indirect fire weapons reflecting the French army's basically offensive doctrine. Each infantry division was supposed to have one foot and one horse company attached to it; each light cavalry division, one horse company, and each heavy cavalry division, two horse companies. Each corps reserve was to include two 12-pounder companies.

The quality of French cast bronze ordnance was excellent; and the Gribeauval system of guns and vehicles was designed with a high degree of interchangeability of parts, which made for efficiency on campaign. Ammunition was virtually the same as that fired by Wellington's gunners – roundshot, common shell and canister, but without shrapnel. As befitted an army whose commander-in-chief had made his name as an artillery officer, the French had skilled crews and officers who made their presence felt on every field, their fire missions integrated as essential parts of the overall plan of battle. The infantry trusted the artillery, believing their gunner comrades to be a match for any enemy, and were heartened whenever they heard the crash of their supporting fire on the battlefield.

The engineer arm of the French Army was far superior to Wellington's. It had a long tradition of siege warfare; the great master of fortification, Vauban, had after all been a Frenchman. It was able to conduct its sieges in a far more scientific manner than the rather haphazard, make-do-and-mend way in which Wellington's few engineers were obliged to proceed. France also possessed a corps of sappers and miners, men skilled in the business of digging parallels and saps, constructing batteries and shoring up defences, whereas Wellington was forced to rely upon the brawn of the ordinary line infantry, who hated the work – and were often short even of suitable picks and shovels.

★ ★ ★

Several other factors conspired to bring about the defeat of the French in the Peninsula. Napoleon himself is often accused of trying to run the war from Paris, which was impossible given the time it took for despatches to reach him. By the time his orders returned to his commanders, the situations in which they found themselves had usually changed, rendering his instructions irrelevant and impossible to implement.

Neither was the French cause helped by the divided regional commands and the absence of any overall commander-in-chief. There were constant disputes between the various French marshals, each jealous of his own command and loth to march any great distance to aid a colleague. It was a situation which often had dire consequences. For example, Phillipon, bravely holding out at Badajoz in April 1812, was finally forced to surrender following an Allied assault which would never have taken place had Soult reacted a little quicker and marched to the city's relief.

The task of subjugating the Iberian Peninsula was an immense one for the French armies, given the vastness of the country, its relative poverty, primitive infrastructure and hostile population. It was simply too large, and the failings of the French system, particularly in the procurement of supplies, were cruelly exposed. Ultimately one is forced to the view that Napoleon was simply asking too much of his men. Although they succeeded in driving the 'hideous leopard' (as he called the British) into the sea in 1809, they could prevent neither their return within the year nor the campaigns that would finally take them over the Pyrenees and into France. One has to admire men like Maximilien Foy for sticking to his task for so long, achieving not a single victory over Wellington. The 14 wounds he received were scant reward for such enduring service; yet he was there again at Waterloo, loyal as ever. It was not for want of trying that the French lost the war in the Peninsula, and on their day they were capable of pushing the British to the verge of defeat. One of those days was 16 May 1811, at the battle of Albuera.

The splendid campaign uniform of an officer of the 5e Régiment de Hussards, in blue faced with white and laced gold, over a gold-laced scarlet waistcoat; his pouch belt and sabretasche are of red leather, and his blue overalls are heavily reinforced with black leather. (Musée de l'Empéri; courtesy the late M.Raoul Brunon)

CHAPTER FOUR

Wellington Clears Portugal: 'Handsome Men Biting the Dust'

After a month of waiting in front of the Lines of Torres Vedras, with little prospect of a breakthrough and with supplies beginning to run low, Masséna pulled his army back to Santarem a few miles to the north, in the hope of finding more provisions. But with the onset of winter his situation grew steadily worse. Starvation took a tight grip on his army, while Wellington continued to be supplied through Lisbon; and by early the following spring Masséna - whose losses from sickness and hunger were counted in hundreds every day - was faced with little option but to retreat. On the morning of 5 March 1811 British piquets, peering out from their positions at their opposite numbers, saw a collection of stiff-looking sentries. Closer inspection revealed them to be straw dummies dressed in French uniforms, left behind to 'man' the outposts while the main army retreated north towards the Mondego river.

Wellington's sojourn behind the Lines, following as it did his stand on the Portuguese-Spanish frontier and his subsequent planned withdrawal to the safety of the Lisbon peninsula, has often been quoted as an example of his defensive-minded nature, one of the most oft-cited qualities of this great commander. However, we must understand that he was fighting his war with an army which was outnumbered seven or eight to one by the 350,000-odd French arrayed against the Allied armies in Spain [1]. The vital part played by the Spanish armies and the guerrillas in preventing a fatal concentration against Wellington's little army has already been pointed out. When he did confront one or other of Napoleon's marshals Wellington's strategy was necessarily based upon fighting the French on his own terms, which meant avoiding any general engagement which favoured his adversaries. Hence, when Masséna retreated north, first towards the Mondego and then - when he was prevented by Portuguese militia from reaching the north bank of the river - towards Spain, Wellington's army emerged fit, well-fed and rested to pursue a French army ravaged by hunger and in poor fighting trim. 'Cautious' is how many historians, particularly French ones, like to describe Wellington; 'sensible', 'competent' and 'far-sighted' might be better choices of adjective. In the criticisms sometimes levelled at him it is tempting to detect the frustrated cry of some out-manoeuvred film villian − 'Come out and fight like a man!' But Wellington fought to win.

The retreat by Masséna and pursuit by Wellington led to a series of small but often sharp fights at Pombal, Redinha, Condeixa, Cazal Nova, Foz d'Arouce and Sabugal. Apart from the latter two actions, Marshal Ney, who commanded Masséna's 6th Corps rearguard, conducted the retreat with great skill. At the first three of these engagements he fought effective delaying actions before burning the towns and continuing his retreat. However, at Foz d'Arouce on 15 March he dallied too long on the wrong side of the Cea river.

Wellington launched his attack late in the afternoon when the troops on both sides were looking forward to halting for the night after a day's hard marching. The French, with the river at their backs, were hit by the Allied 3rd and Light Divisions, and when the former pushed back the French left wing those on the right panicked, fearing that their escape route - a single bridge over the river behind them - would be cut. There followed a flight during which scores tried to swim the river but drowned in the process. The retreat was made all the more chaotic when Ney sent back across the bridge a regiment of cavalry which ran into the retreating infantry head on as they attempted to cross it in the other direction. In the confusion at the river the 39th Line lost its prized Eagle, which was found lying in the riverbed by some Portuguese a couple of months afterwards. It was the second Eagle to be plucked from the French by Wellington's army, the first having been taken at Barrosa by Thomas Graham's men on 5 March 1811 (see Chapter Six).

Sabugal

The final action of the retreat came on 3 April at Sabugal, a town situated on the Coa river. This was a severe engagement in every sense of the word, fought in appalling conditions of fog and rain. Wellington hoped that if he could turn the French right and drive them away from the main road that led back to Spain, Masséna would find himself in the bleak mountainous country of the Sierra de Gata. The French army was already in the grip of starvation; if forced in that direction it faced certain destruction. In the event the French, who were commanded at Sabugal by General Reynier, managed to avoid this by a stroke of good fortune. The Allied attack became disjointed and confused when heavy rain and fog descended on the battlefield prior to the action.

The main fighting on the Allied side was done by the Light Division, which, instead of getting around the French left, lost its way in the fog and hit their flank instead. Initially just a single brigade of the division, under Sydney Beckwith of the 95th Rifles, engaged an entire French division, his men struggling to load and fire their muskets and rifles in the rain, until Drummond's brigade also appeared on the scene. George Simmons of the 95th later recalled the action:

'The company I was leading on pounced upon a column, and, owing to the situation of the ground, came literally within twenty yards of it before we could see it. Guess my astonishment! The most hideous yelling assailed my ears (the same in every direction of our line), the French drumming, shaking their bayonets, and calling out "Long life to the Emperor Napoleon." Luckily the ground was thinly patched with stout trees, which afforded our men good shelter in retiring. Nothing could intimidate our brave fellows, retiring and keeping up a hot and destructive fire upon the

Marshal André Masséna, Duc de Rivoli, Prince d'Essling (17581-1817). The commander of the Army of Portugal was Wellington's most difficult opponent, of whom he was moved to say that he could never relax if the veteran French marshal was in the field against him. Greedy for gold and women, this son of an olive oil merchant from Nice had sailed as a cabin boy before enlisting as a common soldier under the Ancien Régime, and after his discharge as a senior NCO is said to have returned to sea as a smuggler. Small, dark and vividly energetic, he had been blinded in one eye in a hunting accident - some said Berthier fired the unlucky shot, but most knew that it was Napoleon himself. He was tenacious and cool in battle; capable of the bold stroke when opportunity offered, he was never rash like Murat or Ney.

forded the Coa to begin its attack the 3rd Division, under Sir Thomas Picton, was supposed to have crossed the river further north, close to the town. Picton, however, refused to move on account of the dense fog. When it began to clear he finally got his men under arms and ordered them to cross; and when the 5th Division launched its attack at Sabugal itself, the fighting turned in Wellington's favour. When the fog lifted it revealed the perilous position of the Light Division; but at the same time it also revealed to the French the massed ranks of Wellington's entire army waiting on the left bank of the river, prompting a hurried retreat by Reynier. The day ended in victory for Wellington, and marked the final failure of the third French invasion of Portugal.

★   ★   ★

The expulsion of the French from Portugal had cost Wellington only a few hundred men. During Masséna's retreat Allied losses totalled just 594 men, with the heaviest, 206 and 162, being sustained at Redinha and Sabugal respectively[3]. The French limped back across the Spanish border on 8 April in a terrible condition. Losses at Sabugal alone totalled 760, and these were from official figures[4]. Before the retreat even began they had starved for months in front of the Lines of Torres Vedras. Their withdrawal was marked by a series of brutal attacks on the local people and by the destruction of several small towns and villages. The ferocity of the beaten French troops during this hungry, sullen retreat in wretched weather was matched only by the vengeance taken by the Portuguese population whenever opportunity offered. Any French stragglers unfortunate enough to fall into their hands alive were put to death, often with horrifying cruelty. The pursuing Allied troops had little difficulty in following the French army; its path was marked by plumes of smoke from burning farmsteads and villages, and a pitiful trail of outraged corpses. This retreat was one of the most terrible episodes of the war.

When Masséna's Army of Portugal finally arrived back in Spain its losses were estimated at around 25,000 men, or 38 per cent of the force with which he had entered Portugal the previous September. He had started out with 65,000 troops and returned with just over 44,000; but, as Oman pointed out, the loss was not simply the difference between these two figures, for the French had received thousands of reinforcements - Drouet d'Erlon's 9th Corps reached him in January. The starkest revelation was that barely 2,000 of these losses were sustained in battle. Some 8,000 were taken prisoner, while hundreds more were killed by Portuguese

enemy's close column so as to annoy then very materially. I now began to think we were always to have ill-luck on the banks of this infernal river [the Light Division had narrowly escaped destruction on the Coa on 24 July 1810], but fortune, under many circumstances, favours the brave ...

'We retired very steadily about fifty yards into a deep valley, the French firing from a great number of cannon, throwing grape and shells, which splintered the trees and naturally killed several men. Finding the enemy did not advance farther, the Colonel formed part of the 43rd Regiment, our little line of skirmishers moving up at the same time and making a desperate attack upon a gun that was keeping up a very destructive fire. Every one near the gun was bayoneted or shot. We were driven back, attacked again, but were again obliged to retire, when luckily the other part of our division moved up, and the gun was ours. Colonel Beckwith on the second attack, had his horse's side pierced by a grape-shot; a bullet hit him slightly on the eyebrow; as he wiped the blood away he called out, "My brave lads, I am no worse; follow me" ...

'This battle was the most trying and glorious I ever beheld ... The carnage on the enemy's side was dreadful; the most handsome men I ever saw were biting the dust ... One French officer came capering on, to show off to his regiment what a fine fellow he was, and actually made a cut from his horse at one of our men, who shot him. Occurrences of this nature frequently happen. One lieutenant of ours had his head dashed to pieces by a cannon shot - a very brave young soldier'[2].

The fighting at Sabugal took the form of a see-saw struggle, with the Light Division driving back the French only to be repulsed again by superior enemy numbers. During the fight the division captured a howitzer, which became the centre of the struggle. When the Light Division initially

irregulars or peasants during the retreat. The remainder succumbed to 'the sword of famine'[5].

The devastating scale of the French defeat in 1810-11 has never really been appreciated. Wellington knew that he still had an immense task in front of him before he could contemplate even an advance into Spain, let alone final victory. Nevertheless, he had cleared the French from Portugal; and although Masséna would still fight one last battle in Spain, the French commander whom Wellington regarded as his greatest adversary would be recalled to Paris soon afterwards. The size of Masséna's defeat was summed up by the present Duke of Wellington in 1986 in *The Lines of Torres Vedras:*

'If in the course of the history of war a battle had taken place in which one side lost 30,000 men and the other a matter of a few hundreds, it would have echoed down the pages of history as the greatest victory ever won. But that, in fact, is the measure of the decisive nature of Masséna's defeat at the Lines of Torres Vedras. He entered Portugal with 65,000 men in 1810, and although he received 10,000 reinforcements at Santarem during the winter the fact remains that he crossed the frontier on his retreat in the spring of 1811 with only 45,000 left ... it was possibly the most decisive victory that Wellington won during the entire Peninsular Campaign'[6].

With Masséna's field army driven from Portugal there remained only the French garrison at Almeida. Wellington's next move clearly had to be the recapture of Almeida, followed by advances against the two powerful Spanish border fortresses of Ciudad Rodrigo and Badajoz, the so-called 'keys of Spain', without the possession of which any advance into that country could not be contemplated[7]. The operation to take Badajoz would lead to two of the bloodiest episodes of the war.

Drawn in 1810 on the Mondego, this St Clair study of a brigade fording a river gives a good impression of the Anglo-Portuguese army on the move. Note in the foreground Portuguese drivers with one of the infamous ox-carts which played a large part in the Allied logistic arrangements, for lack of anything better available locally.

St Clair's study of Portuguese infantry at Penmacor, 18 March 1811. Note at the head of the unit four pioneers, in bearskins and aprons, with tool cases slung on their hips.

CHAPTER FIVE

Fuentes de Oñoro: 'A Dance of Life'

Commanding the northern corridor between Portugal and Spain were the two fortress towns of Almeida and Ciudad Rodrigo. The latter, situated in Spain, was enclosed within originally Moorish walls which had been modernised in keeping with the principles laid down by the great French engineer Vauban. Embrasures had been constructed for guns, parapets raised, and the height and general strength of the walls increased. Outside the walls ravelins had been built – L-shaped outworks which allowed defenders to bring enfilade fire to bear on attackers approaching the walls. There was also a *fausse braie*, a large bank of earth erected in the ditch which encircled the ramparts, dividing it into two concentric ditches, which would confront stormers who reached the top of the glacis – the long, bare, sloping piece of ground outside the ditch. All these features would increase the difficulties and dangers faced by attackers; but they were not enough to make Ciudad Rodrigo secure against a determined enemy. Importantly, the town was overlooked by a long, rounded hill, the Upper Teson, the top of which was some 16 feet higher than the town's walls – a fact which was not lost on the French or Allies when they besieged the place in 1810 and 1812 respectively.

Almeida, on the other hand, was a perfect example of a Vauban-style fortress. It possessed all of the various elements of defence, such as bastions, ravelins and ditches, and was constructed in such a manner as to make life both very difficult and very dangerous for a besieging army. As already noted, Almeida had fallen to the French in August 1810, but only after the powder magazine blew up when a lucky French cannon shot ignited a leaky powder keg. Now, with Almeida representing the last outpost of the French army in Portugal, it was Wellington's turn to lay siege to the place.

When he approached Almeida in April 1811, Wellington did so in the clear knowledge that he was not strong enough to begin a regular siege. He decided instead to blockade the town and hoped to starve it into surrender. Two factors decided this course of action. Firstly, his siege train of heavy artillery had yet to be landed, despite being aboard transport ships for the past few months; and secondly, Soult's investment of Badajoz had caused Wellington to divide his army in two. In March 1811 Beresford was entrusted with taking a sizeable force south to confront the French marshal. One of the main principles of siege warfare was that any commander contemplating a siege of any town or fortress should first possess a force sufficient not only to carry out the siege itself but also to prevent any interference from a relieving hostile army. Beresford's departure south meant that Wellington did not have this ratio of force, and so a blockade was decided upon. Wellington guessed correctly that it would be at least two or three weeks, possibly even longer, before Masséna could rebuild sufficient strength to attempt a relief of Almeida, by which time he hoped to have starved it into surrender. The garrison had already seen its supplies reduced when Masséna's famished army passed through on its way from Portugal into Spain.

On 28 April Wellington arrived before Almeida, having returned from visiting Beresford whose force lay close to Badajoz. He established his headquarters at Villar Formosa, a small village to the west of Fuentes de Oñoro, where he began to receive reports of a gradual build-up of French troops around Ciudad Rodrigo. Ever since 23 April the

A 'French view' of the hovels and alleyways that form the village of Fuentes de Oñoro today, as seen from close to the Dos Cassos stream. On 3 May 1811 the approaches to the village, lined with high stone walls, became death traps for advancing infantry. The defenders from the British light companies simply had to concentrate their fire upon the lanes, until sheer weight of French numbers eventually drove them out of the village. Apart from the evidence of electricity and television, Fuentes de Oñoro cannot look very different here than it did that day.

The Dos Cassos at Fuentes de Oñoro. Successive French battalions plunged through this shallow stream (usually little more than a trickle) to attack the defenders of the village. The walls and houses on the west bank provided superb cover for the defenders, amongst whom were men of the 5/60th; their Baker rifles took a heavy toll of the enemy as they crossed the stream.

French had been testing the Allied piquets along the Azava river, and intelligence indicated that the Army of Portugal, who had regained their strength surprisingly swiftly considering their ordeal the previous month, were preparing for an attempt to relieve Almeida[1]. Masséna had received reinforcements from Marshal Bessières, although these increased his strength to only 48,500. Wellington could muster only 37,500 men; but their morale was high after the successful campaign of March and early April, and in addition Wellington had 48 guns - ten more than Masséna could field. Although the Allies were outnumbered, therefore, it would demand a great effort from the French to brush them aside and break through to relieve Almeida. In the event, they came very close.

At the time of the Peninsular War the main road from Spain into Portugal ran past Ciudad Rodrigo before turning slightly west-north-west through Marialva, Gallegos, Aldea del Obispo, Fort Concepcion, Val de Mula and finally, Almeida. Fuentes de Oñoro lies about eleven miles to the south-east of Almeida as the crow flies. The road to the village - a small, miserable collection of old stone hovels - was a smaller secondary road in 1811, running from Ciudad Rodrigo and Espeja. It was along this road that Masséna's army approached Fuentes de Oñoro on 3 May 1811.

Wellington had drawn up his army along a twelve-mile front, stretching from Fort Concepcion in the north to Nave de Haver in the south. The distance from Fort Concepcion to Fuentes de Oñoro is about eight miles, although a very steep cliff runs for about two-thirds of this sector, preventing any serious enemy attacks and rendering it possible to defend the northern 'half' of the battlefield with just two of Wellington's six divisions. Fuentes de Oñoro itself formed what might be termed the centre of the line, with the remaining four Allied divisions immediately behind the village.

To the south, at a distance of three miles, lay the tiny village of Poço Velho; and a further two miles to the south was Nave de Haver, held by Don Julian Sanchez's Spanish guerrillas. This marked the southern end of the battlefield. The whole Allied front was covered by a river, the Dos Cassos, which, although deep in some places, was no more than a shallow stream in others; it certainly proved no great obstacle to Masséna.

Masséna's plan was quite simple. He needed to bring enough pressure to bear against the Allied right and centre to induce Wellington to bring either Campbell or Erskine, whose divisions effectively covered Almeida, south to support him. Thus the road to Almeida would be uncovered and the waiting French convoy able to pass through to resupply the place. It was a sound enough plan, but it would take an immense effort for it to succeed. After all, the French had failed to shift Wellington from several defensive positions and battlefields so far in this war.

Conversely, the position at Fuentes de Oñoro was not a particularly strong one; there was no significant reverse slope, for example, although the low ridge behind the village certainly afforded Wellington's infantry a reasonable amount of cover. The Allied left was protected by the cliffs, while Wellington's immediate front was covered by the village of Fuentes itself, which acted like a bastion against repeated French infantry assaults. The weak point was undoubtedly his right flank, a wide expanse of open ground which was particularly good for cavalry and the manoeuvring of infantry. It was in this sector that the Allied troops would face their toughest test. Wellington had little choice but to make a stand at Fuentes de Oñoro, but he did so with the steep chasm of the Coa river at his back. Any French breakthrough would almost certainly result in a desperate fighting retreat down to the river, which was crossed by only two bridges, at Almeida and Castello Bom.

Early on the morning of 2 May, Masséna advanced with Reynier's 2nd, Loison's 6th and D'Erlon's 9th Corps, and Solignac's division of Junot's 8th Corps. The 2nd Corps marched north along the Marialva road in preparation for the hoped-for move into Almeida, while the remaining divisions continued along the more southerly road directly west in the direction of Fuentes de Oñoro. The following morning Masséna continued his advance, and by the afternoon had begun to deploy his men on the low heights opposite the village. Thus it was that the bulk of the two contending armies were concentrated east and west of the village; it is no surprise, therefore, that the bloodiest fighting would occur there. Around 2,200 men, consisting of the light companies drawn from Wellington's 1st and 3rd Divisions, held the village itself. These included four companies of the 5/60th, all of whom were armed with Baker rifles. Commanding the troops in the village was Lieutenant-Colonel Williams, himself of the 5/60th.

The first day: street fighting

Masséna launched his attack at around 2pm on the afternoon of 3 May, when two brigades of Ferey's division from the 6th Corps marched down from the rising ground to the east of the Dos Cassos to make a frontal assault on the village. They did so under heavy fire, both from Allied artillery and from the light infantry companies, who blazed away from behind stone walls and hedges and from inside the houses themselves. The first brigade (IV, V & VI/26th Line, and a battalion each from the Légion du Midi and Légion Hanovrienne) crossed the river and filtered into the alleys and passages, taking possession of some of the houses, but these were quickly cleared when Williams counter-attacked with his reserves. This was to set the tone for much of the fighting in Fuentes de Oñoro itself, with one side taking possession only to be driven out by the enemy.

No sooner had the first brigade of Ferey's division come stumbling back into French lines than his second brigade was sent in (IV, V & VI/66th Line, IV & VI/82nd Line). Again the French advanced under a rain of lead and with shells exploding among them. Some 2,300 infantrymen came noisily on, cheering and shouting the name of their emperor, and on this occasion they were successful. Williams' men were driven steadily back from the river, through the houses and out of the village. They finally retreated to the church, which was situated on top of the rising ground to the north-west. Williams himself was badly wounded; and while his men rallied, Wellington ordered the 1/71st (Highland Light Infantry), 1/79th (Cameron Highlanders) and 2/24th (2nd Warwickshire) into the fray to retake the village. An anonymous soldier of the 71st recalled the action:

'Colonel Cadogan put himself at our head, saying, "My lads, you have had no provision these last two days; there is plenty in the hollow in front, let us down and divide it." We advanced as quick as we could run and met the light companies retreating as fast as they could. We continued to advance, at double quick time, our firelocks at the trail, our bonnets in our hands. They called to us, "Seventy-First, you will come back quicker than you advance." We soon came full in front of the enemy. The Colonel cries, "Here is food, my lads, cut away." Thrice we waved our bonnets, and thrice we cheered; brought our firelocks to the charge, and forced them back through the town.

'How different the duty of the French officers from ours. They, stimulating the men by their example, the men vocif-

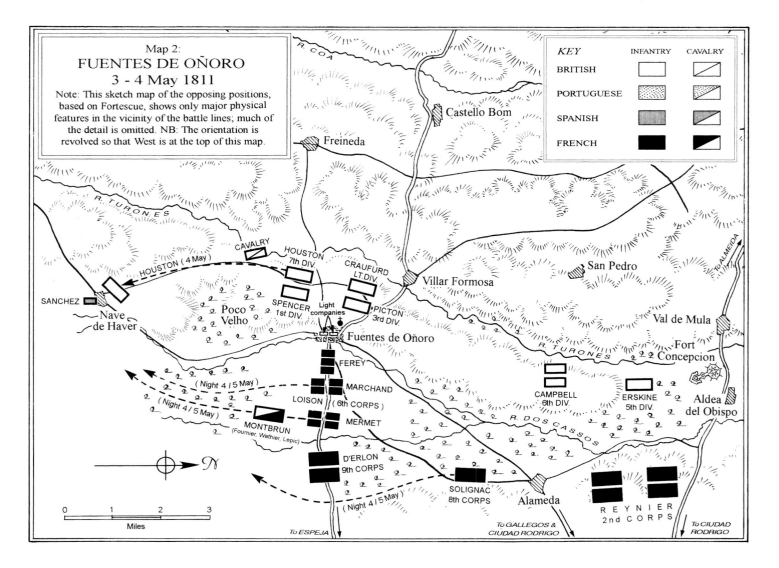

Map 2:
FUENTES DE OÑORO
3 - 4 May 1811
Note: This sketch map of the opposing positions, based on Fortescue, shows only major physical features in the vicinity of the battle lines; much of the detail is omitted. NB: The orientation is revolved so that West is at the top of this map.

A typical alleyway in the village. It was in claustrophobic corners like this that much of the hand-to-hand fighting took place on 3 and 5 May 1811.

erating, each chaffing each until they appear in a fury, shouting, to the points of our bayonets. After the first huzza the British officers, restraining their men, still as death. "Steady, lads, steady," is all you hear, and that in an undertone.

'In this affair my life was most wonderfully preserved. In forcing the French through the town, during our first advance, a bayonet went through between my side and clothes, to my knapsack, which stopped its progress. The Frenchman to whom the bayonet belonged fell, pierced by a musket ball from my rear-rank man. Whilst freeing myself from the bayonet, a ball took off part of my right shoulder wing and killed my rear-rank man, who fell upon me. Narrow as this escape was, I felt no uneasiness; I was become so inured to danger and fatigue'[2].

The three British battalions drove the French through the village at bayonet point, there being little room to manoeuvre in the maze of tiny streets and alleyways. Some of the British troops even crossed the Dos Cassos and for a while fought the French on the eastern side of the river until they were recalled. Soon afterwards a further French attack was made, again by Ferey, this time supported by four fresh battalions from Marchand's division. It met with little success, however, and when night brought a close to the day's fighting there were no French troops on the western side of the Dos Cassos save for the dead, wounded and prisoners.

The second day: truce, music and relaxation

4 May dawned with the two armies still in their positions, facing each other across the Dos Cassas. Apart from a sporadic exchange of fire in the morning there was no real fighting on this day. Instead, parties were sent out from both sides under flags of truce to bury the dead and bring in the wounded – quite a common practice at that date. The lull came as a welcome relief for the men who had fought the previous day and whose efforts had taken their toll. Indeed, our anonymous friend of the 71st, quoted above, discovered that he had fired 107 rounds of ball cartridge, to which his bruised and blackened shoulder bore testimony[3] – the kick of a black powder musket is far less savage than a modern high velocity rifle, but it would only take one careless grip

during those 107 rounds to ensure a memorable bruise.

That 4 May was one of those days when the two sides demonstrated that, when they were not required to kill each other, they were perfectly happy to indulge in their favourite sports and pastimes. The French brought down a few bands of musicians to a level piece of ground between the two armies, while other troops played football or danced to the music[4]. Ensign John Stepney Cowell of the Coldstream Guards, whose diary is full of wonderfully descriptive vignettes, wrote:

'In the cool of the evening a parade took place of the cavalry and infantry of the Imperial Guard. In their rear and on their left flank were considerable woods of cork-trees and of the ilex or southern oak; in front of these our enemy stood out in strong relief and martial array, their bands playing as they passed in review before Marshals Masséna and Bessières. It was a noble sight to behold within our reach these armed men, our nation's foe, surrounded by "all the pomp and circumstance of war" ... On our side we had no reviews; the bands of the German Legion (belonging to our Division) raised their strains in answer to the French, and gave back note for note, as on the morrow we did shot for shot. The moon rose, the bivouac fires were trimmed, the cigar smoked, and our soldiers sank to rest'[5].

The third day: cavalry on the plain

The following day, 5 May, could not have been more different, with some of the bitterest fighting of the entire war. The day began with a shift to the south by Mermet's, Marchand's and Solignac's divisions of the 6th and 8th Corps, supported by Montbrun's cavalry from the 9th Corps reserve. These made a concerted effort against Nave de Haver and Poço Velho, the two small villages on Wellington's right flank. The first of these villages was taken from Julian Sanchez's guerrillas fairly quickly, and the Spaniards were forced to retreat under cover of a few squadrons of the 14th Light Dragoons. The ground here was well suited to cavalry operations, and while Sanchez retired the British cavalry, under Stapleton Cotton – consisting of the 14th and 16th Light Dragoons, 1st Royal Dragoons and 1st Hussars KGL – fought a fine battle with their French

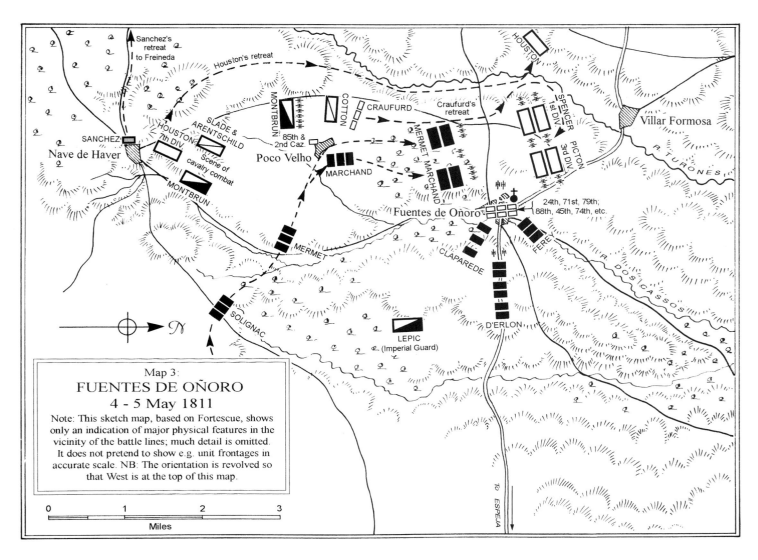

Map 3:
FUENTES DE OÑORO
4 - 5 May 1811
Note: This sketch map, based on Fortescue, shows only an indication of major physical features in the vicinity of the battle lines; much detail is omitted. It does not pretend to show e.g. unit frontages in accurate scale. NB: The orientation is revolved so that West is at the top of this map.

counterparts as they fell back across the plain towards Poço Velho. Indeed, the day was to be one of the most successful of the war for the British cavalry. It was at this point that Captain Norman Ramsay's two guns of Bull's Troop, Royal Horse Artillery, became cut off after the French drove back the British cavalry. In pulling back they were surrounded by French horsemen, forcing them to draw their swords and make a dash through the enemy to reach safety. The episode inspired one of William Napier's greatest passages of prose:

'Men and horses there closed with confusion and tumult towards one point, a thick dust arose, and loud cries, and the sparkling of blades, indicated some extraordinary occurrence. Suddenly the multitude became violently agitated, an English shout pealed high and clear, the mass was rent asunder, and Norman Ramsay burst forth at the head of his battery, his horses breathing fire, stretched like greyhounds along the plain, the guns bounded behind them like things of no weight, and the mounted gunners followed in close career'[6].

Two battalions of General Houston's newly formed 7th Division, which Wellington had sent south the previous day, occupied Poço Velho itself, with the remainder of the division holding some rising ground to the west of the village. While Cotton's cavalry did battle with Montbrun's (the 3rd, 6th, 10th, 11th, 15th and 25th Dragoons), the two divisions of French infantry under Marchand and Mermet (6th Light, 69th Line, 39th and 76th Line; 25th Light, 27th Line, 50th and 59th Line) attacked the village. They drove out the two

battalions from the 7th Division; and these units (the British 85th Regiment and the Portuguese 2nd Cazadores) were badly mauled by French cavalry as they made a desperate run to rejoin the rest of their division. It was only the fire of the Chasseurs Britanniques from the cover of some stone walls on the slope above that checked the progress of the French. (Originally an emigré French royalist unit, the Chasseurs were by now a hard-bitten multi-national 'foreign legion'.)

The Light Division's finest hour

The situation on Wellington's right flank was growing more serious by the minute as Masséna increased the pressure upon it. It was evident that he was trying to force Wellington into shifting his position further south; if he could draw away either or both of the two Allied divisions covering the Almeida road his convoys would get through to the town and the battle would, in effect, be his. However, Wellington was not to be moved. He knew exactly what the French game was and took the decision not to move south, but to refuse his right flank, with the village of Fuentes de Oñoro being the hinge of the new position. The new line faced south and extended from the village itself, to Freneida and on to the Coa. The 7th Division would provide the new 'right flank' close to Freneida.

Wellington would perform a similar operation at Salamanca, just over a year later; but at Fuentes he was risking more by giving up his communications with Portugal via the Coa river at Sabugal. Instead, he left himself just the two small bridges at Castello Bom and Almeida, a retreat across which would be extremely hazardous. But first, he had to deal with the growing threat to the south and to Houston's 7th Division. The resulting manoeuvres would become one of the most famous incidents of the war, and would inspire from the pen of one of its greatest historians, William Napier, some of the most exciting prose in historical literature.

Cotton's cavalry were slowly being driven back, and the 7th Division was in danger of being cut off. (This mixed-nationality formation consisted of Sontag's brigade, with the redcoats of the 2/51st and 85th, the Chasseurs Britanniques, and eight companies of the Brunswick-Oels Jägers – a largely German unit similar in character to the Chasseurs; and Doyle's Portuguese brigade, with the 7th and 19th Line and the 2nd Cazadores.) Just at the moment of crisis, however, Robert Craufurd's Light Division, which had been sent south to extricate the beleaguered 7th, arrived on the scene.

'Black Bob' Craufurd, one of the most controversial characters of the war, had arrived on the battlefield the day before after returning from a period of leave in England. His division of riflemen and light infantry was perhaps the finest in the army – certainly in its own estimation – and had distinguished itself on the Agueda river the previous year. It now consisted of Beckwith's brigade, with the 1/43rd Light Infantry, five companies of the 1/ and 2/95th Rifles, and the 3rd Cazadores; and Drummond's brigade, with the 1/ and 2/52nd LI, four companies of the 1/95th, and the 1st Cazadores.

The 'Light Bobs' were not without their detractors, however, particularly among those officers who had seen little action during the spring and summer of 1810. Instead they

had been forced to wait and watch as the Light Division manned the chain of outposts on the Agueda, shielding Wellington's army from the prying eyes of the French. Indeed, such was the attention which the Light Division attracted during this period, particularly after Craufurd's bungled operations at Villar de Puerco and the Coa river, that one Light Division officer was moved to write: 'Jealousy is a demon which rears its head in all communities and societies, and, I fear, is to be found in military as well as civil life. Amongst a certain number (I hope only a few) of malcontents in the army, the very name of "the Light Division," or "the outposts," was sufficient to turn their ration wine into vinegar, and to spoil their appetite for that day's allowance of beef also'[7]. On their day, however, Craufurd and his Light Division could be dazzling: and 5 May 1811 was one of those days.

When Craufurd arrived to the north of Poço Vehlo he found the 7th Division pulling back. They had been having a desperate time as the French cavalry swept in, cutting at the division's skirmishers as they ran for cover. Craufurd decided that the best course of action was to allow Houston's 7th to continue its retreat while his Light Division covered it, with Cotton's cavalry and Bull's six guns in support. The distance from Poço Vehlo to Fuentes de Oñoro is about three miles and the ground open and rela-

The famous dash by Norman Ramsay's horse artillery section to escape the hordes of French cavalry who swirled around him; this painting by Wollen captures superbly the spirit of the charge. Wellington famously placed this popular officer under arrest after the battle of Vittoria for allegedly moving without orders, thus causing much ill-feeling in the army. Ramsay's career ended on 18 June 1815 when he was killed at Waterloo.

Reconstruction by Gerry Embleton of a private of the 1/43rd (Monmouthshire) Light Infantry, one of the units of Beckwith's brigade of the Light Division which manoeuvred so brilliantly on 5 May. This man carries a New Land Pattern musket, as first issued to the 43rd and 52nd the year before. It differed from the India Pattern in having a simple notched backsight, and a scrolled trigger guard which gave some improvement in grip; the barrel was browned to dull reflections. While creating the training standards for the new light infantry at Shorncliffe Camp, Sir John Moore had achieved five shots a minute. While this remarkable rate of fire can seldom have been achievable in battle, the Light Division did pride themselves on the speed of their musketry.

tively easy for infantry movement. However, that fact also favoured the enemy cavalry; and it was an extremely dangerous operation to retreat on foot across such an expanse of open ground in the face of the overwhelming numbers of French troops opposed to him. Craufurd formed his men into seven squares and, with Bull's horse artillery and Cotton's cavalry supporting him, began the slow and very delicate business of retreating north to the higher ground behind Fuentes.

The French cavalry swarmed around the moving squares, waiting to pounce at the first sign of any disorder, but the opportunity never arose. Whenever Montbrun's dragoons got too close the squares halted; Bull's guns unlimbered, loosed off a few shots and then moved on, having won a few moments' respite. Meanwhile Cotton's cavalry performed prodigies, making several successful charges to prevent the French cavalry from getting too close to Craufurd's men, and the horse artillery from firing on the squares when they were halted. 'Many times Montbrun made as if he would storm the light division squares', wrote William Napier, himself an eyewitness, 'and although the latter were too formidable to be meddled with, there was not, during the war, a more dangerous hour for England'[8].

The Light Division now rose to the occasion and demonstrated why it regarded itself as 'The' Division. As one of Wellington's biographers later wrote, in a wonderfully descriptive piece: 'Now followed under the eyes of the admiring Commander-in-Chief one of the most polished displays in military history. Surrounded by swirling eddies of French dragoons, Craufurd covered the retreat of the 7th with a series of rhythmical evolutions which transformed the deadly orthodoxy of Hyde Park reviews into a dance of life'[9]. The historian of the British Army, Sir John Fortescue, delivered his own verdict on what he called 'the supreme trial of retirement'. He wrote: 'No more masterly manoeuvre is recorded of any general; no grander example of triumphant discipline is recorded of any regiments in the history of the British Army'[10].

The Light Division eventually rejoined the main Allied position with a loss of just 43 men, which speaks volumes for its discipline. Having completed its retreat the division took up a position in rear of the 1st and 3rd Divisions, slightly to the north-west of Fuentes de Oñoro. Evidence of just how closely the French cavalry had pursued Craufurd came in the form of around a hundred casualties among the two battalions of Foot Guards from Spencer's 1st Division - the 1st/Coldstream and 1st/3rd - whose skirmishers were caught in the open by the French as they covered Craufurd's coming in. The Guards formed themselves into a makeshift square until they were relieved from their

ordeal by a charge of the 1st Royal Dragoons and 14th Light Dragoons.

The last act: bayonets in the alleys

Even before Craufurd and his men could congratulate themselves on a job well done, the French had renewed their attacks. Instead of trying to force the right of Wellington's new south-facing line, Masséna continued to hurl his men against the village itself; whoever held it could take either the Allied battleline, or its attackers, in enfilade. These new assaults saw some ten battalions of infantry from Ferey's division (26th, 66th, 82nd Line, Légion du Midi, and the German Légion Hanovrienne) sweep across the Dos Cassos under heavy fire from the defenders. The attackers swarmed into the streets, driving back the men of the 71st and 79th in savage hand-to-hand fighting, with every house and hovel being disputed. 'Down they came,' wrote the soldier of the 71st, 'shouting as usual ... Their stature was superior to ours; most of us were young. We looked like boys; they like savages ... A French dragoon, who was dealing death around, forced his way up to near where I stood. Every moment I expected to be cut down. My piece was empty; there was not a moment to lose. I got a stab at him, beneath the ribs, upwards; he gave back a stroke, before he fell, and cut the stock of my musket in two. Thus I stood unarmed. I soon got another and fell to work again'[11].

During the fighting two companies of the 79th Highlanders were cut off and forced to surrender after they had barricaded themselves into some buildings. Elsewhere, other small groups of soldiers on both sides were wiped out at bayonet point after having got themselves trapped in the maze of alleyways. This phase of the fighting ended with the French holding the lower part of the village close to the river, and the Allies still in control of the upper part.

Masséna had not reached the end of his resources yet, however. A further three battalions, composed of 18 massed grenadier and carabinier companies drawn from the units of D'Erlon's 9th Corps, were thrown into the corpse-choked streets of the village (21st and 28th Light, 40th, 54th, 63rd, 64th, 88th, 100th and 103rd Line; 9th, 16th and 27th Light; 8th, 24th, 45th, 94th, 95th and 96th Line). These elite infantry, set apart by their tall bearskins and red plumes, attacked and drove the defenders back as far as the church situated at the top of the slope overlooking the lower village. The church was in fact separated from the rest of the village by some open ground, dissected by stone walls that afforded good cover for both sides. The 71st and 79th, reinforced by the 24th, again counter-attacked, driving the French back down towards the Dos Cassos; but, reforming, D'Erlon's elite companies surged back up the slope, once more driving the Allies to the church. Wellington himself had taken up a position not far from the church, and for a while he took personal control, feeding in reserves from the 1st and 3rd Divisions. These were hanging on precariously to the ground about the church and to some rocks above it when D'Erlon decided that one final assault should sweep the Allies from the village once and for all.

The old road from Nave de Haver to Poço Velho, looking north towards the latter. It was here, on Wellington's right flank, that Masséna began the turning movement by which he hoped Wellington would be forced to bring the troops which were covering Almeida south to stiffen the Allied line. This open ground was the scene of the repeated clashes between Cotton's and Montbrun's cavalry on 5 May. Cotton's command consisted of the brigades of Slade (1st Dragons, 14th Light Dragoons) and Arentschild (16th Light Dragoons, 1st Hussars KGL).

This is the ground over which Craufurd's Light Division manoeuvred (here, from right to left) during its retirement from Poço Velho on 5 May - for three miles, in the face of constant French cavalry and artillery attacks, and without suffering more than light casualties. The ground is not all as completely open as this photograph might suggest, however; it is intersected in places with low stone walls and is dotted with cork and olive trees.

While the struggle continued between French and Allied troops at the top of the village, as many as ten battalions from Clausel's and Claparede's divisions formed up on the right bank of the Dos Cassos for what they hoped would be the decisive assault. The French columns, or rather masses, picked their way through the ghastly streets of Fuentes de Oñoro before advancing across the broken ground to the west of the village between the houses and the church. As they did so they were lashed by a hail of musketry and canister shot but, undeterred, they fought their way up to the church and drove the defenders from the building and the surrounding ground, until finally they were able to begin establishing themselves on the rocky plateau. Despite a prolonged and desperate defence the outnumbered Allied battalions had been bested.

This was probably the most crucial fulcrum of the battle. Wellington had to drive the French back, or face a potentially disastrous retreat to the Coa river under relentless enemy pressure - the kind of scenario in which armies are not merely defeated, but destroyed. Watching the action taking place below him was William Grattan of the 88th (Connaught Rangers), of which two battalions served with Picton's 3rd Division:

'Wallace with his regiment, the [1st Bn] 88th, was in reserve on the high ground which overlooked the churchyard, and he was attentively looking on at the combat which raged below, when Sir Edward Pakenham galloped up to him, and said, "Do you see that, Wallace?" - "I do," replied the Colonel, "and I would rather drive the French out of the town than cover a retreat across the Coa." - "Perhaps," said Sir Edward, "his lordship don't think it tenable." Wallace answering said, "I shall take it with my regiment, and keep it too." - "Will you?" was the reply; "I'll go and tell Lord Wellington so; see, here he comes." In a moment or two Pakenham returned at a gallop, and, waving his hat, called out, "He says you may go - come along Wallace"[12].

The counter-attack by the 1/88th, a regiment of real Irish beserkers, was delivered with precision, with Mackinnon (the brigade commander), Pakenham and Wallace at its head. Initially the French stood fast, the 9th Light Infantry from Conroux's division in particular fighting with great gallantry; but such was the fury and determination of the 88th to drive back the French that nothing could stop them. With the 45th (1st Nottinghamshire) in support, the men of the 88th, fighting alongside the 74th (Argyle), charged their bayonets and began to get amongst the enemy, driving them back slowly but surely towards the houses at the bottom of the slope. This was one of the few occasions during the war - apart from assaults on the breaches of walled fortresses and towns - when real bayonet fighting took place on any scale.

The experience must have been horrendous, with young, frightened soldiers and veterans alike struggling to find their way through the labyrinth of narrow streets. At one point, it is said that about a hundred French grenadiers dashed down an alley only to find it blocked at the end. As the awful realisation of their predicament dawned upon them, the 88th arrived, maddened by the fury of the fighting. There was no escape as the Connaught Rangers went about their deadly work with the bayonet. It must have been truly terrible for those at the back of the French group, who would have been able to do nothing but watch and listen as their comrades in front of them perished one by one, until

Robert 'Black Bob' Craufurd (1764-1812), one of the most charismatic officers in Wellington's army, who commanded the Light Brigade and later the Light Division from 1808 until his death at Ciudad Rodrigo in 1812. He was a martinet, and his methods were regarded with less than enthusiasm by some of his officers and men; but his corpse was borne to the grave on the shoulders of six battle-hardened veterans, all of them weeping unashamedly. One of his greatest exploits was his leadership of his division on its epic march across the plain from Poço Velho to the high ground above Fuentes de Oñoro on 5 May, moving between the French and Houston's 7th Division retreating west of him.

their own turn came to feel the temper of the 88th's bayonets.

'Mistakes of this kind will sometimes occur,' wrote William Grattan, 'and when they do, the result is easily imagined; troops advancing to assault a town, uncertain of success, or flushed with victory, have no great time to deliberate as to what they will do; the thing is generally done in half the time the deliberation would occupy. In the present instance, every man was put to death'[13].

With the defeat of D'Erlon's last assault on the village the battle effectively ended in a victory, albeit a close one, for Wellington, who later said that if 'Boney' had been there in person the Allies would have been defeated. Some skirmishing continued during the afternoon of 5 May, but the real fighting was over by about 2pm. During the late afternoon and evening flags of truce were sent forward by both sides, which allowed the wounded to be brought in and the dead to be buried. Telling the one from the other must have involved a nightmare process of picking apart bloody heaps

British infantry under attack from French cavalry at the battle of Fuentes de Oñoro, 5 May 1811.

This superb painting by Major Thomas St Clair shows (centre background) Norman Ramsay's RHA troop making their desperate dash through enemy cavalry; (right) wounded being treated, and (centre) one being carried off the field on a comrade's back, while the squad bring in two French officer prisoners; and (left) a light dragoon orderly waiting close to Wellington, while an ADC doffs his hat and speeds off with an order. The picture accurately shows the terrain over which the battle was fought.

of bodies tangled together in the houses and passages.

It was during such episodes that the officers and men demonstrated that strange ability to switch off from the fighting and become human again. Three days after the battle John Mills of the Coldstream Guards wrote to his mother: 'I had some conversation yesterday with some French officers who came out to me as I was employed in burying the dead. They were extremely polite, talked much of their own cavalry, and lamented their being obliged to leave Salamanca, where they said the women were so beautiful'[14]. Elsewhere, burial parties got on with their grim job, cheered only by the opportunies it offered to rob the dead of anything useful or valuable, while other groups from each battalion went around collecting discarded weapons and other items of equipment.

Fuentes de Oñoro was a costly battle for Masséna; he lost 2,844 men, all but 652 of those falling on 5 May. Wellington himself did not get off lightly, losing 1,804 men; nearly 700

of the total were from Spencer's 1st Division, principally the 71st and 79th, who had borne the early brunt of the street fighting.

He did not know it at the time, but André Masséna had fought his last battle in Spain. It was not because his attempt to relieve Almeida had failed; even as he was fighting Wellington at Fuentes de Oñoro, General Foy was on his way to Ciudad Rodrigo bearing a despatch from Napoleon relieving him of command of the Army of Portugal. His dismissal can have come as little surprise; he knew his master well, and was said to be the most cynical man in France second only to the infamous Talleyrand. An incorrigible looter and lecher, Masséna now went home to a quiet job and the enjoyment of his hobbies; and during the Hundred Days in 1815 his brilliant prevarication spared him from taking sides until Waterloo solved his dilemma. Wellington met him after the First Abdication, and paid him the pretty compliment of saying that Masséna had given him sleepless nights. Now the Allied commander-in-chief would face Marshal Auguste Marmont, a well-educated artillery-man but a weaker character with less personal experience of the bloody realities of close combat.

In the meantime, both armies remained in their positions facing each other across the Dos Cassos at Fuentes de Oñoro until, on 10 May, Masséna finally withdrew his forces towards Ciudad Rodrigo. It must be remembered that the battle of Fuentes de Oñoro was essentially an attempt by Masséna to relieve Almeida. The battle to prevent this had been an extremely close call for Wellington; and we can therefore well imagine his wrath when, during the night of 10-11 May, Brennier, the French garrison commander at Almeida, blew up the defences before leading his men through the Allied troops blockading the town, and across the Agueda to the safety of the French lines. It was a failure which Wellington later claimed had turned his victory at Fuentes into a defeat: 'I think the escape of the garrison of Almeida is the most disgraceful military event that has yet occurred to us,' he wrote to Beresford[15]. So enraged was he that he was moved to write two despatches to Lord Liverpool, the second of which he began by saying that he had never 'been so much distressed by any military event as by the escape of even a man of them'[16]. It was, in truth, a bad business, although Wellington could console himself at having taken Almeida without having to lay siege to it.

Having secured the Portuguese end of the northern corridor into Spain, and with the French driven from Portugal, Wellington could feel relatively comfortable in the north. Events in the south, however, were only just coming to the boil. We must leave Wellington, therefore, in order to join the Allied forces in southern Spain, and to examine the events that would lead to the bloody battle of Albuera.

Riflemen skirmishing in the Peninsula. This painting by Dighton is one of the best of all his Peninsular War studies; while it does not purport to show an actual incident, it does portray with remarkable accuracy the sort of skirmishing in which British riflemen engaged. The Baker rifle and its early pattern sword-bayonet are accurate, and so are the uniforms; note the long-tailed coat of the mounted officer, and the fact that the riflemen are wearing standard grey campaign trousers rather than regimental green. Set in convincing terrain, this group of figures make a very believable scene.

CHAPTER SIX

Barrosa: The First Eagle

Any study of the Peninsular War understandably focuses on the operations of Wellington and his field army. This means that other theatres of operations – such as the east coast, the guerrilla war in Navarre, and the war in Andalusia – often attract scant attention. The problem is usually one of how to integrate the story of what we might term the 'peripheral' operations with those carried out by Wellington himself. For example, how did the war on Spain's eastern coast affect the operations of the Anglo-Portuguese army? In truth, it did not, save for the fact that it tied down thousands of French troops who might otherwise have been employed against Wellington. The problem is not as acute, however, when we address the war in Andalusia, for it is an integral part of the Allied operations and, particularly, of the Albuera campaign.

The French had been present in Andalusia since the very first days of the war. Indeed, it was at Baylen, a minor town in the province, that Dupont's catastrophic defeat took place in the summer of 1808. Barely a month after the ragged remains of Sir John Moore's army had arrived home in January 1809 following its traumatic retreat, British politi-

cians were making plans to place a garrison in Cadiz, having appreciated the great significance of this very defensible city as a strategic port. That Britain should turn a thoughtful eye on Cadiz was nothing startlingly new; she had appreciated its importance since the days of Sir Francis Drake. But now, rather than making plans to attack it, Britain was considering garrisoning the place in order to stop it falling into the hands of the enemy. Plans were also made to send a force to Seville, the provincial capital. However, none of these schemes materialised at the time.

It came as no surprise, therefore, that King Joseph – Napoleon's unhappy brother, and his puppet on the Spanish throne – launched an invasion of Andalusia in January 1810. Seville surrendered to the king on 31 January; but when Marshal Victor approached Cadiz the following month his engineers discovered that taking the place by siege would not be as easy as they had first thought. Indeed, the blockade of Cadiz would be prosecuted unsuccessfully by the French for two and a half years, until Soult abandoned Andalusia in August 1812 - yet another example of the way in which French resources were drained by prolonged and often useless operations. It is not that the capture of Cadiz would have brought them a worthless prize - far from it; it is the fact that, after the first few months, one would have expected the French to cut their losses and seal off the drain on men and supplies which could have been far better employed elsewhere in the Peninsula. Just as Wellington's army was supplied by the Royal Navy through Lisbon during its winter within the Lines of Torres Vedras, so the garrison of Cadiz was inserted, supplied, reinforced and kept in consant communication with the outside world by sea.

Cadiz

Cadiz was, in the words of Sir Charles Oman, 'one of the strongest places in the world'[1]. This was not so much due to strong walls as to its unusual geographical location. Cadiz is situated on the end of a long spit of land jutting out into the Atlantic from the Isla de Leon, a triangular-shaped area, which in turn was separated from mainland Spain by the Rio de Santi Petri and, beyond that, by an extensive salt marsh. This made it impossible to conduct regular siege operations. Furthermore, the Rio de Santi Petri was crossed by only one bridge, at Zuazo. Needless to say, Spanish gun

Sir Thomas Graham, later Viscount Lynedoch (1748-1843). Outraged when French Revolutionary Guards desecrated the coffin of his young wife, who died whilst on holiday in France in 1792, Graham raised a regiment at his own expense to fight the French. He became one of Wellington's trusted lieutenants, although ill health forced him to return to Britain for long periods during the war. The victor of the battle of Barrosa on 5 March 1811, he would later became the moving force behind the conception of the United Services Club.

Cadiz today; the object of French designs in 1810 and 1811, the city was highly defensible, surrounded as it is by sea on all sides save for a long spit of land that juts out from the mainland. It was from here that the expeditionary force led by Thomas Graham and Manuel de la Peña sailed for Tarifa in February 1811 prior to the battle of Barrosa.

batteries covered this important approach, as they did other sectors along the river. The only real prospect of French success lay in assault from the sea, and this flank was secured not only by Spanish gunboats but also by the Royal Navy. The capture of Cadiz by the French was, therefore, an almost impossible task. Their cause was not helped by continual requests to Soult from Masséna throughout 1810 for reinforcements for the Army of Portugal.

The problem reached crisis point when Soult invaded Estremadura in January 1811 and turned his attention to the siege of Badajoz. Having despatched reinforcements to Masséna, Soult in turn stripped around 10,000 troops from the French force under Victor that was besieging Cadiz. This left Victor with a serious problem; he had to maintain a force strong enough not only to man the siege lines around Cadiz, but also to prevent interference from any approaching enemy army. The nearest French troops were at Granada and Malaga, some way off. In the event of either a strong sortie from the garrison of Cadiz or an attack by a seaborne force landed in his rear, Victor's 15,000 troops would find themselves seriously stretched.

The significance of the withdrawal of reinforcements for Soult's expedition into Estremadura was not lost on the authorities in Cadiz, who decided that the time was right for an attack upon Victor. Initially, it was proposed that a major frontal attack be launched against the French siege lines. However, after discussions with Major-General Thomas Graham, commanding the British troops in Cadiz, it was decided instead to sail a combined British and Spanish force under the command of General Manuel de la Peña to Tarifa, where they would disembark before marching north to fall upon the French rear. At the same time, 4,000 Spanish troops would make a sortie from Cadiz itself.

La Peña's expedition

General Graham's British contingent consisted of two brigades. Wheatley's brigade had the battalion companies of the 1/28th (North Gloucestershire), the 2/67th (South Hampshire), 2/87th (Prince of Wales's Irish) and two companies of the 20th Portuguese Line - 1,764 men in all. Dilkes's brigade consisted of the 2/1st Foot Guards, a com-

posite battalion of two companies each from the 2/Coldstream and 2/3rd Foot Guards, and two companies of the 2/95th Rifles - a total of 1,361 all ranks. In addition there were two so-called 'flank' battalions. The first consisted of the light infantry and grenadier companies from the 1/9th (East Norfolk), 1/28th and 2/82nd (Prince of Wales's Volunteers); commanded by Colonel Browne, it numbered 536 men. The other 'flank' battalion totalled 644 men under Colonel Barnard, and consisted of two companies of the 2/47th (Lancashire) and four companies of the 3/95th Rifles. Graham also had the services of two squadrons of the 2nd Hussars of the King's German Legion, and two companies of artillery.

Thomas Graham (later Viscount Lynedoch) was one of the most charismatic officers in Wellington's army, and at 62 years of age he was certainly one of the oldest. His young and beautiful wife - the subject of a famous Gainsborough portrait - had died in 1792 while they were travelling on the Continent; and while the heartbroken Graham was taking her body back to Scotland, French Revolutionary Guards broke open her coffin on the pretext of looking for smuggled arms. This desecration so enraged Graham that he personally raised a regiment, the 90th (Perthshire Volunteers), to fight against the French. Graham saw much service between 1794 and 1808, when he arrived in the Peninsula with Sir John Moore, having served with him in Sweden. Graham subsequently served with great distinction under Wellington, and was one of the few subordinates whom the commander-in-chief ever trusted to act in independent command of detached forces. His career was plagued by ill health, however, and he suffered serious problems with his eyes. Nevertheless, when the expedition to Tarifa was conceived this elderly Scottish general was in the best of spirits and eager to get to grips again with the hated enemy.

Graham's force, numbering around 5,000, set sail from Cadiz on 21 February 1811, but bad weather prevented it from landing at Tarifa. The fleet was forced to continue on to Algeciras, a few miles further along the coast, where it disembarked on 23 February. The 10,000-strong Spanish contingent, under Manuel de la Peña, landed five days later. Co-operation between British and Spanish forces was often

A rare contemporary painting of an officer of the 88th Regiment (Connaught Rangers), 1810. This, and the other naïf paintings reproduced here, are part of a set done by Antonio Pereira Pacheco, who found himself at Cadiz in 1810 whilst waiting for a ship to carry him from Tenerife to Peru. The painting shows quite clearly the regiment's yellow facings. The sword is inaccurately painted and the shako is somewhat odd, but overall it is a fairly good representation of a Peninsular War officer. The short jacket and shako are anachronistic for this date, unless he belongs to the light company, which might also explain the curved sabre.

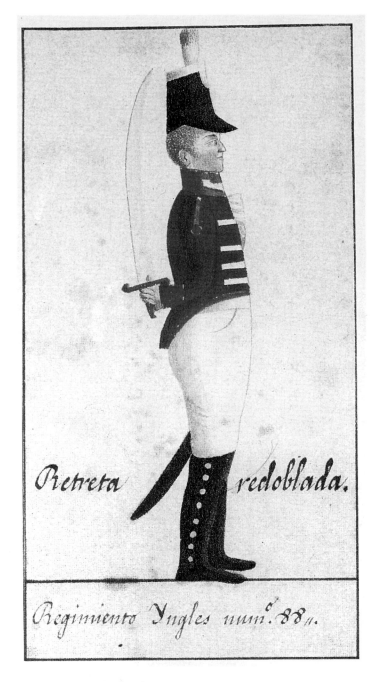

difficult at best, and only showed signs of real improvement in 1813. The 1809 Talavera campaign had set the early tone for the relationship between British and Spanish army staffs, which could only be described as unhappy by even the most sympathetic observer. Barrosa witnessed an equally difficult liaison, hampered by prickly pride on both sides.

The advance towards Cadiz began on 1 March. Two routes lay open to La Peña, each of which had its own particular advantages. The first was along the north-westerly road towards Cadiz, running close to the coast and by far the most direct route. It was also more suited to the transport of wagons, guns and other wheeled vehicles. The other, more easterly route would bring the Allies to the town of Medina Sedonia, whose occupation would not only bring them into Victor's rear but would threaten his communications with the Spanish interior. Indeed, with Medina Sedonia in enemy hands Victor would effectively be penned in against the sea, and would be forced to strip men from his siege lines in order to come out and fight the Allies. This in turn would allow the defenders of Cadiz to emerge and attack while the French lines were in a considerably weakened state.

La Peña initially appreciated the situation and duly ordered an advance upon Medina Sedonia. On 2 March, however, when he had gone only half way towards the town, his advance guards discovered two companies of French infantry at an isolated house called the Casas Viejas. At first La Peña suggested that it would be best to leave them alone and continue the march, whereupon Graham demanded that they be dealt with. The light company of the 1/28th (North Gloucestershire) from Browne's flank battalion was duly sent to flush them out; in the event the French fled before the British infantry could get to grips with them, and it was left to some German and Spanish cavalry to finish them off, killing or wounding virtually all of them. Several prisoners were taken, however, and from these it was learned that the small French force was actually the vanguard of a much larger one, numbering 3,000 men, under the command of General Cassagne.

This news only served to confirm the error which Victor had made; after sending Cassagne so far away from the main French position he would have no choice but to march himself to assist him. It was at this point that La Peña, instead of preparing to face Cassagne, decided to detach a small force to observe the French general's movements while he himself led the main Allied force not on towards Medina Sedonia, but back towards Vejer and the coast to pick up the road to Cadiz.

The subsequent march across the flooded plain of La Landa did nothing to improve relations between Graham and La Peña. The Spanish commander insisted on night marches, which were needlessly hazardous and which result-

ed in the troops losing their way. The Spaniards also had great trouble coming to terms with the watercourses which dissected the plain, stopping to remove socks and shoes before wading them, while their officers crossed on the backs of private soldiers. All of this caused delays, until General Graham himself was forced to lead by example by plunging into one particular river to help extricate a gun which had become stuck. Other British troops crossed without any deviation from the route or delay, until the Spaniards were literally shamed into following them. Despite the delays, however, the Allies reached Vejer on 4 March.

By now Victor was aware that the Allies were moving against him. French scouts had detected La Peña's force at Vejer, while Cassagne had reported the presence of a large body of enemy troops heading for Medina Sedonia – this was, of course, La Peña's column before it changed direction for Vejer. Victor also detected signs of activity in front of him, from the garrison of Cadiz. On 2 March Major-

Fagina regu-   lar:

Regimiento Yngles n.º 87.

Pacheco's painting of a drummer of the 87th (Prince of Wales's Irish) Regiment, wearing half boots and brandishing a sword. The drummer's reversed colours - yellow jacket with red facings - are correct, but the shako is definitely copied from a Portuguese model, with a pointed metal lower band. The 87th captured the eagle of the French 8th Line Regiment at Barrosa.

General Zayas, who commanded the garrison in the absence of La Peña, threw a bridge of boats across the Santa Petri river and moved a battalion to the eastern bank protected by a breastwork which the Spaniards had established there.

Victor, certain that he was about to be attacked, decided with commendable spirit not to wait for his enemies to come to him. Firstly he ordered Villatte's division, barely 3,000 strong, to attack Zayas's force and drive it back across the Santa Petri river; and although Villatte failed to capture the bridge of boats he succeeded in clearing the right bank of enemy troops. Having removed the threat to his siege lines from this direction Victor then ordered Villatte to face his division about and prepare to meet La Peña. He then detached the two divisions of Ruffin and Leval, totalling just over 7,000 officers and men, and had them concentrate at Chiclana, about 20 miles south-east of Cadiz. Here they were to wait until La Peña's force arrived.

If all went to plan, La Peña would be drawn in against Villatte, and while he was engaged here both Ruffin and

Leval would fall upon the Allied right flank. Victor was aware that Zayas still had possession of a bridge of boats and that he might attack Villatte's rear, but this was a calculated risk. If this should happen, Villatte was to engage La Peña until the two other French divisions arrived, whereupon he was to withdraw across the Almansa creek, a tributary of the Santa Petri river.

Meanwhile, La Peña was continuing the pattern set over the previous few days - marching by night across country unknown to him and his staff. The march from Vejer, begun on the evening of 4 March, was intended to be in the direction of Conil, which lay about six miles further on along the road to Cadiz. However, when the first grey streaks of light dawned on 5 March it was discovered that the Allies were, in fact, heading in the direction of Chiclana, where both Ruffin and Leval were waiting. After some animated discussion between La Peña, his staff and Graham yet another change of direction was decided upon, this time to the west, in order to pick up the road to Cadiz once more. Graham was exasperated by the whole situation, and committed his thoughts to paper in his journal:

'Soon after it being reported that our columns were misled and were marching on Chiclana instead of keeping nearer the coast, I halted them and galloped on. Found they had followed the Spaniards, and coming up to the head saw the whole staff in the greatest confusion, from the contradictions of the guides. I could not help exclaiming rather improperly, *"Voilà ce que c'est que les marches de nuit"* ["That's what you get for marching at night ..."]. After some further rather ludicrous scenes of distress, several people of the country agreeing that a path to the left led through the heath towards Santa Petri, and that, the country being dry, the guns could move in all directions over the plain, it was agreed that the march should be continued as I had originally recommended, by a flank movement left in front, forming lines of columns, the cavalry and rearguard on the right in first line, and so on. Our columns closed up, and the army proceeded in this way across the extensive heathy plain of Chiclana, making a remarkably pretty field day'[2].

Shortly after daybreak on 5 March, following the fatiguing march, the vanguard of La Peña's Spaniards reached the coast and the hill known locally as the Cerro de Puerco (Boar's Hill), which stood about 160 feet above sea level at the summit of a low ridge. Standing on top of the hill was an old chapel called the Vigia de la Barrosa; a watchtower, the Torre de Barrosa, stood on the seaward side of the road[3]. This was the key to the whole position, as it commanded the coastal road; and it was here, on what would become known as the hill of Barrosa, that the battle would be fought a few hours later. From the hill of Barrosa the coast road ran directly to the bridgehead over the Santa Petri river and the Island of Leon, which was occupied by

Another of Pacheco's paintings, this time of an officer of the 79th (Cameron) Highlanders, complete with tartan kilt and 'diced' hose and band around the bonnet. Although the details of these Highland features obviously baffled Pacheco - as they did nearly all foreign artists - the green jacket facings are correctly shown.

Zayas's men and from which La Peña hoped the garrison would make a sortie via their bridge of boats.

The left flank of the French siege lines facing the bridge-head was anchored upon the coast at another old watch-tower, the Torre Berjema. The right rested upon the road from Barrosa to the Island of Leon. Therefore, the French flanks were protected on the left by the sea and on the right by an extensive marsh and by the Almansa creek. In the rear of the French lines the road forked inland and ran via a ford across the Almansa creek and on to Chiclana. It was here that Ruffin and Leval were waiting.

The Spanish attack
In spite of the fact that the Allies had been on the march for about 16 exhausting hours, La Peña decided to attack Villatte that same morning with five Spanish battalions under General Lardizabal. The two sides were fairly equally matched in numbers, but the superiority of the French troops proved the difference, and Villatte's men saw off the first attacks without much difficulty. However, six more Spanish battalions under the Prince of Anglona were then thrown in; and Zayas chose this moment to cross his bridge of boats across the Santa Petri river once more and attack Villatte's rear. Faced by an attack from both front and rear the French were forced to retire across the ford over the Almansa creek with the loss of around 330 men, the Spaniards suffering a slightly greater number.

The way through to Cadiz was thus opened, and La Peña was naturally delighted with the way things had gone so far; even Thomas Graham, watching from the hill of Barrosa, conceded that it had been 'a well-conducted and successful attack'[4]. But now, just when things were developing in their favour, La Peña made a grave error that almost cost the Allies everything they had so painstakingly gained.

Having thrown Villatte back across the Almansa creek, the Spanish commander ordered Graham to march his troops down from the hill of Barrosa and occupy the posi-tion previously held by the French at Berjema. Given that the hill was the key to the whole position, it is not difficult to imagine Graham's feelings when he received the order. The occupation by the Allies of both Berjema and Barrosa, he argued, gave them a very strong and secure position; it would take a great effort by the French to shift them from it. Furthermore, it was dangerous to concentrate the entire Allied force close to the Santa Petri river, with just a single bridge of boats as the only escape route, when a strong French force was known to be close at hand. Most impor-tant of all, however, was the fact that by moving his entire force here La Peña was forgetting why the Allies had under-taken the campaign in the first place - namely to open a communication with the garrison of Cadiz. Having made such a great effort to open the road, was La Peña about to throw all of his men back into Cadiz once again? It all seemed absurd to Graham.

Fortunately, his warnings were heeded and La Peña agreed to occupy the hill with three battalions of Anglona's

Spaniards and two under Cruz Murgeon, as well as six squadrons of cavalry - including two King's German Legion squadrons - under Colonel Stamford Whittingham. One British battalion, consisting of the flank companies of the 9th, 28th and 82nd under Colonel Browne, also remained behind. As soon as Graham had reached Berjema the rear-guard was to follow and join him there. Having made this somewhat fragile arrangement, Graham reluctantly marched his British troops off into the Chiclana pine forest in the direction of Berjema, with Wheatley's brigade in the lead followed by Dilkes's brigade and Duncan's guns. Major Amos Norcott's two companies of the 2/95th Rifles brought up the rear[5].

Back on the hill of Barrosa, meanwhile, the Allied rear-guard grabbed some well-earned rest after the exhausting marching of the last few days. Many lay down on the slopes of the hill, lulled by the waves of the Atlantic beating in upon the shore in the distance. Whittingham's troopers stood idly about the Torre de Barrosa, which lay almost on the beach itself. But if they thought they were in for a peaceful afternoon they were sadly mistaken, for even as they began to take their ease a large French force was bear-ing down upon them from the east.

Victor strikes back

Victor had in fact been aware of the Allies' movements since early on the morning of 5 March. He had watched, no doubt perplexed, as La Peña's force had first changed direction, had then attacked Villatte, and finally had apparently abandoned the hill of Barrosa - for the Allied troops resting upon it were, by all accounts, hidden from French view. Victor had sent orders to Cassagne the previous day to join him at Chiclana, but upon observing the Allied movements he decided that the opportunity of first taking the hill and then striking at the Allies while they were still strung out on the march was too good to miss. He therefore issued orders to Ruffin and Leval to prepare their relatively fresh troops to march against the Allies. Victor's force moved off in two columns. The first, under Ruffin, consisted of 2,800 men (9th Light, 24th and 96th Line, and two composite grenadier battalions) with six guns; this passed to the east of the Laguna del Puerco, a large, shallow lake, before making a slight detour to its right, eventually heading straight for the chapel which crowned the highest point of the hill of Barrosa. Leval's column had 4,000 men (8th, 45th and 54th Line, and one grenadier battalion) with a further six guns; this approached the ridge directly from the north-east. Two squadrons of the 1st Dragoons, meanwhile, rode off with orders to skirt the south-eastern side of the hill and cut the coastal road which led to Berjema and Cadiz; they were followed by Ruffin's 9th Light Infantry. If all went according to plan, Victor would occupy the hill at Barrosa before attacking the Allies and driving them back against the Santa Petri river.

Graham's column had been winding its way through the pine forest for about half an hour when he received a report that a large column of enemy troops was on the move in the direction of the hill. A patrol from the ever-reliable 2nd Hussars of the King's German Legion, under Lieutenant von Gruben, discovered the French and duly sent a report back to Major Bussche, who commanded the KGL contingent. By the time Graham received the report Von Gruben's men were embroiled in a sharp skirmish, the sounds of which resonated through the pinewoods and caused Graham to bring his column to an abrupt halt.

Back on the hill, meanwhile, things were becoming decidedly precarious for the Allied troops. First of all, the French 1st Dragoons, sent by Victor to skirt the south-eastern side of the hill, galloped in amongst the Spanish troops guarding the baggage train, causing panic. Fortunately Whittingham, along with the KGL cavalry, managed to hold back the French and prevent them, along with the battalion of the 9th Light, from reaching the coast road and passing round the Allied flank. The French infantry had performed wonders in getting to the hill in such a short time, but were thwarted by Whittingham's resilient defence. The French assault had the desired effect, however, of driving the Allies from the hilltop. This was due not so much to the bravery of Victor's men as to the apparent reluctance of the Spanish battalions to fight. No sooner had the dark blue masses appeared before them than they fled down the north-western slopes of the hill and made off in the direction of Berjema and Cadiz, covered by Whittingham's cavalry.

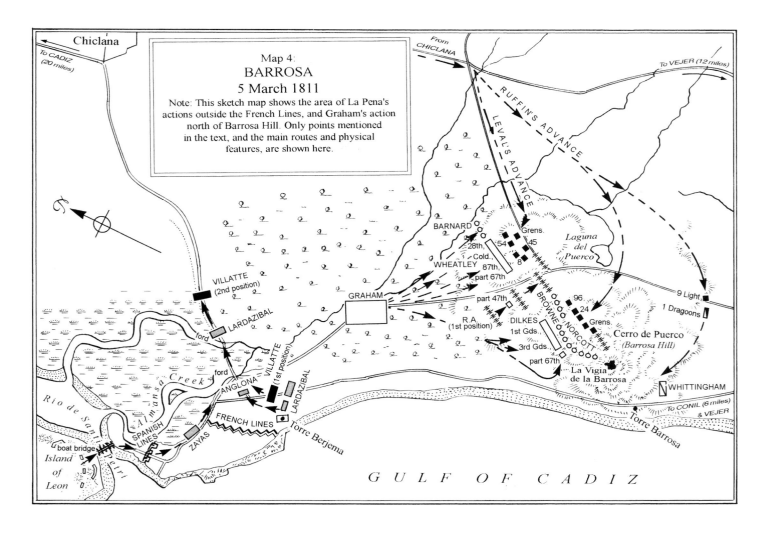

The battle of Barrosa, painted by the officer-artist Baron Lejeune, who served in the Peninsula. This is quite an accurate depiction of the battle, showing the Torre de Barrosa in the left background and Cadiz in the distance. The close-quarter fighting is also accurately shown, although the British troops would have been attacking 'towards the artist' rather than from left to right.

The Torre de Barrosa today, above the beach of the Gulf of Cadiz, with the city just visible in the background. The 2nd Hussars of the King's German Legion fought the French 1st Dragoons close to the tower during the early stages of the battle of Barrosa.

Colonel Browne, along with his six companies of grenadiers and light infantry, was left to fend for himself until, faced with annihilation by Ruffin, he too was forced to retreat[6]. As he did so Ruffin's 1st Dragoons charged, forcing Browne to form square. Fortunately, Bussche's KGL hussars came to their assistance and made several charges, which allowed Browne to gain the relative safety of the woods. As he retreated he no doubt took a backward glance to see hordes of blue-jacketed troops swarming over the slopes of the hill. The key to the entire position was in French hands.

Back in the pinewoods, Graham faced his column about. There was no doubt in the mind of this redoubtable old soldier as to what needed to be done, and when asked what he was going to do he replied simply, 'Fight!' As he rode back to the edge of the woods he could see Ruffin's men gathering in strength on the summit of the hill, while Leval's infantry lapped round its north–eastern edge. There was no sight of the Spaniards; and Browne's men were retreating towards him. Riding up to Browne, Graham apparently exclaimed, 'Did I not give you orders to defend Barrosa hill?' 'Yes, sir,' replied Browne, 'but you would not have me fight the whole French army with 470 men'; wherupon he explained how the Spaniards had run away at the first shot. The French were growing stronger by the minute; Graham needed time to get his men into order, which was no easy task given that his columns were in the depths of a forest. The solution to his problem lay with Browne's battalion of flank companies.

It was not an easy decision to make but it was a necessary and, ultimately, an effective one. Quite simply, Browne had to buy him time with the lives of his men. 'It is a bad business, Browne,' said Graham. 'You must instantly turn round and attack.' Having received this unenviable order Browne rode off to his men and, removing his cocked hat, said simply, 'Gentlemen, I am happy to be the bearer of good news: General Graham has done you the honour of being the first to attack those fellows. Now, follow me, you rascals'[7].

Colonel Browne's forlorn hope

It was indeed a bad business, but it would get far worse unless the British troops acted quickly. Graham's plan was simple. While Browne's flankers returned to engage the French left centre, Dilkes's brigade was ordered to move against Ruffin and Wheatley against Leval. Major Duncan, meanwhile, would get his ten guns forward as quickly as he could to form up in the centre. But if the plan was simple its execution was not, for the woodland restricted movement and visibility. In the confusion of the face-about some of Dilkes's troops mistakenly followed Wheatley's brigade and vice versa, while some of Duncan's guns became completely entangled in the underbrush. It was with no little effort, therefore, that Graham's force finally began to emerge from the pinewoods - much to the consternation of the French, who counted upon an easy afternoon's work. Ahead of the two main brigades four green-clad companies of the 95th, under Andrew Barnard, and two companies of Colonel Bushe's 20th Portuguese threw themselves into skirmishing order and attacked Leval.

Meanwhile, on the lower slopes of Barrosa hill, Browne's composite battalion of flank companies, just over 500 strong, formed into line and advanced slowly up the gentle slope towards Ruffin's division, where eight guns stood primed and ready to receive them. It was one of the most memorable sights of the war, for as he led his men forward, seated upon his horse and with shot and shell flying all round him, Browne broke into his favourite song, 'Hearts of Oak.' As the range closed Ruffin's men and guns opened fire with a tremendous salvo that is said to have dropped over 200 British officers and men at a stroke. Undaunted, the rest of Browne's men continued their stubborn advance, moving up the hill in the face of a hail of lead. Scores more were laid low before Browne finally ordered his men to throw themselves down and take what cover they could

behind bushes or in patches of dead ground. The casualties amongst Browne's flankers totalled around 50 per cent; but their sacrifice had given Graham's two brigades the time they needed to get out of the woods and begin their own advance.

First to emerge from the trees were Norcott's riflemen, who quickly threw themselves into skirmishing order and began moving against Ruffin's left flank. On Norcott's left came Dilkes's brigade, with the 1st Foot Guards on the left and the 3rd Foot Guards slightly to their right rear. In the confusion of the forest the two companies of the Coldstream Guards had followed Wheatley. However, some companies of the 67th (South Hampshire) in turn joined Dilkes's brigade and these followed the 3rd Foot Guards, again slightly to the right rear; thus, Dilkes's brigade could be said to have come on in a sort of echelon formation.

The Foot Guards' attack

Dilkes advanced not against the summit of the hill, crowned by the old chapel, but slightly to the French right of it, where the bulk of Ruffin's infantry were drawn up. Waiting for them were two battalions of the 24th Line, with two provisional battalions of grenadiers and the 96th Line in support. The Foot Guards advanced, slowly but steadily, under a tremendous fire from the French guns, to which Duncan's artillery replied to good effect. These were the proudest redcoats in the British Army, the King's Men, and they were not inclined to let a couple of thousand Frenchmen stand in their way. At last they neared the top of Barrosa ridge with the old chapel away to their right. As they did so, Victor appeared, waving his plumed hat in the air and frantically shouting orders in all directions. As he galloped about the top of the hill the 24th Line, perhaps thinking that the British Foot Guards would not be able to withstand a determined charge, moved down the slope in column to meet the oncoming redcoats. The ensuing firefight halted the French in their tracks, and Ruffin and Victor could only watch in a state of growing anxiety as King George's finest slowly began to edge their way ever upward, forcing the French from their path. In an attempt to stem the advance Victor ordered forward the supporting

A view from the Vigia de la Barrosa looking out over the ground across which Wheatley's brigade advanced - from left to right - against Ruffin. The battlefield is about to disappear (June 2000) beneath a hotel complex; in the background, hotels and golf clubs now cover the site of the pine woods through which Graham returned to meet the French on 5 March 1811.

Although the uniform details are inaccurate (as they are in most later paintings, which usually show British troops in post-1812 shakos), this picture by Granville Baker gives a lively and probably fairly believable impression of British infantry getting to grips with the French at Barrosa.

grenadiers to attack Dilkes's right while the 96th Line moved against his left.

The advance of Ruffin's infantry against the oncoming British provided yet a further example of the superiority of the line over the column. On the slopes of Barrosa hill Dilkes's infantry, around 1,400 strong and formed in line, were able to bring to a halt the French columns of around 2,400 men. The sight of British in line outgunning French columns was nothing new; but the incident was the more striking in that the French were moving down hill with the momentum of the attack firmly in their favour. Added to this was the fact that Dilkes's men had advanced up hill under a terrific fire from Ruffin's artillery. Furthermore, the entire British force had undergone a most fatiguing march from Algeciras over the last few days, whereas the French had enjoyed a relatively easy time at Chiclana. This, perhaps, gives us a valuable insight into the relative morale of the two sides.

Dilkes's infantry began to drive the French up hill in an intense exchange of fire; and the issue was decided when Norcott's riflemen, followed by the companies of the 67th, came swinging round the right flank of Dilkes's line to overlap the French left. Upon seeing this the survivors of Browne's flank companies, who had watched the fight from their cover, suddenly sprang to their feet and formed on Dilkes's left flank. Thus Ruffin's columns were outflanked by a semicircle of British firepower and, assailed from the equivalent of three sides, they suddenly broke and began streaming away to the rear[8]. The Foot Guards reached the top of the hill, cheering and with charged bayonets, and watched as the French fled in some disorder. Both Ruffin and one of his brigadiers, Rousseau, were mortally wounded while attempting to stem the flight from the hill, and were left in the hands of the British[9].

In addition to the 2,400 or so French involved in the main firefight on Barrosa hill there were 599 officers and men of the 9th Light who had been engaged first. Of this total of 3,000 or so French troops involved in the struggle against Dilkes's brigade, no fewer than 36 officers and 840 men were either killed, wounded or taken prisoner; two artillery pieces were also taken. Losses were no lighter in

proportion on the British side. Between them, Dilkes and Browne had attacked with a strength of around 1,900 officers and men, of whom 25 officers and 588 men were either killed or wounded. The only negative aspect of the fight on the British right was the inactivity of Whittingham's cavalry who - apart from the KGL hussars - remained relatively passive, and passed up the opportunity of getting in amongst the fugitives and inflicting greater damage.

Hugh Gough and the 'Faugh-a-Ballaghs'

While Dilkes's brigade was fighting on the French left, Wheatley had gone into action against their right, where Leval's division had deployed on the much lower north-eastern slopes of the ridge. Here another famous episode was to be played out, which resulted in the capture by the British of the first of six Imperial Eagles that they were to take in the Peninsula.

Wheatley's brigade emerged from the pinewoods with the two companies of the Coldstream Guards leading the way, closely followed by Hugh Gough and the 1/87th, the 1/28th and, bringing up the rear, the remaining companies of the 67th, the other wing having gone off with Dilkes's brigade. Once clear of the trees Wheatley formed his 1,400 men into line and prepared to advance against Leval, covered by the three companies of the 3/95th Rifles under Andrew Barnard and the flank companies of the 20th Portuguese under Colonel Bushe. Wheatley's men suffered less from the fire of the French guns as they had less than 300 yards to cover once they debouched from the woods - Dilkes's men had had to cross about 1,000 yards. Like Dilkes, Wheatley benefited enormously from the fire of Duncan's guns, which made great efforts to get forward with the infantry and were eventually firing into the French ranks from as close as 250 yards, protected by two companies of the 2/47th. Once the British line had formed up it comprised, from left to right, the 1/28th, the Coldstream Guards, the 1/87th and 2/67th.

With the main body of Wheatley's brigade formed, the skirmishers of Barnard and Bushe fell back to let them pass and formed up behind them. Like Browne's flankers, they had done their job effectively and had bought time for

Wheatley to deploy his men; and like Browne's men, they had paid a price for it - the 95th suffered 65 killed and wounded, the flankers of the 20th Portuguese over 50 casualties, and both Barnard and Bushe were wounded, the latter mortally.

Opposed to Wheatley was Leval's division - drawn up in columns - with the I/54th Line on the right and on their left the II/54th. On the left of the latter battalion and slightly in front of them were the two battalions of the 8th Line. In reserve were the I/45th along with the remaining provisional battalion of grenadiers. In all, Leval could count upon around 3,800 men to uphold French honour against 2,500 British and Portuguese.

The first British troops to engage the French at close quarters were the 1/87th, confronting the II/8th Line commanded by Vigo-Roussillon. Both sides held their fire until the last moment; then sudden shouts in English and French were heard above the din, and both sides disappeared in a cloud of dirty white smoke as the respective volleys crashed out. Gough's men could have known little of the effect of their fire when they waded into the smoke to get to grips with the enemy. When they did so they found the French reeling backwards after taking the full force of the 87th's volley. The Irishmen had suffered also, but their formation had enabled them to bring three times the number of muskets to bear upon their adversaries.

Like Ruffin's men away on Barrosa hill, Vigo-Roussillon's infantry were not prepared to cross bayonets with the redcoats who now came charging into them. Seeing that his men had reduced the French to a mob, General Graham - leading his men on foot since his horse

had been shot - ordered the infantry to save their powder and attack with the bayonet. Those at the front of the French column could do nothing, hemmed in as they were by those behind; meanwhile those at the back were certainly aware that something unpleasant was happening to their comrades at the front, and began to stream away to the rear. Having discharged their muskets and with nowhere to go, the French front rank men were left with no option but to try to defend themselves as best they could.

It was unfortunate for the II/8th Line that the oncoming troops were from one of the most fearsome units in the British Army, the 87th. Like their brethren of the 88th (Connaught Rangers), the *Faugh-a-Ballaghs* ("Clear the ways") would go on to establish a reputation as one of Wellington's most formidable regiments. As the historian of the British Army so aptly put it, 'They were Irishmen out for a fight'[10]. The 87th cut into the French like tigers, as Gough himself wrote the following day:

'The French waited until we came within 25 paces of them, before they broke, and as they were in column when they did, they could not get away. It was therefore a scene of the most dreadful carnage. I will own to you my weakness. As of course I was in front of the regiment, therefore in the middle of them, I could not, confused and flying as they were, cut one down, although I might have twenty, they seemed so confounded and so frightened. They made, while we were amongst them (about quarter of an hour), little or no opposition.

'We could have taken or destroyed the whole regiment, but at this moment the 47th French regiment came down on our right[11], and General Graham, who was, during the whole of the action, in the midst of it, pointed them out and begged I would call off my men (I will not say 'Halt' as we were in the midst of the French). With the greatest of difficulty by almost cutting them down, I got the right wing collected, with which we came to within about 50 paces of them, they (for us, fortunately) broke and fled, for had they done their duty, fatigued as my men were, at the moment, they must have cut us to pieces. We were, therefore, after they broke, unable to follow them, but took the howitzer attached to them'[12].

Sergeant Masterson's Eagle

In the midst of the chaos, Gough's Irishmen could see the Eagle of the 8th Line held proudly aloft by Sous-lieutenant Guillemain of the I/8th and protected by a strong guard. The British had been seeing these prized birds for the past

'The French Imperial Eagle, Taken by Sergeant Masterman [sic] of the 87th Reg. in the Action at Barrosa, March 5th 1811.' Published as early as May 1811, this is another accurate drawing by Dighton, showing Patrick Masterson shortly after he relieved the 8e Régiment d'Infanterie de Ligne of its standard. Note the 'mosquito' trousers, which are a logical issue to units in the far south; the height of the 'stovepipe' shako; the canteen worn on his right hip and the haversack on his left, with the sword pushed well back and tied down with his sash. The Eagle is correctly shown with a gold wreath round its neck, unique among the eleven Eagles captured by the Allies in Spain; this was presented by the city of Paris to units returning from the victorious campaigns of Austerlitz, Jena and Friedland. (The Eagle was later stolen from the chapel of the Royal Hospital, Chelsea, and has never been recovered. A replica is now displayed in the National Army Museum next door to the Royal Hospital.)

It was somewhere very close to these pine trees, on the sandy hill of Barrosa, that Sergeant Masterson captured his Eagle from Sous-lieutenant Guillemain; he is supposed to have shouted out, 'Bejabbers, boys! I've got the cuckoo!' Lieutenant (later General) Gazan tried to sieze it back, but was wounded in the head. Masterson was rewarded with an ensigncy in the Royal Yorkshire Light Infantry Volunteers, and in later years the 87th (Royal Irish Fusiliers) displayed the Eagle as a badge in various ways.

two and a half years but had yet to bag one of them. Now was as good an opportunity as any, and Ensign Keogh made a dash for it, sword in hand. He actually succeeded in laying a hand on the pole before he was bayoneted twice by its defenders and killed. Then, over the dead body of Keogh, stepped Sergeant Patrick Masterson, who thrust his long sergeant's pike straight into the body of the unfortunate Guillemain. The standard bearer fell to the ground, while his Eagle fell into the grateful hands of Paddy Masterson[13].

The 87th, along with the two companies of Coldstream Guards, had smashed the centre of Leval's division, defeating both battalions of the 8th Line and repulsing the counter-attack by the 45th Line. With the tide turning rapidly against him, Leval ordered forward the two battalions of the 54th Line which had been waiting in reserve. The first battalion of this regiment lay on the extreme right of the French line, and was ably dealt with by Barnard's riflemen and the 20th Portuguese, who drove the French off as they attempted to get round the left flank of the British line. While the I/54th was being driven back, the II/54th advanced against the British 1/28th, who quickly levelled their muskets in anticipation of the order to fire from their commanding officer, Lieutenant-Colonel Charles Belson. Fighting alongside Belson was a young officer, Charles Cadell, who, 24 years later, recalled the fight:

'Colonel Belson then gave orders to fire by platoons from centre to flanks, at the same time "to be sure to fire at their legs and spoil their dancing" – this order was observed for a short time with dreadful effect. The action now became general; twice did we attempt to charge the enemy, who being double our strength (our flank companies being away) only retired a little. Giving three cheers, we charged a third time, and succeeded – the enemy gave way, and fled in every direction ... they had been beaten in every part of the field'[14].

It had been a short but severe battle; but now, after about an hour and a half's fighting, the French were streaming away to the north-east with Ruffin's dragoons covering their retreat. Dilkes's brigade gained the summit and watched, exhausted, as the dark blue masses fell back before them. Away to Dilkes's left Belson and the 28th were firing into the retreating ranks of the enemy to keep them on the move, for they still retained some order. 'There they are, you rascals,' Belson shouted, 'if you don't kill them, they will kill you; so fire away!'[15]. In the centre, meanwhile, the tireless Duncan had got his guns up on to the summit of the ridge and was sending shot and shell into the French as they fell back.

Victor's men were beaten, but they still turned every now and then to fire defiantly back at their British tormentors. Their withdrawal was ably covered by the French 1st Dragoons, who made several effective charges, forcing the 3rd Foot Guards to form square several times. It was at this point that Whittingham failed by not sending his own cav-

alry forward to complete Graham's victory; he might have inflicted severe damage on the retreating French, but instead held his men in check and fumbled the chance. It was Frederick Ponsonby, Graham's aide-de-camp, acting on his own initiative, who eventually brought forward a squadron of the KGL 2nd Hussars to charge the French rearguard.

Victor's troops continued their retreat until they reached Chiclana. The victorious British were too exhausted by their efforts both at Barrosa and during the marches of the previous days and nights to make any effective pursuit. Instead, they halted and returned to the hill of Barrosa to tend to their wounded, before marching to the bridge over the Santa Petri river and from there on to Cadiz. Graham had suffered 1,238 killed and wounded, against a French loss of 2,062. The battle of Barrosa had been a great success for Graham and his men but, not for the first time, relations between the British and Spanish commanders soured what should have been a far more significant victory. After the battle La Peña did nothing but write an overboiled despatch in which he justly claimed credit for defeating Villatte at Berjema, but attempted to pour scorn over Graham's much greater triumph. The results of a successful Spanish pursuit might have brought the blockade of Cadiz to an end, but in the atmosphere after the battle co-operation became impossible. Graham, livid with rage, withdrew into Cadiz with his men, while La Peña contented himself with his small victory. He was known even to his own troops as 'Dona Manuela', implying an old-womanly character, and he certainly lived up to this reputation after Barrosa. As the historian of the British Army put it, 'he gathered his skirts about him on this fateful day, and with quivering anility sat still'[16].

★   ★   ★

The ill-feeling between La Peña and Graham lasted for some time, during which the astonished French gladly took advantage of Allied inactivity to resume their blockade of Cadiz – which they were to prosecute unsuccessfully for a further 17 months. Everything the Allies – and in particular Graham – had worked for was lost in the course of this acrimonious quarrel. It would not be the last time that the two Allies squabbled amongst themselves. Fortunately an even greater and bloodier battle, fought just two months after Barrosa, was to prove that co-operation, while often difficult, was not impossible.

CHAPTER SEVEN

Campo Mayor: 'Undisciplined Ardour'?

Six days after the battle of Barrosa, Marshal Soult captured the fortress of Badajoz, thus strengthening his grip on Estremadura. However, news of Graham's victory caused him to retreat to Seville - the only repercussion of that battle upon French operations, due to the failure of La Peña's and Graham's disunited command to exploit it. As mentioned earlier, the French siege of Badajoz in March 1811 had caused Wellington to send Beresford south with a detached corps; his choice for this independent command was due to the temporary illness of the reliable Rowland Hill. Beresford was given 18,000 troops, mainly the 2nd and 4th Divisions, as well as Hamilton's Portuguese division and the excellent King's German Legion light infantry brigade. Soult's retirement to the south allowed Beresford's force to approach Badajoz without the possibility of facing strong French resistance, or not at least until Soult chose to come forward again to meet him.

Badajoz fell to the French on 11 March, and the news reached Wellington a few days afterwards. However, he saw no reason to countermand his orders to Beresford, who was now faced with the task of laying siege to the place in his turn. But even before Beresford could approach Badajoz he found himself embroiled in one of the greatest controversies of the entire war: the charge of Robert Ballard Long's cavalry at Campo Mayor on 25 March 1811.

Beresford's army approached Campo Mayor on the morning of 25 March. The town is situated just inside the Portuguese border and is about ten miles from Badajoz. It was a weakly defended place, with crumbling fortifications - although its poor defences, stoutly manned by a garrison under Major José Talaya, had kept Marshal Mortier's troops at bay for seven days, between 15 and 21 March, before being obliged to capitulate. The loss of Campo Mayor was not a particularly serious blow to the Allies, as the French had no real intention of defending it. Instead, they were set upon dismantling the works and preventing the Allies from using it as a base during the forthcoming siege of Badajoz, which town occupied all of the French effort and resources. Fortunately for the Allies, Talaya's brave defence of Campo Mayor had bought valuable time for Beresford's advance; his army arrived just four days after its capture by the French, and before General Latour-Maubourg's men had done any real damage to the place. In fact his arrival caught the French unawares, suggesting a distinct lack of vigilance by their cavalry piquets. It was only when Latour-Maubourg

was himself visiting the outposts that Beresford's advance was detected.

The French force numbered around 2,400, including 900 cavalry. With some 15,000 men at his disposal - the 4th Division was marching some way in the rear - Beresford was presented with a wonderful opportunity of capturing the whole, as well as 16 heavy guns that had set off for Badajoz earlier that morning. The consternation in Campo Mayor can well be imagined, with officers hastily trying to form their men, the cavalry attending to their mounts, and commissaries trying to get supplies and wagons collected and started off along the road to Badajoz - all in the knowledge that a strong Allied force was bearing down upon them. Latour-Maubourg hoped to get away before Beresford's force came up, but Beresford quickly grasped the situation. He had with him two cavalry brigades, heavy and light, and he planned to get them forward in order to detain the French column long enough for his infantry and artillery to come up. Then, in theory, it would be a simple matter of mopping up, and counting the French prisoners and booty.

Before Beresford had begun his march south Wellington had given him precise instructions, placing particular stress on the need to keep his cavalry together. 'I recommend to you to keep your troops very much en masse', he wrote. 'I have always considered the cavalry to be the most delicate

Robert Ballard Long (1771-1825) commanded a cavalry brigade in the Peninsula from 1811 to 1813. An argumentative man, he nevertheless voluntarily gave up his command of the Allied cavalry before Albuera to William Lumley in order to avoid it passing to a more senior Spanish officer. Historians such as Oman have tended to malign Long, unjustly portraying him as an incompetent dismissed from command by Beresford.

The northern end of the road from Campo Mayor to Badajoz, as seen from the glacis of the former. The French artillery and baggage train retreated away from the camera towards Badajoz, but were caught by the 13th Light Dragoons who charged over the heights to the left. Beresford, under the impression that the dragoons had been lost, halted the heavy cavalry brigade on the far side of the road, and thus deprived Robert Long of vital support.

arm that we possess. We have few officers who have practical knowledge of the mode of using it, or who have ever seen more than two regiments together; and all our troops, cavalry as well as infantry, are a little inclined to get out of order in battle. To these circumstances add, that the defeat of, or any great loss sustained by, our cavalry, in these open grounds, would be a misfortune amounting almost to a defeat of the whole; and you will see the necessity of keeping the cavalry as much as possible en masse, and in reserve, to be thrown in at the moment when an opportunity may offer of striking a decisive blow'[1].

Nevertheless, in the circumstances of that morning Beresford did indeed divide his cavalry. He despatched Long, with the light horse, away on a wide sweep around Campo Mayor with the intention of cutting the road to Badajoz. The heavy cavalry under De Grey was still coming forward, with the infantry still farther back. A great responsibility was thus placed upon Long.

The charge of the 13th Light Dragoons
No sooner had he arrived at the top of a hill overlooking the road than the French cavalry reacted. The 2nd and 10th Hussars maintained their position on the road, escorting the retreating infantry, while the 26th Dragoons formed for the charge. Long duly formed up his own troopers to meet them, with the two and a half squadrons of the 13th Light Dragoons in the centre, flanked on the left by two squadrons of the Portuguese 7th (Alcantara) Cavalry Regiment under Otway, and on the right by three squadrons of the 1st (Lisbon). Long's orders to the commander of the 13th Light Dragoons were succinct: 'Colonel Head, there's your enemy. Attack him', adding, 'and now, Colonel, the heavy brigade are coming up on your rear, and, if you have an opportunity, give a good account of these fellows.' Head replied simply, 'By gad, sir, I will'[2].

The French 26th Dragoons duly set off towards the 13th Light Dragoons, who had formed in front of the supporting Portuguese cavalry on their flanks before charging down against the approaching lines. The two lines - the British in blue jackets and black leather helmets, the French in green coats and brass helmets - came together in a fearful clash, passing through each other before turning for a second charge, this time leading to a general mêlée in a welter of individual swordplay. It was at such moments that the training methods of John Gaspard Le Marchant paid dividends. He had also designed the fearsome 1796 pattern light cavalry sword, a deadly sabre with a pronounced curve and a cleaver-like edge. French commentators considered that the British cavalry relied far too much on slashing with the edge rather than stabbing with the point, but they conceded that when wielded with skill the British sabre was capable of inflicting terrible, dismembering wounds. (It is interesting to remember that this fight was against adversaries armed with the straight French dragoon sword, wielded by men who had presumably been trained in the importance of the point rather than the edge.) An officer of the 13th described the action in *The Courier* for 20 April 1811:

'The French certainly are fine and brave soldiers, but the superiority of our English horses, and more particularly the superiority of swordsmanship our fellows showed, decided every contest in our favour; it was absolutely like a game at "prison bars", which you must have seen at school ... The whole way across the plain was a succession of individual contests, here and there, as the cavalry dispersed ... it was certainly most beautiful'[3].

It was during this fight that one of the most famous sabre cuts of the war was delivered. If the most celebrated shot was that fired by Tom Plunkett of the 95th Rifles at Cacabelos which killed General Auguste Colbert, then the blow by which Corporal Logan of the 13th Light Dragoons put paid to the career of Colonel Chamourin of the 26th Dragoons at Campo Mayor is probably the most famous exploit with the 'white weapon'. It was an incident that was again witnessed by our correspondent from the 13th Light Dragoons:

'Yesterday, a French Captain of Dragoons brought over a trumpeter, demanding permission to search among the dead for his Colonel; his regiment was a fine one, with bright brass helmets, and black horse hair, exactly like the old Romans are depicted with; the Captain was a fine young man, and had his arm in a sling. Many of us went with him - it was truly a bloody scene, being almost all sabre wounds, the slain were all naked, the peasants having stripped them in the night; it was long before we could find the French

The uniform and green caped riding mantle of an officer of French dragoons; the leopardskin turban on the brass helmet was an officer's distinction – the troopers had cowhide instead. Note also the long, straight sword of dragoon pattern. This is similar to the uniform which would have been worn at Campo Mayor by Col Chamourin of the 26th Dragoons. (Musée de l' Empéri; courtesy the late M. Raoul Brunon)

Colonel – he was lying on his face, his naked body weltering in blood, and as soon as he was turned up, the Officer knew him, he gave a sort of scream, and sprung off his horse, dashed his helmet on the ground, knelt by the body, took the bloody hand and kissed it many times in an agony of grief; it was an affecting and awful scene ...

'The French Colonel I have already mentioned, was killed by a corporal of the 13th; this corporal had killed one of his men, and he was so enraged, that he sallied out himself and attacked the corporal – the corporal was well mounted and a good swordsman, as was also the Colonel – both defended for some time, the corporal cut him twice in the face, his helmet came off at the second, when the corporal slew him by a cut which nearly cleft his skull asunder, it cut in as deep as the nose through the brain'[4].

It is as well for us to be reminded occasionally of the medieval realities of combat with cold steel.

The French dragoons were scattered in all directions before making off along the road to Badajoz, pursued vigorously by the 13th. Robert Long himself was following up behind, and described what happened next:

'I followed as rapidly as I could to support this attack, still supposing the heavy brigade in my rear, occupying the attention of the remaining part of the enemy's force, but, to my utter astonishment, when, at the point where I first met the Badajoz road, I halted, and looked round to see what

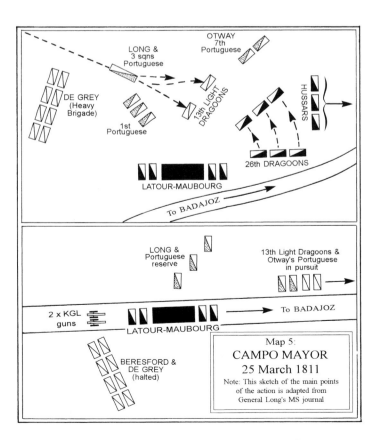

Map 5:
CAMPO MAYOR
25 March 1811
Note: This sketch of the main points of the action is adapted from General Long's MS journal

was next to be done, I found they had quitted altogether the line of direction I had pointed out, and at the suggestion of one of Marshal Beresford's aides-de-camp, had marched by their right to the other side of the valley and road, and were halted a mile and a half off, on the opposite and elevated ground, quite abandoning me to myself, and completely oversetting all my plans'[5].

It was true. Instead of coming forward in support of Long, De Grey's heavy dragoons were halted by the side of the road. It was from this point that the dire results of poor communications began to unfold.

Having placed himself at the head of the three reserve Portuguese squadrons, Long could not see what had happened to the 13th Light Dragoons after they disappeared from view over a hill in front of him as they set off in pursuit of the French. Although his position prevented him from getting a decent view, he did nevertheless manage to despatch Otway and his two Portuguese squadrons that had been covering the 13th's left flank, to support and rally the British regiment. Otway also disappeared over the hill and out of sight, following hard on the heels of the 13th. With the British heavy cavalry halted, the French infantry and hussars were allowed to move off unmolested towards Badajoz. There was little Long could do but send for the heavy brigade; in the meantime he determined to advance with his three Portuguese squadrons in order to detain the

Another view looking north along the road from Campo Mayor to Badajoz. It was along this road that Colonel Head's 13th Light Dragoons galloped to capture the 16 heavy siege guns from the French, only to be forced to relinquish their prizes when the French cavalry and infantry, who had been allowed to escape through Beresford's neglect, came marching along the same road after him.

French long enough for the heavy cavalry, along with the British infantry and artillery, to get forward. However, a few shouts and some carbine shots from the French were enough to put the Portuguese to flight; they turned tail and fled, despite Long's personal attempts to rally them, in which he was assisted by Captain Doyle of the Quartermaster General's Department. It was apparently this officer who was sent by Long to get the heavy brigade forward.

Tripp's false report

Doyle was met by an alarmed Beresford, who came forward and enquired somewhat angrily as to the whereabouts of the 13th. Doyle told him that they had scattered the French and that it was imperative that the heavy brigade be brought forward to ensure the surrender of the French infantry. However, Beresford was under the impression that he already knew what had become of the 13th – he had been told that the regiment had all been taken prisoner. This false information had been brought to him by one of Long's aides, a Dutch émigré officer named Baron Tripp who, upon seeing the 13th disappear, thought that they had been captured wholesale by the French, and so returned to inform Beresford, who in turn ordered the heavy brigade to halt. Doyle meanwhile returned to Long and told him who was responsible for halting De Grey's brigade. 'For the first

time', wrote Long, 'I learned from Captain Doyle that Marshal Beresford himself was with the brigade of heavy cavalry, and had himself halted them in the situation I have described. I had nothing further to say'[6].

Although unable to substantiate Tripp's panicky claim, Beresford nevertheless believed that the 13th Light Dragoons had been lost, and so ordered the heavy brigade to move to their right, whereupon they crossed the road, formed up to the west of it with their left flank upon it, and simply halted. By now Colborne's infantry were fast approaching, as were Cleeve's KGL artillery[7]. In fact, Cleeve managed to get two of his guns forward under Captain Hartmann, who threw a few shells into the midst of the retreating French. Hartmann wanted to get the guns even closer to the enemy, but Beresford ordered him to halt and remain where he was. The French infantry, meanwhile, were allowed to continue along the road to Badajoz.

While all of this had been in progress, Head and the 13th Light Dragoons caught up with the section of the French convoy drawing the 16 siege guns towards Badajoz. They were almost certainly in the vicinity of Fort San Cristobal, which is situated on the northern bank of the Guadiana. As well as the guns themselves there were a number of wagons and an immense quantity of stores, baggage, provisions, horses and mules – in fact, the whole camp equipage which had been sent off from Campo Mayor towards Badajoz earlier that morning. When the light dragoons caught up with the convoy the gunners and drivers, with no other mounted supports, surrendered without a fight, but as they neared Badajoz they tried to escape and most of them were sabred. British troopers were then mounted on the mules in order to bring the guns back to Campo Mayor.

Colonel Head rallied the 13th, some of whom had been

wounded by artillery fire from Fort San Cristobal[8]. These were joined by Otway's two squadrons of the Portuguese 7th Cavalry, which had arrived on the scene, and together they organised the return towards Campo Mayor of the guns, stores, equipment and the French prisoners they had taken. But if they thought that they were to return as heroes to the Allied camp their hopes were to be quickly dashed. After having got about half way along the road they were met by a trooper of the 13th with a message from Lieutenant Holmes, also of the 13th, who had been wounded during the initial charge and had stayed behind. The message to Colonel Head told him that the French hussars and infantry were approaching him and that there were no Allied infantry or cavalry to give him support.

One can imagine Head's astonishment at this message, for it was apparently concluded that it must be mistaken – that the reported French infantry were, in fact, Portuguese, who also wore dark blue uniforms. However, as Head and his men continued along the road a second courier from Lieutenant Holmes galloped up, confirming his first warning. Furthermore, this second message also informed Head that the French dragoons who had earlier surrendered had regained their arms and horses and were even now approaching him. This second message confronted Head with an impossibly difficult choice.

Colonel Head's dilemma

He had altogether fewer than four and a half squadrons of British and Portuguese cavalry, most of whom were blown after their exertions and would be no match for some 1,200 French infantry supported by a superior body of French cavalry. And yet, he had with him 16 precious heavy guns as well as the large quantity of wagons and supplies captured from the French. Was he now, after his officers and troopers had made such heroic efforts to secure them, simply to abandon these prizes? Sadly, he had little option; and indeed, his men had barely remounted their own horses and left behind the captured convoy before the French columns hove into view, marching hurriedly and unmolested along the road. As the French approached, Head and his men rode off to their right, making their way across the rolling plain

and leaving their trophies standing by the roadside. The French could not believe their luck. When the column came up the guns and wagons were secured, while Mortier sent out from Badajoz a force of 2,000 infantry and one cavalry regiment to assist in bringing them inside the town.

Of the 232 officers and men of the 13th Light Dragoons who took part in the fight at Campo Mayor, twelve men were killed, and three officers and 26 men wounded; 15 others were recorded as missing, presumably taken prisoner by the French close to Badajoz[9]. Total Portuguese casualties were one officer and 13 men killed and 35 men wounded; a further 55 were recorded as missing.

There is no record of what happened when Colonel Head met Beresford after returning to the British camp. The historian of the 13th, however, records that Head was received with 'coldness and somewhat bitter sarcasm'[10]. Given the stern warning that Wellington had issued to Beresford prior to the operation, one can easily imagine Wellington's feelings when he received the report of the fight. In fact, the commander-in-chief was so enraged that he was moved to issue a strong reprimand to Head and the 13th; but his despatch to Beresford shows quite clearly how little he knew of the true facts behind the fight:

'I wish you would call together the Officers of the dragoons', he wrote, 'and point out to them the mischiefs which must result from the disorder of the troops in action. The undisciplined ardour of the 13th [Light] dragoons, and 1st regiment of Portuguese cavalry, is not of the description of the determined bravery and steadfastness of soldiers confident in their discipline and in their Officers. Their conduct was that of a rabble, galloping as fast as their horses could carry them over a plain, after an enemy to whom they could do no mischief when they were broken; and the pursuit had continued for a limited distance, and sacrificing substantial advantages, and all the objects of your operation, by their want of discipline. To this description of their conduct I add my entire conviction, that if the enemy could have thrown out of Badajoz only one hundred men regularly formed, they would have driven back these two regiments in equal haste and disorder, and would probably have taken many whose horses would have been knocked up. If the 13th

An atmospheric depiction of a British light dragoon on active service in the Peninsula, wearing the Tarleton helmet and laced jacket which were replaced from 1812 by a French-style bell-topped shako and kurtka. The light dragoons were the real workhorses of the cavalry, whose contribution to operations involved a wide variety of vital, though often unglamorous tasks.

[Light] dragoons are again guilty of this conduct I shall take their horses from them, and send the Officers and men to do duty at Lisbon. I beg that you will tell De Grey how well satisfied I was with the conduct of his brigade'[11]. He also issued a General Order which again censured the 13th 'for their impetuosity' and want of discipline, although he did give the regiment credit for its 'bravery and resolution'[12].

The charge that they galloped like a rabble cannot be substantiated, nor can that of their want of discipline. As to the 'sacrificing substantial advantages, and all the objects of your [Beresford's] operation', this was clearly Beresford's own fault for not supporting the 13th with the heavy brigade. The praise of De Grey's conduct simply emphasises Wellington's ignorance of the facts; after all, the heavy brigade, through no fault of its own, did nothing whatever at Campo Mayor but sit and watch. This naturally angered Robert Long, who said of Wellington's praise for De Grey: 'The Heavy Dragoons and Col.Grey have received his particular thanks for having, under the Marshal's personal directions, done nothing but look on, and suffer that enemy to escape unmolested from their swords who in ten minutes might have been annihilated!'[13]

The officers of the 13th were understandably stung by the rebuke, not only for its tone and content, but by the obvious misrepresentations contained within it. The upshot was that they wrote a letter containing the full and true facts of their action which was signed by all of the regiment's officers; this was given first to Long and then passed on to Wellington himself. After reading it the commander-in-chief apparently said that had he known the full facts of the fight at Campo Mayor he would never have issued the reprimand. However, as he had already issued it he characteristically refused to withdraw it. The 13th's historian also wrote that Beresford himself later 'changed his opinion as regards the conduct of the regiment at Campo Mayor'[14]. Long, meanwhile, read out Wellington's General Order, censuring the conduct of the 13th, to all of the assembled officers of the regiment – although he went on to say that he would never allow it to be entered in the regiment's Orderly Book.

★   ★   ★

The cavalry engagement at Campo Mayor was one of the most controversial actions of the war. A brilliant cavalry charge followed by the capture of 16 heavy guns had been upset by Beresford's refusal to allow De Grey's brigade to go forward in support. Given that the bulk of the 2nd Division's infantry were also coming forward at speed, such support would almost certainly have completed the victory and secured considerable spoils. Although Robert Long bears some of the responsibility for not maintaining touch with the 13th after their initial charge, the blame for the entire fiasco rests squarely upon the shoulders of Beresford. He acted upon false and uncorroborated information; failed to support his light cavalry; and in turn blamed both Long and Head for the failure to secure the guns and for allegedly charging on recklessly, which it is patently clear that they did not.

Campo Mayor became the central issue of a vitriolic pamphlet war, fought out during the years following the end of the Peninsular War by the various participants. It would be wearisome and unilluminating to retrace here all the arguments advanced by the partisans of the various actors in the drama. What should be said, however, is that the success of Colonel Head's charge at Campo Mayor set the future tone of combats between the British and French cavalry, the latter being forever wary of their opposite numbers. It has also been the subject of much faulty analysis and interpretation by historians over the years, which has left the British cavalry with an undeservedly poor reputation[15]. In terms of our own story of the 1811 campaign, Campo Mayor was simply an introductory move to the first siege of Badajoz.

COLOUR PLATES A – D

A1: Sergeant, 1/71st Regiment (Highland Light Infantry)

The 1/71st formed part of Howard's brigade of Spencer's 1st Division at Fuentes de Oñoro and, as recounted in the text, saw much hard fighting in the houses and alleyways of the village. The battalion suffered 52 casualties on 3 May and a further 127 on 5 May. Light infantry training laid more stress on open-order fighting than was the case in the line battalions, which relied upon rigid obedience to orders to perform massed manoeuvres and co-ordinated firing. Although they too often fought in the line of battle, light infantry battalions and companies were frequently sent forward to form the advanced skirmish line, separating into smaller groups to deliver harassing fire on an advancing enemy from behind cover. Detaching light units to defend the village was conventional practice, since this sort of fighting demanded initiative and quick reactions. The 71st had until very recently been named as a Glasgow regiment, although like most British units it would also have had in its ranks men from all parts of the British Isles (and occasionally, beyond).

The short red jacket or coatee, cut straight across the waist with short tails, was standard issue to British line and light infantry 'other ranks'; for sergeants it was of a better quality, brighter red cloth. The tufted 'wings' at the shoulders were a distinction of light infantry units and of both 'flank' companies of line units. It is faced here at collar, cuffs, shoulder straps and turnbacks with the buff of the 71st, and a patch of this colour also backs the sergeant's three chevrons of rank, which in light infantry units were worn on both upper sleeves. Another distinction of sergeants was the use of plain white worsted tape on the coatee, rather than the regimental pattern - for the 71st, with a red line at the outer edge - worn by privates and corporals. Buff-faced regiments were also distinguished by wearing their leather equipment straps in that shade, rather than pipe-clayed white.

The regimental headgear was unique: a blue Scottish bonnet with a diced band, formed into a shako shape over cardboard, with a laced-on black leather visor; the green toorie or tuft and the buglehorn badge were references to the light infantry role. The loose trousers worn for Peninsula campaigning are nearly always depicted as white, and were probably made up locally. (Variations on the grey trousers which later became general wear were tested by the 4th, 20th and 28th Foot at Walcheren in 1809; the type worn by the 28th stood up best, and according to Charles Cadell they were generally adopted. The 28th may therefore have worn grey in the Peninsula.) Short black spat-type gaiters were worn over the low shoes. In the heat of battle the sergeant has pulled off his black leather neck stock, but no doubt this is safely stowed in his haversack. Since 1808 the hair was ordered cut close to the head and neck and was worn unpowdered.

In light infantry units the sergeant's crimson waist sash, with a central stripe of facing colour, was retained, but the sword and pike carried by sergeants of centre and grenadier companies in line battalions were discarded. Full musket equipment was carried instead: the 0.75in India Pattern 'Brown Bess', a crossbelt supporting a heavy 60-round cartridge pouch behind the right hip, and a second for the bayonet scabbard. The blue-painted 'Italian' water canteen and rough linen haversack for rations and small necessaries were also slung over the shoulders. Surprising as it may seem, contemporary pictures almost invariably show British troops in action wearing their full marching order, including the knapsack and rolled greatcoat and/or blanket.

A2: Private, Portuguese 6th Cazadores

It was some time before Portuguese troops were accepted by their suspicious British comrades as being fit to fight alongside them; however, beginning with their fine showing at Busaco in September 1810, they came to be warmly respected as full equals by the redcoats, and Wellington famously called them 'the fighting cocks' of his army. (Indeed, he requested a Portuguese brigade at the outbreak of the Waterloo campaign, although this was not forthcoming.)

On 5 May 1811 Ashworth's independent Portuguese brigade (8th and 18th Infantry Regiments, and 6th Cazadores) seems to have been deployed in the south-facing line at Fuentes d'Oñoro between Spencer's and Picton's divisions. The 6th Cazadores were certainly one of the units sent down - with the British 1/88th and 74th - to retake the village, and distinguished themselves during that bloody action.

This light infantry branch of the reorganised Portuguese Army was formed from autumn 1808; cazadores means 'hunters', echoing the French chasseurs and German Jäger. The 6th Battalion was raised in Minho province among

The so-called 'universal' brass plate worn on the British line infantry shako from c1800 to c1812. In fact individual regiments were permitted to add their own 'ancient badges' and other devices; this example has a scroll around the royal cypher embossed 'King's Own Infantry', identifying the 4th Regiment, which fought at Corunna in 1809. (Peter Joslin / Lancaster City Museum)

hardy highlanders from the north-east border regions, although it was assigned to Oporto. The small, 628-man battalions had only five companies, including one of tiradores, 'sharpshooters'. The latter seem to have had Baker rifles (since between 100 and 200 were apparently available for issue to each battalion), while the rest carried the standard British India Pattern smoothbore musket. The Cazadores quickly earned a reputation as elite troops, and at the time of the May 1811 battles their expansion from six to 12 battalions had just been ordered. Their uniform was brown with black cord and tape embellishments and battalion-coloured facings, here the yellow collar and cuffs of the 6th; all had the characteristic Portuguese broad shoulder straps tufted with black. British accoutrements were supplied, in blackened leather. The shako from about 1810 was of the British felt 'stovepipe' shape with leather top and peak, brass numeral and buglehorn badge, the national cockade and a green tuft (black for sharpshooter companies).

B1: Company officer, 1/3rd Regiment (East Kent – The Buffs)

The Buffs had been in the Peninsula since September 1808; they were first across the river at Oporto in May 1809, where they held the vital Seminary, and had taken 152 casualties at Talavera. The Buffs suffered the highest casualties of any battalion at Albuera - 643 out of 755 officers and men; but earned a second nickname, 'The Resurrectionists', for the speed with which they were brought up to strength again. This figure does not pretend to be a portrait of Lieutenant Matthew Latham, famous for the terrible wounds he suffered while successfully defending the King's Colour of the Buffs against the French cavalry attack on Colborne's brigade at Albuera; it is merely an impression of such an event. (It is pleasant to be able to repeat the fact that the heroic Latham was able to continue his army career, although one-armed and disfigured; a special medal was struck for him, and his face was partially repaired by a surgeon at the expense of the Prince Regent.)

The infantry officer's scarlet coat was long-tailed and double-breasted at this date, and faced with regimental colour at collar and cuffs; the Old Buffs took their ancient nickname from their facing colour. They were an 'unlaced' regiment, i.e. the officers did not wear bullion lace buttonhole loops on the faced areas of the coat, but only lines of sewn 'twist'. Ensigns and lieutenants were distinguished by a single lace epaulette on the right shoulder; the Buffs wore silver lace. The crimson silk net waist sash was the universal distinction of British officers; it is tied on the hip to keep the sword belt with its frogged scabbard from flapping. The straight 1796 pattern infantry officer's sword was an elegant but flimsy weapon. The types of breeches and boots illustrated were conventional, although officers enjoyed a wide latitude for personal choice. The regulation headgear was still the broad black felt bicorn hat.

B2: Private, Spanish Regimiento de Infanteria Imperial de Toledo

The Buffs and the rest of Colborne's brigade from Stewart's 2nd Division were brought south on 16 May to relieve the pressure on the strong Spanish brigade commanded by the energetic General Marquez de Zayas. Like Lowry Cole later that day, Zayas seems to have taken it upon himself to deploy his troops where they were obviously needed, ignoring his superior officer's lack of activity. The weight of the French attack by Girard and Gazan on the right wing thus fell first upon the 2nd and 4th Battalions of the Guardias de Infanteria Española, 4th Guardias de Infanteria Walonna, Voluntarios de la Patria, Legion Estranjera, and Regimientos Irlanda, Ciudad Real and Imperial de Toledo. They behaved admirably, and their stubborn stand in the face of this attempt to roll up the Allied line was one of the keys to the eventual Allied victory. (Indeed, an officer of the Walloon Guards - Captain Carlos Favre d'Aunoy, who was born in Louisiana - became a national hero for his behaviour at Albuera, and enjoyed rapid promotion to general rank thereafter.)

Spanish infantry regiments were supposed to muster three battalions, each with six companies - four of fusiliers and one each of grenadiers and cazadores, light infantry; the regimental establishment was 2,554, giving a battalion strength of about 850 all ranks. In practice unit strength in the field was far lower than these figures suggest. The Toledo Regiment had served alongside the British before; it had fought at Talavera in 1809 and was in the Lines of Torres Vedras in 1810. Spanish uniforms were enormously varied at this date, much clothing being provided by the British, but that of the Toledo was locally procured and is interpreted from a painting by Dighton. The soldier is shown here with a captured French An IX/An XIII musket and cowhide knapsack, a local blanket, and British-supplied blackened leather accoutrements.

C1: Trooper, French 1er Chevau-Légers Lanciers de la Légion de la Vistule

In March 1808 a Polish corps entitled the Légion Polacco-Italienne was transferred from Westphalian to French service and renamed the Légion de la Vistule. It originally consisted of one lancer and three infantry regiments; second lancer and fourth infantry regiments joined it in the Peninsula in 1809. The Poles spent much of the war in eastern Spain, and particularly distinguished themselves during both sieges of Saragossa. It was Colonel Jan Konopka's 1st Lancers which led the devastating charge out of the rainstorm against Colborne's brigade at Albuera, though at a cost of about a quarter of their own strength; many eyewitness accounts speak of their brutality towards British wounded and prisoners. Soon afterwards the regiment would be broken up to form the French 7e and 8e Chevau-Légers Lanciers, when their own success and that of the Polish Lancers of the Imperial Guard prompted Napoleon to raise this whole new branch of his cavalry. (Within the year, most would be on their way to perish in the snows of Russia.)

The trooper wears two classic features of Polish lancer dress which would later be copied by other armies: the square-topped, cane-stiffened czapka headgear and the short kurtka jacket; for the Vistula Lancers the latter - like the buttoned riding overalls - was dark blue with yellow facings and piping. On campaign it was usual for the cap to be covered with oilskin to protect it from rain, and the chest of the jacket was buttoned across to hide the yellow plastrons. A striped canvas girdle is worn over the belt which supports the light cavalry sabre. As a front rank man this trooper carries a 9-foot lance (an eyewitness account mentions the pennants fluttering loose, rather than rolled and tied as usual on the march); he also has one or a pair of flintlock pistols, their holsters hidden here by the front of his sheepskin saddle cover.

Tacticians of the day, both British and French, were unanimous that although the lance was an effective weapon for the first shock, if sabre-armed cavalry could get inside the lancers' reach then it became a positive hindrance. It was for this reason that only the front of a regiment's two ranks were so armed; the rear rank carried carbines, like the other light cavalry. Against unprepared infantry, of course, the lance was lethal.

C2: Officer, French 2e Régiment de Hussards

The second regiment sent against Colborne and Zayas by General Latour-Maubourg was the French 2nd Hussars from Briche's brigade. Veterans of Jemappes and Friedland, Colonel Vinot's regiment had led General Lasalle's brigade in the charge which smashed Cuesta's Spanish army at Medellin in March 1809. They won another victory at Torrijos in July 1809, and later operated against Andalusian guerrillas from a base at Ronda. At Albuera they lost 73 men when they charged Colborne's brigade to continue the deadly work begun by the Vistula Lancers; but eyewitness accounts suggest that they showed far more humanity towards their wounded adversaries and prisoners.

The traditional features of hussar uniform - the lavishly braided dolman jacket and fur-trimmed pelisse overjacket, the 'barrel' sash and tight braided breeches - were worn in a wide variety of colours by the various regiments of this branch; the colours of the 2nd were brown and light blue with silver lace. This figure in campaign dress is largely based on a portrait of the interestingly-named Lieutenant

John de Rocca, who served in Spain from 1810. His baggy riding overalls are typical of the many variations in detail from regulation practice; officers in particular could indulge their personal whims. Shako covers were often worn to protect the expensive coloured cloth and lace ornaments from the weather and dust.

D1: Lieutenant-Colonel, 1/57th Regiment (West Middlesex)

Although this is not a portrait, this figure - based on paintings from life of a number of contemporary infantry officers - probably gives a reasonably close impression of the appearance of William Inglis, whose heroic conduct at Albuera is recounted in the text. In Napoleonic times the battalion's commander and the two majors who seconded him were expected - like the junior officers - to share every danger of battle with their men. Memoirs are rich in accounts of officers deliberately exposing themselves to fire in the front rank to lift the spirits of their soldiers at moments of crisis; whatever the other faults recorded against individuals, it is rare indeed to find any hint that an officer was 'shy'. Such behaviour was simply intolerable, to their social equals and to their men.

The uniform of field officers was only distinguished from that of company officers by the two bullion epaulettes; in the 57th these were of gold lace, and for the rank of lieutenant-colonel they bore crown badges in the opposite colour. The lapels of the scarlet coat were very often worn with the upper triangular area of one or both lapels folded back to display the facing colour, which was yellow for the 57th; note that like the 3rd, this was an 'unlaced' regiment. Shirt collars and black silk stocks were worn high, with a ruffle at the throat. Field officers were mounted, and he wears spurred boots; he also has a small 'spyglass' (telescope) slung in a leather case. His bicorn hat is embellished with the regulation black national cockade held by a gold lace loop, and a cut-feather plume of white over red. The 1796 pattern officer's sword was normally blued and gilded for part of its length. As remarked above, it was flimsy for a serious battlefield weapon; but a senior officer's role was to direct and encourage rather than to indulge in hand-to-hand fighting.

D2: Private, battalion company, 1/57th Regiment (West Middlesex)

The 1/57th, from Hoghton's brigade of the 2nd Division, suffered casualties second only to the Buffs - 428 of its 647 officers and men, or 67 per cent, the battalion being led off the field by a lieutenant. They would forever afterwards be known as 'the Diehards', from their fallen Colonel Inglis's exhortation to them. This is the uniform which would have been worn by Thomas Hitchcock, who survived the battle and lived at least until 1848, when the retrospective institution of the General Service Medal saw him granted eight clasps, for Busaco, Albuera, Vittoria, the Pyrenees, Nivelle, the Nive, Orthes and Toulouse.

The reloading drill for a flintlock musket was time-consuming. After each shot the soldier had to take a paper cartridge from his pouch, bite off the end, pour powder into the priming pan, and close its cover; then ground his musket, tip the rest of the powder and the ball down the muzzle, draw his ramrod, ram the charge home, and return the ramrod to its pipes under the barrel; then bring the butt to the shoulder, cock the hammer, and fire. Even so, experienced infantry were expected to keep up a rate of one shot every 20 seconds, at the orders of their company officers; and French accounts often mention admiringly the steadiness and control of British volley fire. The inherent inaccuracy of the smoothbore musket meant that co-ordinated fire by whole battalions was essential to achieve effective results, and even against similarly massed targets the number of hits above a range of about 50 yards seems to have dropped off dramatically. In encounters like that endured by Hoghton's brigade at Albuera, however, the effects were murderous.

This soldier has dropped his pack - of the earlier canvas 'envelope' type - after a musket ball has cut one of its straps and grazed his chest; contemporary accounts often mention lucky escapes when bullets passed through men's clothing and equipment. Note the brass wire brush and 'picker' carried attached to a buttonhole; these were essential for keeping the lock of the musket free from the burnt powder fouling which built up after a few shots. His other field equipment is the same as that worn in Plate A1.

The dull red coatee is decorated down the front, on the cuffs and false rear pockets, round the turnbacks (and, hidden here, round th collar and shoulder straps) with worsted tape in the regimental 'lace' pattern - for the 57th, with a central black line, the loops set in pairs, square ended. Some campaign trousers had buttoned openings down the sides. The felt 'stovepipe' shako worn since c1806 has the universal pattern brass plate, and added chin tapes; tufts were white-over-red for battalion companies, white for grenadiers and green for light companies.

A2: Private, Portuguese
6th Cazadores

A1: Sergeant, 1/71st Regiment
(Highland Light Infantry)

PLATE B

B2: Private, Spanish Regimiento de
Infanteria Imperial de Toledo

B1: Company officer, 1/3rd Regiment
(East Kent – The Buffs)

PLATE C

C1: Trooper, French 1er Chevau-Légers
Lanciers de la Légion de la Vistule

C2: Officer, French 2e Régiment de Hussards

PLATE D

D1: Lieutenant-Colonel,
1/57th Regiment (West Middlesex)

D2: Private, battalion company,
1/57th Regiment (West Middlesex)

PLATE E

E2: Company officer, 1/23rd
Regiment (Royal Welsh Fusiliers)

E1: Private, 2/7th Regiment
(Royal Fusiliers)

F1: Voltigeur, French 88e
Régiment d'Infanterie de Ligne

F2: Bugler, chasseur company,
French 12e Régiment
d'Infanterie Légère

PLATE G

G1: Cornet, 4th (Queen's Own) Dragoons

G2: Sergeant, battalion company,
2/31st Regiment (Huntingdonshire)

PLATE H

H1: Company officer, 2nd
Light Battalion, King's German Legion

H2: Private, 5/60th
Regiment (Royal American)

E1: Private, 2/7th Regiment (Royal Fusiliers)

This reconstruction must be something like the appearance, after the fight of Myers's Fusilier Brigade against Werlé's brigade at the climax of the battle, of Private John Spencer Cooper, who would - at the age of 81 - sit down to write his famous memoir Rough Notes of Seven Campaigns. Cooper fought in a number of great actions between 1809 and 1815; in later life his General Service Medal would bear the clasps for Talavera, Busaco, Albuera, Ciudad Rodrigo, Badajoz, Vittoria, the Pyrenees, Orthes and Toulouse, and he also took part in the ill-fated expedition to New Orleans in 1815. At Albuera the two battalions of the Royal Fusiliers went into action with a strength of 1,282 all ranks, and lost 706 dead and wounded - a casualty rate of 55 per cent.

Fusiliers took their title from the 17th century, when 'fusils' - flintlock muskets - first replaced matchlocks as the armament of artillery guards. By Napoleonic times the title was purely honorary, but was still marked by certain detailed differences of uniform of the kind beloved within the 'tribal' culture of the British regimental system. Fusiliers wore white shako tufts - the colour of the Board of Ordnance - and the cockade was secured by a small brass 'bomb' badge rather than a button; and all ranks and companies wore shoulder wings on the coatee. Like all infantry regiments granted the title 'Royal' the 7th Foot wore dark blue facings; their regimental lace had a central blue line, and their buttonhole loops were set on singly, square-ended.

Many Peninsula memoirists remark on the dirty, patched appearance of uniforms on campaign. Even though Albuera was fought fairly early in the season the men had already been marching and bivouacking in the open, without tents, for two months. This also took a toll on the men's shoes, which were often supplied by unscrupulous contractors and wore out quickly. Lieutenant Harrison of the 23rd wrote of the 110-mile forced march to Portalegre as the Fusilier Brigade hurried to join Beresford's army: 'It was the most fatiguing day I ever felt. We marched 30 miles and had no meat for two days before or spirits, only a small portion of biscuit and water to support us … The men were in a poor way, as most of them were barefoot'. Even those who were shod had been issued with locally-produced shoes, 'very clumsy and of dirty buff colour, their rough seams made their wearers hobble like so many cripples.'

E2: Company officer, 1/23rd Regiment (Royal Welsh Fusiliers)

The 23rd were a 'laced' regiment, and this officer's expensive coat of scarlet superfine cloth shows heavy gold braid loops on the dark blue faced areas. As a Fusilier he wears a pair of bullion-fringed shoulder wings instead of a single epaulette, worked in gold on padded scarlet cloth and bearing a 'bomb' badge. (Such items were very costly, and were just one of the expenses which demanded that a regimental officer have a reasonable private income in addition to his pay.) This captain chooses to wear non-regulation blue breeches - quite commonly seen - and a striped civilian waistcoat peeps out under his sash. Tucked into the latter is a small flintlock pocket pistol, a personal weapon of last resort. An experienced combat officer, he has also provided himself with a non-regulation sabre - though such weapons were regulation for flank company officers. There are several references to officers buying themselves haversacks, of leather or other sturdy materials, to carry some of the necessities of campaign life. His bicorn hat has an oilskin cover.

One of the company officers who served with the 23rd at Albuera was Captain John Edward Humphrey Hill, whose career is worth summarising. Commissioned in 1796, he served two years later at Ostend, where he was taken prisoner. Released in Holland the following year, he was sent home aboard the ship Valk; but the vessel was wrecked in a storm, and Hill was one of only 25 survivors out of more than 400 souls, having apparently saved his life by tying himself to the forecastle with his braces and a handkerchief. He subsequently saw service at Ferrol and Cadiz, in Egypt, Hanover, and at Copenhagen (where he was accidentally bayoneted by one of his own men). In 1808 he sailed for North America and Barbados, and commanded the light company at Martinique. He served in the Peninsula from Albuera onwards. At Waterloo his horse was killed; and while standing in the front rank of his regiment's square he was wounded by a splinter of a comrade's bone driven into his eye, two stone splinters through his cheek, a musket ball in his jaw, and finally by a grapeshot in the left breast which passed out through the centre of his shoulderblade. When he left the regiment in 1823 he could boast that he had been present at every single battle honour then emblazoned

on his regiment's Colours save only Minden. He died in 1835.

F1: Voltigeur, French 88e Régiment d'Infanterie de Ligne

The 88th of the Line was a typical French infantry regiment; it had been present at Austerlitz, Jena, Eylau, Eckmuhl and Wagram, and saw much service in the Iberian Peninsula, fighting at Saragossa, Ocana, the Gebora, Albuera, Badajoz, Vittoria, Nivelle, and the Pyrenees. While two battalions served at Albuera a third was on garrison duty at Badajoz (where, coincidentally, the 88e de Ligne would be defending the castle the following spring while Wellington's 88th Regiment, the Connaught Rangers, were fighting their way into it). At Albuera the I and II/88th formed part of Girard's division for the massed French attack on the Allied right, facing first Zayas's and then Hoghton's and Abercrombie's brigades. This soldier would have been lucky to survive Albuera unscathed; the 88th lost 405 men out of 899 all ranks - at 45 per cent, the highest casualty rate of any French regiment present.

Apart from the green and yellow distinctions marking the voltigeur (light infantry) company of his battalion, no part of this soldier's regulation uniform is visible; contemporary sources make clear that the French soldier in the field was a law unto himself in such matters. On the march his blue uniform coat is stowed away, and he has transferred his voltigeur epaulettes from it to his white sleeved waistcoat - issued for drill, fatigue and barracks dress. His felt and leather 1810 pattern shako is protected by a cloth cover, bearing the painted regimental number and with a hole exposing the company pompon. His baggy campaign trousers are made from local brown cloth. His crossbelts support a cartridge pouch behind the right hip, and on the left combined frogs for a bayonet and the simple brass-hilted sabre which was a distinction of both flank companies of line battalions. French soldiers were issued cowhide knapsacks and greatcoats, but not haversacks or water canteens; contemporary pictures show an enormous variety of personal acquisitions and improvisations.. The French An IX/An XII Charleville musket was essentially similar to the British 'Brown Bess' and had a comparable performance.

F2: Bugler, chasseur company, French 12e Régiment d'Infanterie Légère

With three battalions present the 12th Light Infantry was one of the strongest French regiments on the battlefield; they were veterans of Austerlitz, Friedland, Vimeiro and Talavera. The regiment formed half the strength of Werlé's brigade, and suffered the highest casualties among his units - 769 from 2,164 all ranks, or 35 per cent - when it was pitted against the 1/7th (Royal Fusiliers) at the climax of Albuera.

The four centre companies of a Light Infantry battalion were termed chasseurs, the heavy company carabiniers and the light company voltigeurs. Only the latter were supposed to have buglers (cornets) instead of company drummers, but a contemporary picture clearly identifies this man with a chasseur company of the 12th. Although he wears a broadly 'regulation' coat (habit-veste) it has the kind of regimental variations typically seen - in this case, longer tails, broad white tape edging instead of piping, and curious 'swallow's nest' ornaments at the shoulders which were presumably the mark of buglers. Non-regulation shako plates were also common, and this eagle-and-shield type anticipates the 1812 model. The rest of his dress is improvised, and he has acquired a carbine (mousqueton) in place of the heavier musket.

G1: Cornet, 4th (Queen's Own) Dragoons

Although Albuera is famous for being mainly an infantry affair, the Allied cavalry played a valuable part at various key stages. They were active against the cavalry supporting Godinot's attack on the village; they saw off - somewhat belatedly - the attack by Latour-Maubourg's cavalry; and they fulfilled an important role in supporting the advance by Cole's 4th Division at the decisive stage of the battle. One of the most entertaining Peninsula memoirists is Cornet John Luard, who served with the 4th Dragoons in De Grey's heavy brigade; he had also been present at Campo Mayor, which he described as 'a mismanaged affair by Beresford'.

This junior troop officer wears the archaic cocked hat which was still the official headgear of the heavy cavalry, often worn over a protective skullcap of iron strapwork. It was difficult to keep on, and some officers and men fitted chinstraps, sometimes with metal scales to give a little protection against slashes to the face. The scarlet coatee has the regiment's green facings at collar and cuff, and silver lace; heavy cavalry officers wore shoulder 'wings' of metal chain or scales which were both decorative and gave some protection against sword cuts. Riding overalls with leather reinforcement were popular among mounted officers of all branches, often with lace side stripes or rows of buttons. The straight heavy cavalry sword was suspended from the waistbelt on two slings; a white pouchbelt was worn over the left shoulder, supporting a small black pouch - officially for pistol ammunition - in the small of the back. The 4th's mounts were chestnuts; the saddlery is typical of field use, with a sheepskin cover, two pistol holsters with the tops covered with fur 'flounces', and instead of a valise the officer's red cloak (with green regimental lining) neatly rolled at the crupper.

Luard tells us that officers in the Peninsula 'ran into great extremes of fashion; and as there was a difficulty frequently in procuring articles of dress exactly according to regulation, considerable latitude was of necessity granted ... The hair was worn very long, and the waists longer, the sash being tied over the hips, the pantaloons tight about the waist, and very large at the lower part of the legs' - his accompanying sketch makes clear that he is referring here to overalls.

G2: Sergeant, battalion company, 2/31st Regiment (Huntingdonshire)
The 2/31st were the left hand battalion of Colborne's brigade, and as it advanced in echelon they found themselves to the rear and furthest from the point of contact when the Vistula Lancers and 2nd Hussars struck from the right flank. The battalion thus emerged relatively unscathed from this disastrous encounter; but it was therefore called forward to link up with the right flank of Hoghton's brigade when the rest of the 2nd Division advanced to engage the French 5th Corps in the terrible short-range firefight. The battalion went into action with 20 officers and 398 men, of whom 155 became casualties, most of them during the great musketry duel.

If a wounded man was capable of walking it was up to him to make his own way back to the surgeons in the rear - sometimes a long way in the rear. Many collapsed from shock and bled to death before they reached attention; and even when they found the place they often had to wait for many hours among the overwhelming numbers of casualties after a major action. This hard-bitten NCO has dropped his knapsack (the infamously uncomfortable Trotter pattern, of tarred canvas over a wooden box frame) has, bandaged his leg with a torn-off shirt tail; and is starting his long journey to try to find where his battalion's surgeon has set up his rudimentary dressing station.

The sergeants of all except the light companies within infantry battalions were distinguished partly by their armament: a pike with a 9-foot ash staff and a footlong blade with a crosspiece like a boar spear, and a brass-hilted sword slung from a single crossbelt. The pike could be useful in combat, particularly against cavalry, but was more often used to direct and push the ranks into alignment. The sergeant's sash was tied over the sword belt - which is buff here, since the 31st's uniform facings were that colour - to keep the scabbard from tripping him. The three rank chevrons were displayed on the right arm only, and like all the other jacket lace were plain white for sergeants. The felt shako was sometimes lacquered to make it waterproof, and a rain flap was often added to the back.

H1: Private, 5/60th Regiment (Royal American)
The 60th was unique among the numbered regiments of the British line, being raised in America in 1755 to fight in the French-Indian War and later rising to a strength of eight battalions. By the Napoleonic Wars the American title was purely traditional; it was a 'foreign legion' of many nationalities, always particularly strong in Germans and Swiss. The 5th Battalion was a rifle-armed unit, raised in 1797 and given the green jacket which would become traditional for Rifle regiments, distinguished by red facings; the pantaloons were at first light and later dark blue, but grey trousers were probably much in evidence in the Peninsula. The black leather accoutrements for the 0.62in Baker rifle included a waistbelt supporting the long brass-hilted sword-bayonet and a pouch of loose balls, as well as a conventional crossbelt pouch for made-up cartridges, and a powder flask. When the tactical situation allowed the rifle was loaded with patched ball and an individually measured charge of powder, for greater accuracy.

The 5/60th served with distinction throughout the Peninsular War, but not as a formed unit; its companies were dispersed among the different line brigades and divisions to improve their skirmishing capability. Six companies were present at Fuentes de Oñoro, and three with Stewart's 2nd Division at Albuera, where they fought in the front line against the French 5th Corps. In their ranks was a rifleman named Daniel Lochstadt, who achieved two notable distinctions. Firstly, he was one of only a handful of men who fought at both Fuentes de Oñoro and Albuera; and secondly, he lived to be awarded the General Service Medal with no fewer than 15 clasps, a total matched only by Private James Talbot of the 45th Regiment (apparently six survivors claimed that they had been present at 15 relevant battles, but only Lochstadt and Talbot could make good their claims).

H2: Company officer, 2nd Light Battalion, King's German Legion
After the Electors of Hanover inherited the British throne early in the 18th century links of alliance were naturally formed between the two nations. In 1803 Napoleon occupied Hanover and disbanded its small army; but King George III invited former soldiers and other volunteers to Britain, and a steady stream of clandestine recruits would continue to make the journey for years to come, aided by a sophisticated 'underground railway' of secret agents. Under their own officers the Hanoverians formed a corps which became the King's German Legion, eventually of some 14,000 men in eight line and two light infantry battalions, five cavalry regiments and five artillery companies. Much of the KGL fought in the Peninsula, earning a high reputation for professional excellence.

The KGL light battalions wore green 'rifle'-style uniforms, although they were in fact equipped with muskets apart from a strong 'sharpshooter' element in each unit which carried Bakers or similar German-made rifles. In these elite corps the officers' uniforms echoed light cavalry styles to some extent; note the shako with a squared folding visor and long retaining cords, recalling the traditional mirleton cap of German hussars, and the lavish black cord braiding on the jacket. The 'whip sash' is that worn by British light infantry officers, who also carried sabres. Officers of all corps frequently wore lace side stripes on their campaign overalls.

Captain George Baring (1773-1848), here in the uniform of an officer of the 1st Light Battalion, King's German Legion; this differed from that of the 2nd Battalion (Plate H2) in having an unbraided chest with two converging rows of ball buttons, and silver chain shoulder wings. The 38-year-old Baring was ADC to Charles von Alten, commanding the brigade defending the village of Albuera, and was wounded during the fighting. After surviving the Peninsular War and the ill-fated expedition to Walcheren in 1809 he found himself in a far more desperate situation in 1815 when, as major commanding the 2nd Light Battalion, he was given the task of defending the farm of La Haye Sainte at Waterloo. The second portrait shows him in old age. (Courtesy Michael Tänzer)

CHAPTER EIGHT

Albuera: 'A Storm of Lancers'

The end of April 1811 saw Wellington engaged in his blockade of Almeida, having driven Masséna from Portugal the same month. As we have seen in Chapter Five, he was about to fight that disgraceful but rather attractive personality at Fuentes de Oñoro in what would prove to be 'The Fox's' last battle in Spain before his recall to Paris. In the south, meanwhile, the strategic border fortress of Badajoz was in French hands, while Marshal Soult waited with his Army of Andalusia around Seville for the expected Allied move against him – a move which never came, due to the disagreement between La Peña and Graham after Barrosa. Attention therefore focused, not for the first or last time, upon Badajoz, the immensely strong medieval fortress that was to be the death of so many soldiers on both sides during the war.

Having brought an end to the brief period of French occupation of Campo Mayor the previous month, Beresford's Anglo-Portuguese force was preparing to lay siege to Badajoz. Beresford knew that it would be a difficult task, for neither he nor Wellington possessed many officers skilled in the art of siege warfare. It was an art that belonged largely to the previous two centuries and was certainly not one which commanded much attention from his engineers. Indeed, not since Drogheda in 1649 had a British army successfully stormed a regularly fortified town in Europe. The strong but irregular fortresses in far-off India, taken by Wellington himself, were the only such successes of late; while Montevideo, taken by Sir Samuel Auchmuty in February 1807, hardly rates as a strong fortress and was certainly not besieged in what might be termed a regular fashion. Wellington himself had not yet undertaken any sieges during the Peninsular campaigns; so Beresford faced what might be described as an interesting challenge when he approached Badajoz at the end of April 1811.

Beresford possessed few heavy guns or suitable tools; his engineers were inexperienced; and, more importantly, he had no specialist units of sappers or miners, and had to depend upon the unskilled and unwilling infantry for the physical labour in the trenches and batteries. With only some 18,000 men Beresford also lacked sufficient strength to prosecute a siege while also covering himself against the interference of a relieving army.

Although Beresford had taken Campo Mayor on 25 March, he suffered many delays in getting across the flooding Guadiana river. At Jerumenha the trestle bridge proved

unequal to his needs. Once across he had become embroiled in an irritating siege of Olivença, held by just 400 Frenchmen, which nevertheless obliged him to wait while heavy guns were brought from Elvas to batter its walls. To cap it all, on 6 April his cavalry had suffered an embarrassing setback, again at Jerumenha, when a piquet of the 13th Light Dragoons had been surprised with the loss of 50 men and 65 horses. The only real success during this period came on 16 April at Los Santos when the 13th LD and the heavy cavalry brigade scattered a French cavalry force and inflicted heavy casualties. It was not until 20 April that Beresford was finally able to approach Badajoz; and all these delays allowed Soult to prepare the force with which he intended marching to its relief.

On 20 April Wellington himself arrived at Elvas, much to everybody's surprise. The commander-in-chief was satisfied with affairs in the north, and with his army blockading

Gordon Browne's depiction of British troops constructing the bridge over the Guadiana in April 1811, close to the fords at Jerumenha. With Badajoz in enemy hands the bridge was the only way of ferrying men, guns, equipment and suplies across the Guadiana. This was a risky business, for should the bridge be swept away by rising flood waters - which happened in 1812 - the besieging troops on the south bank would be isolated.

William Carr Beresford (1764-1854), wearing his uniform of a Portuguese marshal. Remembered for his successful reorganisation and training of the Portuguese Army, and an officer whose previous career attested to a personal bravery which he was to demonstrate again on 16 May, he was not a gifted tactician. At Albuera he was paralysed by indecision, which would have cost him the battle had it not been for the energy of Henry Hardinge and the moral courage of Lowry Cole.

Almeida he took the opportunity to ride south to inspect Badajoz for himself. On 22 April he rode round the fortress making copious notes during a thorough reconnaissance, and the following day he produced a series of detailed memoranda regarding the forthcoming siege and arrangements for the other Allied forces in the area. One of the points mentioned by Wellington concerned Beresford's movements in the event of an offensive by Soult. Wellington thought this a distinct probability, and authorised Beresford to withdraw across the Guadiana if he did not consider himself in a strong enough position to fight. If he did, he was to abandon the siege of Badajoz temporarily and to march south to meet Soult. He also suggested a suitable place for such an engagement: Albuera[1].

Meanwhile, Beresford pressed on with his preparations for the siege. Standing on the southern bank of the Guadiana river, and with its eastern front covered by the Rivellas stream, the town of Badajoz commanded the southern corridor between Portugal and Spain. It was enclosed within strong walls, in places 40 feet high and as

many thick, linked by nine bastions (see page 107). Unlike the relatively weak walls of Ciudad Rodrigo, which commanded the Spanish end of the northern corridor, the fortifications of Badajoz had been improved and modernised as the science of siege warfare evolved. The north-eastern part of the town, where the old Moorish castle dominated the area, stood some 130 feet above the Rivellas and was an extremely strong sector. The northern side was covered by the Guadiana itself and required only a relatively low wall to protect it. Four outworks had also been constructed. The Pardaleras covered the south-western side and the San Roque and Picurina the eastern approaches. On the northern bank of the Guadiana stood Fort San Cristobal, an extremely strong position approachable from only two sides; the fort's rear was covered by steep cliffs, at the foot of which ran the Guadiana. It was also protected by a very effective glacis which hid the fort from view until any attacker was actually standing on the edge of the deep ditch which completely encircled the fort.

When Beresford arrived in late April he found the town in a fine state of defence, even allowing for the damage done to the place when the French besieged it the previous month. In addition to the bastions there were numerous ravelins covering the curtain walls between them; ditches had been deepened, outworks strengthened, and everything possible done to ensure that when the Allies attacked they would do so at extreme cost to themselves. The governor of Badajoz was Baron Armand Phillipon, who commanded a garrison of some 3,000 men. Phillipon was to prove a superb exponent of the art of aggressive defence, for he was not content to simply sit back and hope that a friendly relief force would arrive. He continually encouraged his men, ordered sorties to be made, saw to it that debris was cleared away from the ditches, and ensured that damaged defences were repaired as quickly as possible. In this way he was able to maintain morale throughout the siege - often a very difficult task. He was to prove even more proficient during Wellington's siege in March and April 1812, but that is another story.

Satisfied with the arrangements he had made for the siege, Wellington left Beresford and rode north on 25 April. Bad weather hampered Beresford's operations, and with the Guadiana in full flood the transportation of men and supplies across the river proved a lengthy and hazardous business. In fact it was not until 8 May, almost two weeks after Wellington's departure, that Beresford was able to complete the encirclement of Badajoz. Towards evening of the same day his engineers began tracing out ground, while the infantry began the laborious and hated task of digging the trenches ('parallels'). Soon afterwards the first batteries began to be constructed for the Allies' guns. The available artillery did not inspire much confidence; the 32 guns which had been assembled were a mixture of British ordnance and outdated Portuguese pieces taken from fortresses - many of them dating from the 17th century. Although the resources for conducting sieges would be improved later in the war, this type of operation was always to expose the Achilles heel of the Allied field army in the Peninsula.

Hardly had the first guns opened fire on the walls of Badajoz when Beresford received news on 10 May that Soult was approaching from the south, intent on relieving the place. It was an unwelcome, if half-expected development. Two days later he gave orders for the entire siege

Marshal Nicolas - Jean de Dieu Soult, Duke of Dalmatia (1769-1851), pictured in old age. In the Albuera campaign he showed all his renowned skill in moving armies across the map, but little flair in moving brigades across the battlefield. In November 1812 his advance forced Wellington to raise the siege of Burgos and retire to Portugal once again. In July 1813 he was named commander-in-chief of the Armies of Spain and the Pyrenees; he welded together this tattered command, and led it in delaying operations, with considerable skill, but was unable to halt Wellington's advance into southern France. During the Hundred Days he was appointed chief of staff of the Army of the North, but did not shine in this role. After a brief period in disgrace Soult was restored to his rank under the Bourbons, and held senior appointments until 1847. When he visited London in 1838 as an ambassador to Queen Victoria's coronation he was cordially received as a respected former enemy. At the age of 78 he attained a rank held by only three men before him: like Turenne, Villars and Saxe, he died a Marshal-General of France.

train, including all stores and artillery, to be withdrawn to the northern bank of the Guadiana for safety. The first siege of Badajoz came, therefore, to a swift end, while Beresford turned his attention to the threat from the south.

The commanders

Soult himself had arrived at Seville on 14 March, having retired there in the wake of Graham's victory at Barrosa on the 5th of that month. Although he had been aware since the end of March of Beresford's advance against Badajoz he took no steps to begin collecting his relieving force until 25 April. This may well have been on account of the problems and delays Beresford had encountered during April; Soult, realising that Badajoz was under no great immediate threat, knew that there was no need for any undue haste. Under normal circumstances the governor of a besieged fortress would conduct an aggressive defence in order to buy time for a relieving force to arrive to break the siege. Had Beresford been able to approach Badajoz at the beginning of April things might well have been more serious for the French, with Soult having to get forward much earlier and with a much weaker force than he was eventually to lead. In the event, the difficulties encountered by the Allies meant that Soult's apparent tardiness was not to prove fatal to the garrison - although, as we shall see in Chapter Eleven, their salvation in 1811 would be due not to any intervention on the part of Soult but to their own skill and tenacity.

The two opposing commanders at Albuera - Marshal Nicolas-Jean de Dieu Soult, Duke of Dalmatia, and Marshal William Carr Beresford - were both in their early forties, had both been soldiers since their teens, had both seen wide-ranging service, had both been injured and both captured. They also possessed rather similar military skills and weaknesses; both were excellent organisers of armies but indifferent commanders in battle in the absence of specific orders from their brilliant commanders-in-chief. Wellington once said that Soult certainly knew how to get his men to the battlefield, but once there he did not know what to do with them. This may have been rather harsh as a summary of a whole career; but equally, Napoleon's praise of Soult after Austerlitz as the ablest tactician in Europe was even further off the mark.

Like Wellington, Napoleon and Ney, Soult was born in 1769; he was of humble background, and an early ambition was to be a baker. Instead he enlisted in the Régiment

Royal-Infanterie in 1785, two weeks after his 16th birthday. A corporal at the outbreak of the French Revolution, five years later he was commanding a brigade. His rapid promotion continued during several campaigns between 1794 and 1804, including service as a divisional commander under Masséna; in 1800 he was wounded and captured by the Austrians in Italy. In May 1804 he was one of the first group of generals created Marshals of the Empire by Napoleon. At Austerlitz in December 1805 it was Soult's 4th Corps which Napoleon launched in the decisive frontal attack on the Pratzen Heights which won him the battle. His service in the Jena and Eylau campaign of 1806-07 brought him further honours and huge financial rewards (which were important to him: like Masséna he was a rapacious plunderer, though he did not share his old chief's sexual voracity). Sent to Spain in 1808, Soult chased Moore's army to the coast the following winter, but was himself driven out of Portugal by the future Lord Wellington in 1809. In September he was made chief-of-staff to King Joseph, and two months later he routed a much stronger Spanish army at Ocaña. Moving south in January 1810, he invaded Andalusia and set up his headquarters at Seville in February. His response to Beresford's incursion into Estremadura was to be his first test against British troops since Wellington bundled his men out of Oporto in May 1809.

William Carr Beresford was the illegitimate son of the Marquess of Waterford. A year older than Soult, Beresford had been purchased a commission in the Army in 1785; a year later he lost his left eye in a shooting accident. In 1793 he attracted praise for his behaviour as a junior officer in the doomed Toulon operation; and just two years later this tall, burly 27-year-old Anglo-Irishman became commanding officer of the 88th Foot - the famous Connaught Rangers.

Since then he had seen service in India, Egypt and the Cape of Good Hope before becoming embroiled in the ill-fated attack on Buenos Aires in 1806 as a brigade commander. This audacious but badly thought-through operation, which began with a measure of success, provoked a full-scale rising by the outraged locals, who defeated the small British force in August 1806. Beresford was taken prisoner, although he escaped after six months and returned to England.

In 1807 he captured Madeira in the name of Britain's Portuguese allies, beginning to learn the language (which defied all but the most capable and dedicated British officers) and forming an admiration for the stoic military qualities of the Portuguese. He took part in Moore's campaign in the winter of 1808-09; and commanded a brigade at Corunna in January 1809, when Soult's advance to prevent the British embarkation was checked. On 2 March that year Beresford was appointed Marshal of the Portuguese Army and charged with its reorganisation. In this task his grasp of the language, his tireless energy and his great administrative and organisational skills brought excellent results.

These gifts, however, were not matched by leadership skills on the battlefield; and it was Beresford's tactical ability and talent for exercising command and control under pressure which were about to be put to the most severe test possible. Physically brave, with a good mind for detail, William Beresford secretly knew his own limitations, and lacked confidence when exercising independent command; his main problem was anxiety.

The Duke of Damnation marches north

On 10 May, Soult's army lumbered into motion and began its march north from Seville towards Badajoz - around 19,000 infantry and 4,000 cavalry of the 5th Corps, with 48 guns[2]. The distance from Seville to Badajoz is around 120 miles by the direct route passing through Zafra and Albuera. Soult, however, took a more easterly route and, passing Zafra, continued north to Villafranca and Almendralejo in the direction of Merida. During the march the French advanced guard encountered several isolated Spanish patrols, which quickly turned and fell back. The first encounter

between British and French troops came on 13 May in front of Villafranca, where Long's light cavalry were watching the road. These too fell back towards Santa Marta and Almendralejo in the face of the oncoming French force.

Meanwhile, Beresford had marched south from Badajoz and on 13 May arrived at Valverde. He had with him the 2nd Division and Hamilton's Portuguese division, around 7,000 men altogether, and three batteries of guns. With events moving ever quicker, Beresford had to make some important decisions. First, he had to decide where to position his army. There were three roads Soult might take to reach Badajoz. The first, the western road, lay through Valverde itself; the central road lay through Albuera; and the third, the more easterly route, lay via Almendralejo. The problem was solved when the French followed Long's cavalry to Santa Marta. From here the logical and most direct route to Badajoz lay through Albuera; and Beresford moved his troops the eight miles or so east from Valverde to that town.

The other important issue to be decided was that of overall command. The force gathering at Albuera was, for once, truly an Allied one. Up until now Wellington had been operating with a mainly Anglo-Portuguese army, with the various Spanish armies acting under the orders of their own generals, of which there were two at Albuera - Blake and Castaños. There were in excess of 15,000 Spanish troops converging upon Albuera, twice the number of British troops; but, after a brief conference, it was decided that Beresford should command the entire Allied force. On 15 May, Beresford reached Albuera and waited for the arrival of the Spaniards and the Allied cavalry, who came in throughout the afternoon and evening, as did Alten's King's German Legion light brigade and a further Portuguese brigade under Collins. There only remained Myers's brigade of the 4th Division, which was marching south from Badajoz, along with just three companies of Kemmis's brigade, one each from the 2/27th, 1/40th and the 97th, these being all that had been able to cross to the south bank of the Guadiana before its flooding prevented the rest of the brigade from getting across. If he had moved faster, Soult might have caught Beresford at Albuera before the Allies

An impression of street fighting in the village of Albuera on 16 May. The actual fighting never reached the level of intensity portrayed in this typically spirited painting by Caton Woodville; Godinot's attacks were intended to be more of a feint than a full-blooded blow. The village was defended by the Light Battalions of the King's German Legion rather than the British line infantry depicted here; and as usual, the artist incorrectly shows the uniforms as the post-1812 pattern.

Captain Julius Hartmann, who served with the King's German Legion horse artillery at Albuera. Hartmann also fought at Talavera, Campo Mayor, Salamanca, Vittoria, San Sebastian and the Nive, and was wounded during the sortie from Bayonne on 14 April 1814. (Inset) Hartmann's gold medal, with clasps for Albuera and Salamanca. (Courtesy Michael Tänzer)

had concentrated, and indeed his despatches show that he had intended to attack Beresford before Blake, marching up from the south, arrived at Albuera. However, although he got part of his force to within striking distance of Albuera on the 15th, the bulk of Soult's infantry had only reached Santa Marta, where they camped for the night.

The Albuera campaign was to provoke heated arguments between various participants and non-participants after the event. One of the controversies surrounded the replacement by Beresford of Robert Long as commander of the Allied cavalry. Long had been commanding the Allied cavalry outposts south of Albuera and had pulled back in the face of heavy French opposition. However, Beresford's aide Benjamin d'Urban considered that Long had given up ground rather too quickly and easily. It will be remembered that Beresford and Long, a naturally argumentative man, had already clashed following the fight at Campo Mayor two months earlier. Now, with his staff complaining bitterly about Long, Beresford seems to have taken the opportunity of having him replaced and appointed General William Lumley to command instead, with Colonel Abercrombie - son of Sir Ralph, the much-loved old hero of Alexandria in 1801 - assuming command of Lumley's old brigade of the 2nd Division.

In fact, however, Long's removal from command owed more to his own concerns on behalf of the army than to any spite on the part of Beresford. Long, aware that there were Spanish cavalry officers present who were senior to himself, was concerned lest one of these demand to be placed in command of the Allied cavalry. (This was not a question of petty rivalry; the prejudice of British officers against Spanish leadership was solidly based on experience of its very variable quality. The Spanish themselves acknowledged the urgent need for professional officer training and took steps to improve it, but the results of this effort were inevitably slow to arrive. It was only in 1811 that a law requiring all officers to be from the nobility was repealed.) The situation was brought to the attention of Beresford by Long himself; and therefore, to ensure that overall command was retained by a British officer over whom no Spanish officer could claim seniority, Long stepped aside and Lumley was placed in command[3]. Far less explicable,

however, is that Beresford chose make these changes only on the morning of 16 May just as the battle was about to begin. Long was removed from command when he was in the very act of forming the cavalry, leaving a bemused Lumley very little time to adjust to his new responsibilities.

The field and the deployments

The battlefield of Albuera has at its centre the village itself, through which runs the road to Badajoz; in fact it was the junction of roads to Talavera, Valverde, Almendralejo and Santa Marta. Today's visitor will not notice any feature that stands out as being particularly dominant, with a range of low hills running north-south parallel with the road which runs south from Albuera to Torre de Miguel. The hills, then covered with a mixture of vineyards and rough meadowland, lie to the west of the road while a small stream, the Chicapierna, lies to its east. Another stream, the Nogales, lies even further to the east, running alongside the road to Santa Marta. The two streams begin at Albuera itself, for it is here that the Albuera river, which itself is little more than a large stream, divides into two; the lower slopes rising from the watercourse were dotted with olive groves. The Albuera river is crossed in two places by small stone bridges which carry the roads from Santa Marta and Almendralejo into the village. Beyond the Nogales stream and the road to Santa Marta is an undulating plain, extensively planted with vineyards, bordered to the east and south-east by a large wood. To the south of the battlefield there is a further range of low hills, in 1811 planted with vines on the slopes beneath crests of scrubby meadowland, through which run the roads to Santa Marta, Nogales and Torre de Miguel. These hills, too, were covered with olive groves in 1811. To the west of the hills upon which Beresford had drawn up his army there lies an even more extensive plain.

These hills afforded Beresford's men a good reverse slope position, although it appears that the Allies were drawn up in full view of the French, for they were easily observed by Soult as he approached from the east. The main weakness of Beresford's position lay in the fact that the low hills running south from the village had no apparent end: no matter how far south he deployed his men, there was always a further hill that dominated his right flank. He had to place his right flank somewhere, but wherever he chose to do so it was in the knowledge that it might come under threat from any hostile force which took possession of the next height to the south.

In March 1812 John Mills, of the Coldstream Guards, passed across the old Albuera battlefield on his way to Santa Marta when the Guards formed part of the covering force during the third siege of Badajoz. After seeing the position for himself, Mills wrote: 'He [Beresford] had the choice of two positions 200 yards distant from each other, chose the worst and lost his men in taking up the other after he had perceived his error'[4]. Beresford himself later claimed that he was not unaware of this dilemma but literally had to draw the line somewhere[5]. Commenting on this error, Major Roverea, Lowry Cole's ADC, wrote in his journal: 'Five hundred paces from the right of the Spanish line was a hill which dominated our position, the possession of which was essential to our safety, which should have been strongly fortified or at any rate held very strongly. The Marshal [Beresford] thought it sufficient to occupy it with 500 Spanish light troops. Under cover of a false attack on the bridge, screened by their numerous cavalry, the French occupied the fatal hill in force'[6].

Beresford's 35,000 troops were arrayed along a front of about two and a half miles upon the range of low heights running north to south to the west of the roads from Badajoz to Albuera and from Albuera to Torre de Miguel, with the village of Albuera at the centre of his position. Hamilton's Portuguese were deployed on the left, or furthest north, with Collins behind him. On Hamilton's right was William Stewart with the 2nd Division and on his right came the bulk of the Allied infantry - the Spaniards, with Lardizabal and Ballasteros in the front line and Zayas in the rear. Loftus Otway's Portuguese cavalry occupied a position about half a mile to the north of Albuera, at the foot of the heights occupied by Hamilton and Collins, while Long's cavalry were the best part of a mile directly west of Albuera, behind Beresford's main infantry line. Alten's two light battalions of the King's German Legion held the village of Albuera itself. The Allied artillery, of which there were 36 guns, were judiciously placed at various parts of the battlefield.

To an enemy approaching from the east Beresford's position could not have looked particularly strong; and the weakness of its right flank must have been clearly apparent to a man of Soult's experience. The one saving grace was almost certainly the reverse slope which shielded Beresford's infantry from enemy view, though this does not seem to have given Soult any great pause. In September 1811 a great French opportunity to defeat Wellington would go awry at Fuenteguinaldo mainly because Marmont, fearful that

Captain Augustus Wahrendorff of the 1st Light Battalion, King's German Legion. He served throughout the Peninsular War and was severely wounded twice: at Villafranca, three days after Vittoria, and during the crossing of the Bidassoa on 7 October 1813. He would be wounded again at Waterloo. (Courtesy Michael Tänzer)

Wellington had great numbers hidden from view, refused to attack quite a perilous British position, enabling vital reserves to get forward. At Albuera Soult seems to have had no such misgivings, and quickly formed his plan of attack regardless of what might lie behind the crest.

With just under 25,000 troops, Soult was fighting at Albuera with 10,000 fewer men than the Allies. We must assume, therefore, that he was unaware of the arrival after dark on the 15th of Blake's Spaniards. His plan involved a feint in strength against Albuera village, while the main bulk of his infantry crossed the Nogales and Chicapierna streams further south under cover of the woods and groves. Then, after deploying on the hills to the south of Beresford's line, they would advance against the Allied right flank and, if all went according to plan, would simply roll up the line. It was a sound enough plan, and it almost succeeded. Indeed, as we shall see, it was only the staying power of the British infantry that saved Beresford's skin.

The first phase: Godinot at the village

The battle of Albuera began at round 8am on 16 May when, with storm clouds gathering overhead, 3,500 men from Godinot's brigade (16th Light and 51st Line), flanked to the north by Briche's brigade of light cavalry, marched forward to assault the village of Albuera. Two batteries of artillery supported them but these, along with the attacking columns, quickly came under fire from Captain Arriaga's Portuguese battery, situated just behind the village. The Albuera river is not much of an obstacle even to infantry, but it was enough to make Godinot's men make for the bridge which lay just to the south of the village. Here, with round-shot and canister ripping great holes in their ranks, the French attack floundered, while Alten's German marksmen opened up a galling fire from the cover of the village's out-buildings. Godinot's skirmishers threw themselves under cover, loading and firing and exchanging shots with the green-clad Hanoverians. (Alten's experienced troops of the 1st and 2nd KGL Light Battalions included Captain George Baring who, just over four years later, would find fame defending the farm of La Haye Sainte at Waterloo.) The French continued to pour forward. The situation intensified when a body of Polish lancers crossed the stream and formed up on the western bank. Fortunately, Long brought forward the 3rd Dragoon Guards and 13th Light Dragoons, who cut and hacked their way between the sabres and lances of the enemy to send them flying back across the water. At this time the French army did not have lancer regiments; the Polish unit - the 1st Lancers of the Vistula Legion - normally operated in eastern Spain, and this was the first occasion when British cavalry had come face to face with this weapon in the Peninsula[7].

The French attacks on the village were to continue throughout the day; but the fighting on this northern sector was really only a diversion, intended to draw more Allied troops into the centre. To this end the plan worked well, for with the fight at the village intensifying Beresford decided to bring forward Colborne's brigade of the 2nd Division and Cleeve's 6-pounder battery of the KGL artillery. Two of Lardizabal's Spanish battalions were also sent forward to support those fighting against Godinot's men. A further KGL battery, under Captain Braun, which was attached to Hamilton's Portuguese division, also opened fire on Godinot's men. At about this stage Beresford was reassured

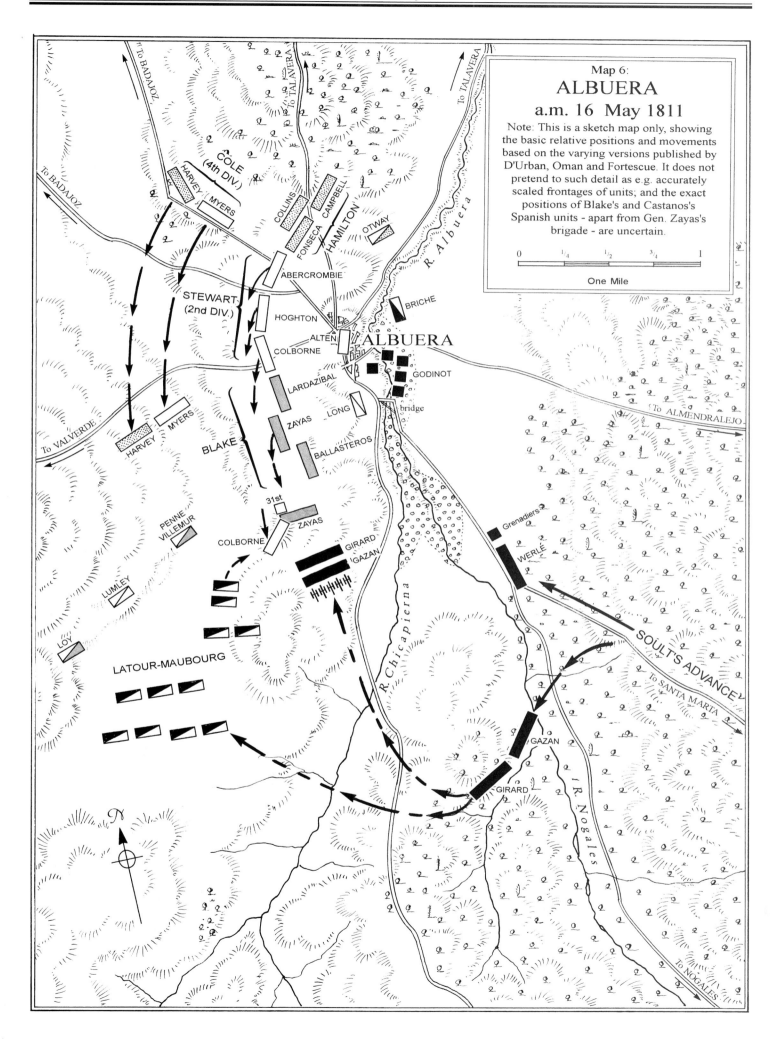

Map 6:
ALBUERA
a.m. 16 May 1811

Note: This is a sketch map only, showing the basic relative positions and movements based on the varying versions published by D'Urban, Oman and Fortescue. It does not pretend to such detail as e.g. accurately scaled frontages of units; and the exact positions of Blake's and Castanos's Spanish units - apart from Gen. Zayas's brigade - are uncertain.

| 0 | ¼ | ½ | ¾ | 1 |

One Mile

by the arrival on the field of Myers' brigade of Lowry Cole's 4th Division, along with the three companies from Kemmis's brigade. These troops took up a position to the west of Albuera, along the road leading to Valverde. Here they were to wait until they were brought into action.

While the guns barked and musketry crackled around the village of Albuera, in the woods to the south the two French divisions under Gazan and Girard began snaking their way west and north, crossing the Nogales and Chicapierna streams, and finally emerging from cover to appear just over a mile away from the Allied right flank, supported by Latour - Maubourg's strong cavalry division. Blake's Spaniards, safe on the reverse slope of the Allied position, had been listening intently to the fighting at the village. This had been in progress for about an hour and a half when one of General Zayas's aides suddenly rode up and reported movements away to the south. British cavalry patrols also saw these movements, which were duly reported to Beresford. A hasty dash by Blake and other Spanish officers to one of the hills to the south was all that was needed to confirm the fact that, whilst Godinot's men were attacking Albuera, a much larger enemy force had crossed the two streams and was rapidly approaching the Allied right.

The second phase: Girard and Gazan on the right

It did not take long for Beresford to grasp the situation once it had been reported to him, and he ordered Blake to quickly realign his forces. Blake was to wheel his line to his right, creating a new east-west front facing to the south, and to advance to occupy the low height next to the one he had previously occupied, which now became his second line. It was a similar manoeuvre to that adopted by Wellington at Fuentes de Oñoro, when he had been forced to 'refuse' his right flank and adopt an inverted L-shaped line. By shifting to his right and facing south across the new height, Blake would create not so much an inverted L but more of a T-shape, with his own divisions forming the crosspiece. To support Blake, Beresford instructed Stewart's 2nd Division to form the second line to this new front. It was at this point that the old failings of the Anglo-Spanish alliance resurfaced once more. General Blake, believing that the enemy flank march was nothing more than a demonstration, and convinced that Soult's real intention was a frontal attack, refused to move his battalions. Instead, he rejoined his men and despatched a messenger to inform Beresford of his intention to stay where he was. Fortunately, General Zayas's grasp of the situation was more in keeping with reality; and this officer took it upon himself to face four battalions of his division to their right, along with his single battery of divisional artillery.

Beresford, meanwhile, was north of Albuera supervising Hamilton's Portuguese division, when Blake's message arrived. There was no time to lose; leaving Hamilton with orders to act as he saw fit, he galloped off to find Blake. When he arrived he found Zayas's four battalions forming up with two in line and two in column behind them, all facing south. In the distance, a mass of French infantry supported by cavalry and artillery were coming straight at them, and coming on fast. Beresford quickly gave orders for the three remaining battalions under Lardizabal (the other two having been moved north closer to the village) to be brought forward on Zayas's right, and two of Ballasteros's

Francis Schaumann, 2nd Light Battalion, King's German Legion. Francis was the brother of Augustus Schaumann, author of the hugely entertaining memoir On the Road with Wellington. *(Courtesy Michael Tänzer)*

battalions on his left – a move that was barely accomplished before French skirmishers came within range[8]. Thus, Beresford stood waiting to oppose this massive French attack with what can best be described as troops of uncertain abilities who had barely had time to settle into their new position.

In his classic book *Wellington in the Peninsula* Jac Weller described the French infantry attack at Albuera as 'the most massive single attack of the Peninsular War'[9]. Ahead of the infantry rode some 3,500 cavalry under Latour-Maubourg, who had little difficulty in driving back Loy's 1,100 Spanish cavalry and De Grey's 700 British heavy dragoons. Following behind came Girard and Gazan, who had formed their infantry divisions into a massive formation that came on like a juggernaut, driving noisily towards the Allied line. Between them the two divisional commanders had 19 battalions. The exact formation was set down by an anonymous French officer, and is worth quoting in full, in order to appreciate the sheer size of this mass of men:

'The line of attack was formed by a brigade in column of attack. To the right and left the front line was in a mixed formation, that is to say, on each side of the central column was a battalion deployed in line, and on each of the two outer sides of the deployed battalions was a battalion or regiment in column, so that each end of the line was composed of a column ready to form square, in case the hostile cavalry should try to fall upon our flanks – which was hardly likely, since our own cavalry was immensely superior to it in number'[10].

An idea of the great size of the French attacking force can be gained from the fact that the above description is of Girard's division only. Immediately behind Girard came Gazan's division, arrayed in four regimental columns, two consisting of four battalions and two of three, each battalion following one behind the other. In all, there were some 8,400 French infantry advancing in a formation which, given that were between 400 and 500 men in the front rank, must have been at least 500 yards wide, by at least 60 to 70 yards deep. (Although this was not a solid formation, since at least two battalions advanced in line, nevertheless once the fighting began it must have been extremely difficult for the officers to maintain its shape, with casualties occurring and with men continually closing ranks.)

To the Spanish troops facing the men of Soult's 5th Corps the French formation must have appeared as a single, solid mass, and it can only have been when the front ranks advanced on to the forward slopes of each successive low hill that it was possible to see over their heads, thus revealing not only the large columns but also the open spaces between them. Not that this was any sort of encouragement to Zayas's men as they prepared to meet this intimidating blue tide, outnumbering them at least two to one, in an attempt to hold on long enough for Stewart's 2nd Division to get forward in support. Before long Zayas's men began to drop as French skirmishers crept forward to harry the Spanish line. Girard's horse artillery, too, began to take its toll, opening fire from the crest of the hill opposite Zayas.

To their immense credit, Zayas's four battalions stood firm, loaded their muskets and began to return fire. Amazingly, the great French mass halted in its tracks. While its rear ranks shuffled and stood patiently, waiting to get forward, the front ranks opened fire at the thin line of Spaniards arrayed across the slope facing them. The terrible killing match of Albuera had begun in earnest.

The two slopes were quickly covered by Spanish and French troops, while the dip in the ground between them filled with thick, grey-white smoke as volley after volley was fired. To the north, meanwhile, Stewart was hastily bringing forward the 2nd Division, the leading brigade of which was commanded by Colonel John Colborne. The four battalions - the 1/3rd (Buffs), 2/31st (Huntingdonshire), 2/48th (Northamptonshire) and 2/66th (Berkshire) - made good time, passing easily over the deep reddish-brown earth of the undulating terrain. In the distance they could see powdersmoke rising above the skyline, below which Zayas's units were exchanging volley for volley with Girard's men.

Overhead, meanwhile, the inky black clouds that had been gathering all morning blotted out the sun to create an eerie and menacing atmosphere, the air becoming thick and oppressive while at the same time a cold rain began to fall. Galloping past Colborne's men in a jingling, thundering rush came Cleeve's battery of the King's German Legion; the leading four guns unlimbered on the extreme right of the Spanish line, and at a range of about 90 yards began to open fire on the enemy columns[11]. At this very short range the ammunition of choice was light canister, spreading 85 musket-size balls with every shot, and quite possibly double-loaded with a roundshot. Thus assailed from both front and flank, by artillery and infantry, Girard's men began to draw back.

It was at this point that Colborne's brigade finally arrived in the firing line. The brigade had moved forward in echelon, with the 1/3rd on the right, followed closely by the 2/48th and the 2/66th, with the 2/31st furthest from the line to the left rear. It should be remembered that Colborne had been ordered by Beresford to form up behind Zayas, to form a second line. However, Stewart appears to have acted upon his own initiative and brought the brigade up on the right flank of Zayas instead, with the intention of attacking Girard's left flank. No sooner had the front three battalions passed Zayas's men than Stewart formed them into line, and they opened up with a blaze of musketry against the French left flank. Major William Brooke of the 2/48th later recalled the moment when the brigade finally got to grips with the enemy:

'On gaining the summit of the hill we discovered several heavy columns of French troops ready to receive us. The British line deployed, halted, and fired two rounds: the heads of the French columns returned the fire three deep, the front rank kneeling. Finding these columns were not to be shaken by fire, the three leading battalions of the brigade prepared to charge with the bayonet, by order of Major-General the Hon. William Stewart, who led them on in

The 1/3rd Regiment (Buffs) at the battle of Albuera; a small group of officers and men fight to save the Colours while Polish lancers move in for the kill. Only inaccuracies of uniform detail mar Wollen's otherwise superb painting. It was during this episode of the battle that Lieutenant Matthew Latham lost an arm and half of his face while defending the King's Colour.

person to the attack in the most gallant manner. The charge being delivered, the French 28th Léger gave way, as did also the front ranks of the Grenadiers. In the latter we could see the officers trying to beat back the men with the flats of their swords'[12].

It was a devastating attack. Girard's men, already reeling from the fire of Zayas's infantry and from the blasts of canister and roundshot from Cleeve's battery, certainly returned fire for a while, and inflicted significant losses on Stewart's battalions (see the letter quoted below from Lieutenant Crompton of the 2/66th). Soon, however, they began to turn and stagger backwards, whereupon Colborne's men cheered and prepared to hasten them on their way with the bayonet. But even as the cheers rose from their throats, the dark clouds above opened up and a torrential storm of rain and hail came lashing down into the faces of the redcoat infantry, rendering their muskets useless and making it almost impossible to see anything more than a short distance away. Then, out of the blinding sheets of rain, large dark shapes came looming straight for them, the ground shaking beneath their pounding weight. For infantrymen formed in line, this was the worst of all nightmares: cavalry.

The destruction of Colborne's brigade

General Latour-Maubourg had been watching the infantry duel developing in front of him, while at the same time keeping his eye on the Allied cavalry arrayed on the plain to his left front, beyond which lay part of Cole's 4th Division – Myers's brigade and Kemmis's handful of companies. The sudden downpour gave him the opportunity of charging the flank of the British infantry nearby, and he was quick to seize it. The French cavalry commander had two regiments with him, the Polish 1st Lancers of the Vistula Legion and

the French 2nd Hussars – about 800 riders in all. They had been hidden from sight by the hill upon which Girard's men had formed, the same hill which so many Allied troops thought should have been occupied by themselves. Now, with Colborne's men blinded and almost disarmed by the rain and strung out in line almost end-on to their front, these two regiments were launched against the brigade's unprotected right flank and rear in one of the most devastating cavalry attacks of the Peninsular War.

As Colborne's men advanced into the storm the shout went up, 'Cavalry!' Apparently it was assumed that they were Spaniards, but the first few piercing screams of pain dismissed that illusion. The British infantrymen were left almost helpless as the Polish troopers went about their grim work. Under normal circumstances, infantry under cavalry attack would form square, four ranks deep and bristling with bayonets; but here, caught without warning in the confusion of the storm, strung out so that they could not protect each other by massed action, each individual soldier or little knot of men offered easy prey. It is impossible to reload and fire a flintlock musket in heavy rain; the loading process involves pouring powder from a torn-open paper cartridge into an open priming pan, where raindrops will turn it into a useless black slurry. The fact that the front rank of the Poles were armed with nine-foot lances (see Madden's comment at the end of this chapter) made it almost impossible to escape their reach, or to fight back effectively with fixed bayonets. By throwing himself upon the ground an infantryman could usually avoid the cut of an enemy cavalryman's sabre, although he risked injury under the horse's hoofs. Against enemy lancers, however, even this was futile - the trooper had only to lean over to one side and stab downwards.

The first unit to feel the power of Latour-Maubourg's charge was the 1/3rd. Caught in line on the right flank of Colborne's front, the Buffs virtually disappeared as the enemy cavalry rode them down. Small groups of soldiers formed up and tried to defend themselves as best they could, but there was little they could do against such a long-armed enemy. Mounted British field officers fared little better; indeed, of the 27 officers present with the Buffs, only seven came through the battle unscathed; the rest were killed, wounded or taken prisoner. The episode was the more horrific for the fact that the Poles went about their business giving no quarter even to wounded men. Captain Gordon was one of those struck down during the attack:

'I was knocked down by a horseman with his lance, which luckily did me no serious injury. In getting up I received a lance in my hip, and shortly after another in my knee, which slightly grazed me. I then rose, when a soldier hurried me to the rear a few yards, striking me on the side of the head with his lance. He left me, and soon another came up, who would have killed me had not a French officer came up, and giving the fellow a blow told the fellow to spare the English, and to go on and do his duty with those of my unfortunate comrades. This officer conducted me to the rear of the French lines and here, the sight that met the eye was dreadful! Men dead, where the column had stood,

This somewhat stylised representation by Stanley L. Wood of the 1st Lancers of the Vistula Legion attacking Colborne's brigade does have the virtue of conveying the lethal impact of a lance charge against a line of infantry.

The small house on the skyline marks the site of the Buffs position when the Vistula Legion lancers overran them. The lancers attacked under cover of the hailstorm, and swept around the slopes of the hill to appear suddenly in rear of Colborne's brigade. It was also here, in the light-coloured field on the right, that the left flank of the Fusilier Brigade linked up with the right flank of the 2/31st to begin the final advance against Werlé - see Chapter Nine.

heaped on each other; the wounded crying out for assistance and human blood flowing down the hill! I came to where the baggage was where I found a vast number of my own regiment, with a good proportion of officers prisoners, like myself; numbers of them desperately wounded even after they were prisoners!'[13].

Amongst the prisoners was another captain of the Buffs, named Cameron, who had been shot in the neck and wounded in the chest by a lance. In spite of his wounds he managed to escape from the French and was back with his regiment by the end of the month. In fact, scores of the prisoners taken on the 16th escaped during the next few days and rejoined their regiments.

The 1/3rd's Colours were, predictably, the focus of particularly savage fighting. Ensign Charles Walsh was holding proudly aloft the King's Colour, the staff of which had been cut in two by a roundshot. Walsh was wounded and in danger of losing the Colour when Lieutenant Matthew Latham rushed over to him and took the Colour himself. In one of the most famous incidents of the Peninsular War, Latham defended the colour furiously, fighting off the enemy cavalry with his flimsy 1796-pattern infantry officers' sword. One enemy sabre cut took away his nose and half of his face, while another severed his left arm; but still Latham refused to give up the Colour. So many enemy cavalrymen tried to get at him that, ironically, this jostling press of riders almost certainly saved his life, by hampering one another so that no one man could deal him the fatal blow. Cut down and trampled on, Latham was left for dead. That night, when the dazed survivors of the regiment were scouring the field, he was found terribly maimed and disfigured but still alive, with the King's Colour hidden beneath his body.

Carrying the Buffs' Regimental Colour was 16-year-old Ensign Edward Thomas. The Polish lancers surged round the Colour, stabbing and hacking at those who defended it. When summoned to surrender the Colour the boy replied, 'Only with my life!', and was immediately cut down, mortally wounded. Captain Stevens saw the Colour captured, and later wrote of young Thomas: 'He rallied my company after I was wounded and taken prisoner, crying out, "Rally on me, men, I will be your pivot." He was buried with all the care possible by a sergeant and a private, the only two survivors of my company, which consisted of sixty-three men when taken into action'[14]. The Regimental Colour of the Buffs did not remain long in the hands of the enemy, however; it was recovered by Sergeant William Gough of the 1/7th Royal Fusiliers towards the end of the battle fol-

lowing the successful advance of the Fusilier Brigade.

The recovery of the Colours was small comfort for the scores of men who were cut down or speared by the enemy cavalry. The Buffs suffered appalling casualties of four officers and 212 men killed, 14 officers and 234 men wounded, and two officers and 177 men taken prisoner - a total of 643 casualties out of a strength of 27 officers and 728 men, or just over 85 per cent of the Buffs' strength. The disproportionate ratio between killed and wounded tells us much about the ferocity of the Poles' attack; conventionally, one expects around three or even four times as many wounded as killed, not these virtually equal numbers.

Although the Buffs took the full force of the attack by Latour-Maubourg's cavalry, two of Colborne's remaining three battalions suffered almost as high casualties. Major William Brooke, fighting with the 2/48th, was another officer to experience the brutality of the Vistula Legion:

'Part of the victorious French cavalry were Polish Lancers: from the conduct of this regiment on the field of action I believe many of them to have been intoxicated, as they rode over the wounded, barbarously darting their lances into them. Several unfortunate prisoners were killed in this manner, while being led from the field to the rear of the enemy's lines. I was an instance of their inhumanity: after having been most severely wounded in the head, and plundered of everything that I had about me, I was being led as a prisoner between two French infantry soldiers, when one of these lancers rode up, and deliberately cut me down. Then, taking the skirts of my regimental coat, he endeavoured to pull it over my head. Not satisfied with this brutality, the wretch tried every means in his power to make his horse trample on me, by dragging me along the ground and wheeling his horse over my body. But the beast, more merciful than the rider, absolutely refused to comply with his master's wishes, and carefully avoided putting his foot on me!'[15]. Fortunately, Brooke was saved by two French infantrymen who took him to the rear, guarded by a dragoon.

The 2/48th suffered 343 casualties from a strength of 452 (75 per cent), while the 2/66th lost 272 of its 441 officers and men (61 per cent). The two battalions also lost both their King's and Regimental Colours. Only the 2/31st, bringing up the left rear, had time to form square before the riders reached their part of the line, and beat off the enemy cavalry attack with relative ease. Of 2,066 officers and men of Colborne's brigade, no fewer than 1,413 became casualties (68 per cent); and although it is impossible to determine what percentage occurred during Latour-Maubourg's attack and what percentage became casualties during the remainder of the battle, we can be fairly certain that the great majority did occur at this moment. However, Lieutenant George Crompton of the 66th, in a letter to his mother two days later, certainly suggests that a good part of his battalion's loss was incurred before the cavalry appeared:

'... I think it was about 10 o'clock a.m. when the French

menaced an attack on our left; we immediately moved to support it. It proved, however, to be a feint, and the right of the line was destined to be the spot (Oh, never to be effaced from my mind) where Britons were to be repulsed; 3 solid columns attacked our regiment alone. We fought them till we were hardly a Regiment. The Commanding Officer was shot dead, and the two Officers carrying the Colours close by my side received their mortal wounds. In this shattered state, our Brigade moved forward to charge. Madness alone would dictate such a thing, and at that critical period Cavalry appeared in our rear. It was then that our men began to waver, and for the first time (and God knows I hope the last) I saw the backs of English soldiers turned upon the French. Our Regiment once rallied, but to what avail! we were independent of infantry; out-numbered with Cavalry. I was taken prisoner, but re-taken by the Spanish Cavalry.

'Oh, what a day was that. The worst of the story I have not related. Our Colours were taken. I told you before that the 2 Ensigns were shot under them; 2 Sergeants shared the same fate. A Lieutenant seized a musket to defend them, and he was shot to the heart; what could be done against Cavalry? ...'.

Crompton signs himself 'a miserable Lt.of the unfortunate 66th Regt.' - though he does add a postscript: 'The Fuzilier Brigade afterwards came on, also the other Brigades in the Division with some Spaniards and Portuguese beat back the French and gained a complete Victory'[16].

Having accomplished the virtual destruction of Colborne's brigade, Latour-Maubourg's lancers and hussars continued to penetrate into the Allied lines. They rode along the rear of Zayas's men, cutting and stabbing as they went. They also overran Cleeve's KGL battery, which had been firing into Girard's men from the left of Colborne's position. Such was the speed of the enemy attack that the Hanoverians were unable to limber up and get their guns away before the Poles were on them. The gunners were helpless against the cavalry and fared little better than their infantry comrades, to which a casualty figure of 48 officers and men testifies. During the struggle two sergeants, Hebecker and Bussmann, managed to limber up two of the guns and were getting them away when one of the shaft horses fell wounded and the leading driver of another was shot and killed. Seeing the riderless horse, a corporal named Fincke jumped from his own and, mounting it, managed to bring the gun safely away. (In later campaigns such an action might have won a Victoria Cross, but in 1811 Fincke had to content himself with a hundred Spanish dollars presented by Wellington himself. For a soldier in Wellington's army, however, this was almost certainly the greater reward.) The remaining guns were taken by the French, although all except one howitzer were recovered later in the day.

Latour-Maubourg's cavalry continued to run amok behind Zayas's battalions while others herded away hundreds of dazed, wounded and badly shaken British prisoners from Colborne's brigade. Despite the damage they had inflicted upon the Allies, Latour-Maubourg's men did not escape unscathed themselves; the brigade suffered just over 200 casualties, which represented almost a quarter of their strength. Roughly two thirds of these casualties were suffered by the Polish lancers, who also lost one of their guidons; taken by a Spanish infantry regiment, this rests today in the cathedral of Seville.

The long list of Allied casualties almost included Beresford himself, for after the Poles had ridden down Colborne's brigade some of them rode at Beresford and his staff. Beresford may not have possessed any of Wellington's skills on the battlefield, but he was a brave man and he possessed immense strength, all of which was needed when an enemy lancer came straight at him. Beresford did not draw his sword, but parried the lance thrust with his bare hands and, grabbing the Pole by the collar, heaved him from the saddle and threw him to the ground. Beresford's staff meanwhile drew their swords and defended themselves until Lumley sent forward two squadrons of the 4th Dragoons, who finally drove away the exhausted but exultant enemy cavalry. However, the British dragoons were in turn set upon by fresh French cavalry that had been sent forward to cover the retreat of the lancers. Lieutenant Charles Dudley Madden charged with the 4th Dragoons, and entered his experiences in his diary:

'The charge of our right wing was made against a brigade of Polish cavalry, very large men, well-mounted; the front rank armed with long spears with flags on them, which they flourish about, so as to frighten our horses, and thence either pulled our men off their horses or ran them through. They were perfect barbarians, and gave no quarter when they could possible avoid.'

The destruction of Colborne's brigade was not the only tragedy to occur during this phase of the battle, for in the confusion of the French cavalry attack Zayas's men became the unfortunate victims of what today would be termed 'friendly fire.' It occurred when the cavalry, who were riding across the back of Zayas's line, came under fire both from the Spaniards and from Hoghton's British brigade, which was coming forward rapidly from the north. With so much smoke and confusion in front of them, Hoghton's men apparently mistook the Spaniards for French troops and opened fire upon them, shooting many of them in the back. In fact it was only the intervention of Robert Arbuthnot, one of Beresford's aides, that brought a halt to the firing; he rode bravely between the two formations, waving his hat in the air and shouting to Hoghton's men to cease firing. He was fortunate not to be shot himself, but his courage prevented the unnecessary deaths of many more Spanish soldiers.

★　★　★

With the final repulse of Latour-Maubourg's cavalry the second phase of the Battle of Albuera can be said to have come to an end. Colborne's brigade had effectively ceased to exist, but the remaining two brigades of the 2nd Division, under Hoghton and Abercrombie, had arrived in front of Girard's infantry and were now to take their place in the firing line. The third phase of the battle, which saw the most awesome exchanges of musketry of the entire Peninsular War, was about to begin.

CHAPTER NINE

Albuera: 'That Astonishing Infantry'

Colborne and Zayas had between them suffered a terrible mauling, which had left the former without a brigade and the latter with men on the verge of breaking, having suffered 30 per cent casualties. But the fighting had taken its toll of the French too, and of Girard's infantry in particular. It will be remembered that before the intervention of Latour-Maubourg's cavalry Colborne's brigade had dealt Girard's division, already clawed by the Spanish infantry and KGL gunners, a second savage blow, which had driven his troops back in some disorder. Had it not been for the success of the French cavalry charge the outcome of the battle of Albuera might have been resolved much earlier and with far fewer casualties. As it was, Girard's battered division remained on the slopes opposite Zayas until Gazan's division got forward to take its place.

The confusion which reigned as the two divisions attempted to pass through each other's ranks can best be imagined. Sweating and cursing, the officers must have had great difficulty in manoeuvring their battalions and companies around one another. Those who had been fighting at the front of the massive formation, now dazed and bloodied, must certainly have been relieved to get out of the firing line for at least a brief respite – for a long pull from their flasks to ease the thirst brought on by continuous tension, and the biting of black-powder cartridges; and perhaps a chance to light up the pipes many of them carried in their pockets or shakos.

The men of Gazan's division, meanwhile, were probably cursing just as hard as they tried to shoulder their way forward to get to grips with the enemy, and in particular the Spaniards, for whom they had no liking and little respect. In the confusion, it is thought that the two divisions virtually became one massive formation with no real internal order, presenting a column that must have been at least 200 files wide by 40 ranks deep[1]. It was simply a case of thrusting as many men forward into the firing line as was humanly possible. Girard's 34th, 40th, 64th and 88th Line had all fought in the terrible siege of Saragossa and at Fuentes de Oñoro, and between them their Eagles bore honours won at Austerlitz, Jena, Eylau, Friedland, Essling, Eckmuhl, and Wagram; those of Gazan's 21st and 28th Light and 100th and 103rd Line boasted many of the same. These were veteran battalions, none facing the British for the first time; surely they could be trusted.

It was fortunate for Beresford that Girard and Gazan encountered so many problems in reorganising their com-mands. The lull gave the Allied staff time to get Hoghton's and Abercrombie's brigades from the 2nd Division forward to join the 1/31st, this last of Colborne's battalions having alone survived Latour-Maubourg's cavalry. Hoghton's brigade consisted of the 29th (Worcestershire), 1/48th (Northamptonshire) and 1/57th (West Middlesex); Abercrombie had the 2/28th (North Gloucestershire), 2/34th (Cumberland) and 2/39th (Dorsetshire). As the 1/48th hurried towards the firing line, and just beyond it the ground where their sister battalion had been slaughtered by the Polish lancers, many in the ranks must have sworn to take a bloody revenge.

The arrival of the two British brigades allowed Zayas's four shattered battalions to pass through their red-coated comrades and make their way to the rear. They had performed superbly in holding the Allied line until the arrival of Colborne's brigade, suffering terrible casualties as a consequence. The Spanish armies in the Peninsula had an

An impression of the fall of Ensigns Vance and Furnace, of the 29th (Worcestershire) Regiment, both cut down during the terrible firefight between Hoghton's Brigade and Soult's 5th Corps infantry. The regiment's Colours were both found on the evening of 16 May, one of them wrapped around young Vance's dead body.

A spirited and probably accurate depiction of Hoghton's brigade in the firing line. Soldiers load and fire into the smoke while dead and wounded continue to pile up around them.

unfortunate reputation for being ill-led and untrustworthy in battle, to which many incidents testify; however, there are few examples of greater steadfastness under such trying conditions than that of Zayas's men on the field of Albuera. They had earned their chance to fall back into the second line behind the British. Such was their pride that, as they fell back, some Spanish officers were anxious for their British comrades to understand that they were not retreating but merely retiring under orders to let the British through[2]. Stewart, meanwhile, took off his hat and, calling for three cheers, led the two British brigades to the crest of the hill, his skirmishers driving back their French counterparts. These voltigeurs fell back to the bottom of the slope to wait for the renewed onslaught.

It was now around 11am, and the right flank of Beresford's line, facing south, was organised with Hoghton's brigade on the right and Abercrombie's on the left. The exact order was as follows: on the extreme right of the line was the 1/31st, the surviving battalion of Colborne's brigade, and then, from right to left, the 29th, 1/57th, 1/48th, 2/28th, 2/39th and 2/34th. Altogether there were around 3,600 officers and men, deployed in their traditional two-deep line.

Staring down the barrels of their muskets were the best part of 8,000 French troops, arrayed in their massive formation. This had certainly begun as a formation from 400 to 500 men wide; exactly how it stood following the attempt to pass Gazan's division forward through Girard's is unclear, but there is little doubt that the French were fighting under a severe handicap, with a possible maximum of about 1,000 muskets being able to fire at any one time, these being the front two ranks and, possibly, those on the flanks. This, of course, is assuming that the French formation was still at least 400 files wide. If its earlier casualties had diminished it even more – to, e.g., the 200 files wide by 40 ranks deep suggested by Weller – then the total effective firepower of the column might have been as few as 400 to 500 muskets. It was the same old story of the mathematical superiority of the line over the column; for arrayed against this formation were no fewer than 3,300 muskets, allowing for the officers and sergeants present in the two British brigades.

On the face of it one does not need to be a genius to predict the outcome of such a fight. However, the French had two advantages which greatly compensated for this drawback. They had 24 guns with them, well up in the firing line; while the British had only four, of Hawker's company on Hoghton's left flank, and whatever may have been left of Cleeve's, on the right. The French also had plenty of infantrymen to take the places of the fallen: when one man was shot down there were as many as 40 waiting to step into his place. The British had no such luxury; when comrades fell they simply closed up the gaps, shuffling ever inwards towards the centre, and carried on fighting.

A contest in butchery: Hoghton and Abercrombie

The rain had ceased by the time that Hoghton and Abercrombie led their men forward in silence from the crest of the hill to the slope in front of it. They advanced to within 60 yards of the great French mass before they halted, easily outflanking the French on both sides, and made ready to fire. The French artillery gunners must have relished the prospect of being able to wreak havoc in the red ranks without much danger from counter-battery fire. The battle lines being thus drawn, the two sides were immediately engulfed in thick clouds of powdersmoke as the first volleys crashed out to 'open the ball' – a murderous duel of close range musketry that was to last the best part of an hour.

The superiority of the long British line quickly began to tell as volley after volley was unloaded into the massed blue ranks, reducing their confused formation to even greater depths of chaos. One should never overestimate the efficiency of 'Brown Bess' even at 60 yards. There will have been a surprising number of high shots, some low, some misfires, some ramrods shot away, some bewildered men rhythmically ramming load after load down the muzzle but never actually firing; but despite all this, against such a massive target those three volleys per minute must have done dreadful execution. Those on the far ends of the British line blazed away at the flanks of the French column. The battalions on the right of the British line, from Hoghton's brigade, suffered three times more casualties than Abercrombie's during the fight, which suggests that

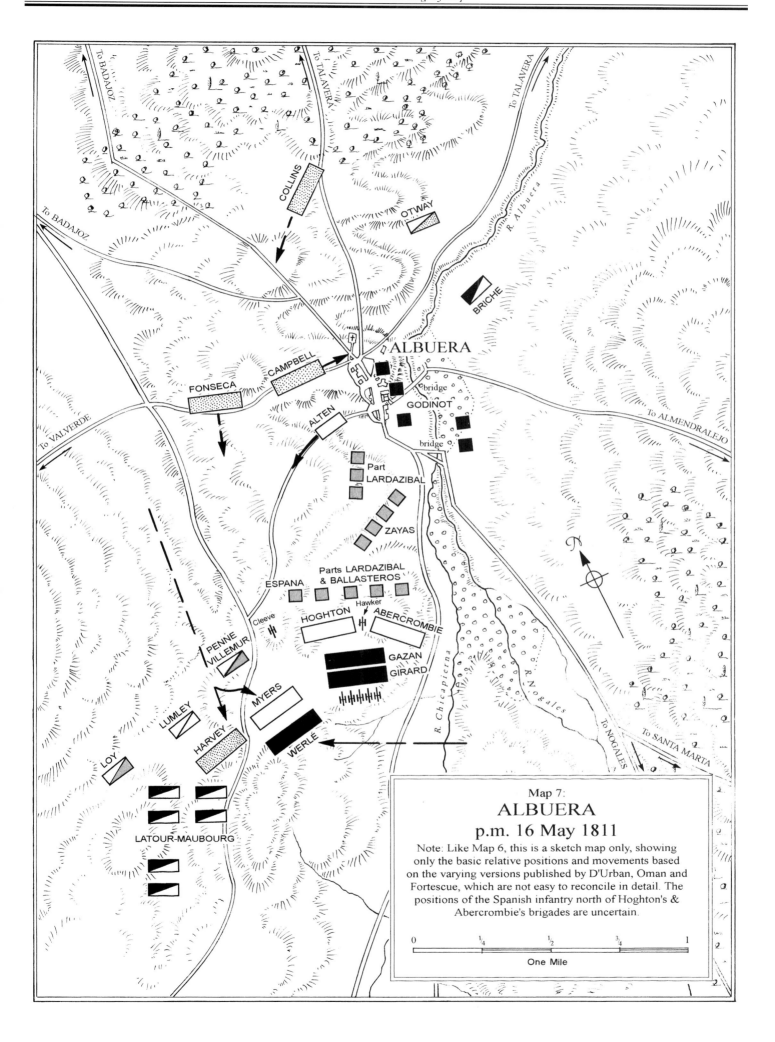

Map 7:

ALBUERA
p.m. 16 May 1811

Note: Like Map 6, this is a sketch map only, showing only the basic relative positions and movements based on the varying versions published by D'Urban, Oman and Fortescue, which are not easy to reconcile in detail. The positions of the Spanish infantry north of Hoghton's & Abercrombie's brigades are uncertain.

One Mile

Hoghton's men were right in front of the French formation with Abercrombie's to the left. Nevertheless, the latter brigade still had to endure its fair share of punishment, as Captain Moyle Sherer of the 2/34th[3] later wrote:

'Just as our line had entirely cleared the Spaniards, the smoky shroud of battle was, by the slackening of the fire, for one minute blown aside, and gave to our view the French grenadier caps, their arms, and the whole aspect of their frowning masses. It was a momentary, but a grand sight: a heavy atmosphere of smoke again enveloped us, and few objects could be discerned at all, none distinctly. The coolest and bravest soldier, if he can be in the heat of it, can make no calculation of time during an engagement. Interested and animated, he marks not the flight of the hours, but he feels that, "Come what come may, time and the hour run through the roughest day." This murderous contest of musketry lasted long. We were the whole time progressively advancing and shaking the enemy. At the distance of about twenty yards from them, we received orders to charge; we had ceased firing, cheered, and had our bayonets in the charging position, when a body of the enemy's horse was discovered under the shoulder of a rising ground, ready to take advantage of our impetuosity. Already, however, had the French infantry, alarmed by our preparatory cheers, which always indicate the charge, broke and fled, abandoning some guns and howitzers about sixty yards from us. The presence of their cavalry not permitting us to pursue, we halted and recommenced firing on them. The slaughter was now, for a few minutes, dreadful; every shot told; their officers in vain attempted to rally them; they would make no effort. Some of their artillery, indeed, took up a distant position which much annoyed our line; but we did not move, until we had expended every round of our ammunition'[4].

And so the killing-match ground on, with both sides simply firing into each other at ranges of between 20 and 60 yards, in a duel described by Fortescue, the historian of the British Army, as having few parallels in the annals of war. In fact the fight inspired him to write one of the most memorable passages of his great work:

'The survivors who took part in it on the British side seem to have passed through it as if in a dream, conscious of nothing but of dense smoke, constant closing to the centre, a slight tendency to advance, and an invincible resolution not to retire. The men stood like rocks, loading and firing into the mass before them, though frightfully punished not so much by French bullets as by grapeshot from the French cannon at very close range. The line dwindled and dwindled continually; and the intervals between battalions grew wide as the men who were still on their legs edged in closer and closer to the colours; but not one dreamed for a moment of anything but standing and fighting to the last'[5].

It is difficult to imagine the ordeal that both sides went through, with iron and lead flying through the air like hail. The wounds made at such close range by big, slow, soft lead musket balls were massive, while those of heavy canister shot could be dismembering, smashing off heads and limbs and opening up the body cavity. Even against infanty drawn up in two lines a roundshot could mangle a man and his rear-rank mate in an instant, splashing their staring comrades to left and right with apalling human debris. It was at times like this that the men's training took over, enabling them to prime, load and fire without thinking - the sort of drill they had carried out dozens of times before during bland field exercises. Now, on the slopes of this anonymous Spanish field, they were doing it for real, in a nightmare battle that was pushing them to the very limits of their endurance. They simply loaded and fired, reloaded and fired, often blindly into the smoke opposite, for as long as their cartridges held out; and when their ammunition pouches were emptied there were plenty more to be found in those of the dead and wounded who lay in ever-increasing piles all around them.

Daniel Hoghton had brought his brigade on to the field dressed in a green frock coat, but he had no sooner reached the firing line than his servant rode up bringing him his scarlet coat. An officer of the 29th Regiment wrote: 'He immediately, without dismounting, stripped off the green and put on the red one; and it may be said that this public display of our national colour and of British coolness actually was done under a salute of French artillery, as they were cannonading us at the time'[6]. Hoghton was in the thick of it, cheering on his men, when his horse was shot beneath him. He got to his feet and continued to call out orders and encourage-

On 16 May 1811 these peaceful summer fields were the main fighting area at Albuera. Abercrombie's brigade fought immediately to the right of the photo, while Hoghton's engaged the French 5th Corps infantry - advancing up slopes from the right - in and to the right of the area marked by the trees on the near skyline. This ground witnessed the greatest infantry confrontation of the Peninsular War.

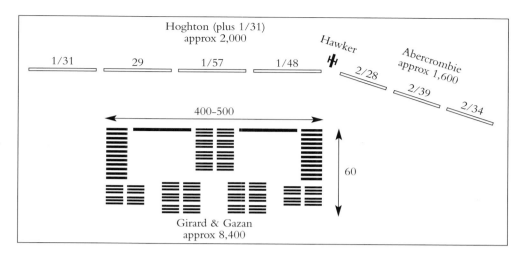

A representational sketch of the confrontation between the British 2nd Division and the French 5th Corps infantry. Once engaged the French formation quickly became a surging mass, but it is shown here drawn up as described by a French eyewitness, and in its original strength at the start of the battle. This was certainly diminished by the time the 2nd Division came up, but by how much it is impossible to say. Abercrombie's brigade wheeled forward only towards the end of the fight.

ment until he was struck down again, and killed.

Not far from Hoghton was Ensign Benjamin Hobhouse of the 1/57th, a battalion that now found itself at the very centre of the storm. The day after the battle he wrote to his father and described his battalion's part in the fight:

'During our advance in column the incessant and well-directed fire of the French artillery mowed down many of our poor fellows. Of course, our object was, and should have been sooner, to deploy into line, which we did about twenty yards in the rear of the right of a small body of Spaniards, who were supporting and returning the enemy's fire with the greatest bravery. We immediately passed in front of them, and received a most raking and continued cross-fire of musketry from a large body of the enemy's infantry whose heads were scarcely exposed above the brow of a hill. At this time our poor fellows dropped around us in every direction. In the activity of the officers to keep the men firm, and to supply them with the ammunition of the fallen, you could scarcely avoid treading on the dying and the dead. But all was still firm. In passing the Spaniards, the different regiments of our brigade were separated, and fought alone during the remainder of the action. Tho' alone, our fire never slackened, nor were the men the least disheartened. Tho' by closing to the right we appeared to be no more than a company, we still advanced and fired; and the Spaniards moved upon the left with the greatest bravery. Just before this, our Colonel, Major, every Captain and 11 subalterns fell; our King's Colours were cut in two; our regimental ones had 17 balls through them, many companies were without Officers, and as the light company was next to me, I could not do otherwise than take the command of it which I did, until it was my turn to take up the shattered colours'[7].

In its position in the centre of Hoghton's brigade the 1/57th found itself in the most dangerous place of all, with the French mass firing directly into it at extremely short range. The two ensigns carrying the Colours, Jackson and Veitch, were both shot down and badly wounded and the Colours themselves ripped to shreds. In fact Hobhouse understated the case: the Regimental Colour was shot through with 21 bullets, whilst the King's Colour had its staff shattered and was pierced by 17 shots.

Captain Ralph Fawcett was only 21 years of age but had already been in several actions. He was cheering on his company when he was mortally wounded, but his men placed him on a hillock from where he watched the action,

still encouraging them to the last, and ordering them to fire low and not waste their ammunition. Such was the punishment taken by the 1/57th that only eight officers of 31 came through the battle unscathed.

The battalion commander, Colonel William Inglis, had his horse shot dead beneath him while he was in the act of dressing his men, but after shaking his feet clear of the stirrups he continued to lead his battalion on foot. With Hoghton dead Inglis assumed command of the brigade, but remained with his battalion throughout the action. He was cheering on his men when he was flung to the ground by a grapeshot which struck him in the left breast and lodged in his back. In spite of this dreadful wound he refused to be carried from the field, but remained amongst the dead and wounded of his beloved battalion, in front of the Colours, waving away those who wished to help him. He continued to shout out to encourage his men, using a phrase that was destined to become one of the most famous not only of the Peninsular War, but in British military history: "Die hard, Fifty-seventh, die hard!" he cried, time and time again. And die hard they did, until barely 200 of them were left standing; and still they continued, biting and loading cartridges, furiously plying their ramrods, and discharging volley after volley into the French as their own ranks continued to dwindle, and move inwards towards the Colours, and dwindle again.

Elsewhere similar acts of heroism were taking place. Fighting furiously on the right of the 1/57th was the 29th Regiment under Colonel White, who was wounded early in the action. Command then passed to Major Way, who was also wounded. The 29th blazed away at the French, taking fearful casualties, their frontage diminishing by the minute. In the centre of the carnage stood Ensign Edward Furnace, proudly holding the King's Colour, while at his side stood Ensign Richard Vance with the Regimental Colour. These two young men could do little but watch as their regiment was torn apart around them. The French onslaught reduced the 29th to a quarter of its original strength, with the survivors steadily closing ranks around the Colours, the spiritual home of the regiment. As the fight intensified Ensign Furnace was badly wounded but refused to relinquish the Colour, and remained in the midst of the fight, aided by a sergeant. He was still holding it when he was killed outright, and the precious, bullet-riddled rag passed into the hands of a brother officer. When Edward Furnace fell Ensign Vance was still there, probably half-deaf-

Galbraith Lowry Cole (1772-1843), the hero of Albuera. It was Cole's decision to advance with Myers' brigade, without orders from Beresford, that almost certainly saved the day. Cole commanded Wellington's 4th Division for the greater part of the Peninsular War. He would have served at Waterloo in 1815 but missed the battle on account of getting married.

ened, blinded and choking from the smoke, but proudly bearing the weight of the Regimental Colour. Like Furnace, this was his first action. The boy had been with the regiment for just seven weeks, but that was long enough for him to understand the importance of the huge, awkward piece of silk that hung heavily from its staff in his arms. As the numbers of desperate soldiers still on their feet around him dwindled further Richard Vance, fearing the Colour might be lost to the enemy, tore the silk from its staff and hid it under his tunic. Like Furnace, Vance was killed; but the reeking flag was still wrapped round his corpse when it was found on the battlefield later that evening.

Beresford's crisis of confidence

It seems extraordinary that, given the carnage that was engulfing the Allied right, Beresford made no effort to help the two British brigades which were fighting like devils to block the French advance. The French artillery continued to pound away opposed by only a handful of Allied guns; although one officer of the King's German Legion actually got forward with three guns, apparently he could find no superior officer alive to tell him where to deploy them. To his credit, he unlimbered them anyway and brought some relief to the beleaguered British infantry.

Eventually, Beresford was moved to send orders to Charles Alten to evacuate the village of Albuera and bring

his KGL light infantry into the front line in support of the 2nd Division. This was not an easy task, given that Godinot's brigade was pressing very hard at the time. However, Alten somehow managed to break off the action and extricate his men, whereupon they began to hurry away to the south to support Hoghton's and Abercrombie's brigades. This, of course, was the signal for Godinot to thrust his men into the village, a development which might have spelt disaster for the Allies had it not been for Campbell's Portuguese brigade, which prevented any further incursions on the Allied left. (In the event, Alten's support on the right flank was not needed, as the crisis there was over before he arrived. Instead, he faced his men about and returned to the village where, after some hard fighting, he ejected Godinot's men from it and threw them back across the Albuera river.)

The initial withdrawal of Alten from the village marked the crisis point for Beresford. On the slopes away to the south his infantry were being steadily slaughtered, and while the French were taking great punishment themselves they still possessed large reserves, particularly Werlé's strong brigade with nearly 5,500 men. Latour-Maubourg's cavalry still hovered menacingly, while to the north Godinot still pressed against the village. Beresford had few options, and the one he appears to have considered most strongly at this point was retreat. In a letter to the Quartermaster General, Major Alexander Dickson of the artillery wrote: 'The Marshal himself, for a moment, thought he was defeated, as I received an order to retreat, with my Artillery, towards Valverde and Baron Alten absolutely, by order, quitted the village for a moment. All this was, however, soon countermanded and rectified'[8].

Beresford's reluctance to call forward the 4th Division appears to have been based on the assumption that it was covering the road from Valverde to Badajoz, which was the main Allied communication route – and along which he would have to try to retreat if he were defeated. If this was uppermost in his mind, it is strange that he should choose to open a path for the enemy towards this point by withdrawing Alten's Germans from the village. Yet at this critical stage, when Beresford seriously considered himself beaten and a retreat the only option, he still had thousands of Portuguese troops, including Hamilton's division, which had yet to play any real part in the battle. Taking some kind of a grip on his resolution, he duly ordered these units to advance south in support of the 2nd Division. He also attempted to get Carlos de España's brigade forward as well, but these simply would not budge. Indeed, Beresford was moved to grab hold of a Spanish colonel with his own hands and try to haul him forward, but his grip slipped and the Spaniard ran off to join his men. Unlike Zayas's heroic battalions – and probably because they lacked such stout leadership – they simply did not have the stomach for a fight.

Soult, meanwhile, faced slightly different problems. He had begun the battle with fewer troops, although he was apparently unaware that Blake's Spaniards had arrived during the previous night. Thus he was fighting under the assumption that the two sides were fairly evenly matched. Girard and Gazan had found the uncompromising British infantry unwilling to yield a single inch of ground. However, if the two sides continued to blaze away at the rate they were going it would simply be a matter of time before the British finally broke, not through any irresolution, but through sheer lack of strength. It was a battle of attrition. And yet, with Soult poised for a victory which must surely have come had he launched Werlé's brigade, the French commander wavered and did nothing. He later declared that he was unaware of the presence of Blake's Spaniards until informed of the fact by a Spanish prisoner. This, he said, determined the future course of the battle, and instead of considering the potentially battle-winning strike he shifted from offence to defence and simply allowed his men to continue their bloody struggle against the ever-dwindling British infantry line. Here, if at any moment in his career, Soult surely earned Wellington's jibe that he often performed wonders in getting his men to the battlefield, but did not know what to do with them once they were there.

And so the slaughter continued, with ammunition running lower and lower and the piles of agonised bodies growing higher and higher. Moyle Sherer of the 2/34th was still on his feet:

'To describe my feelings throughout this wild scene with fidelity, would be impossible: at intervals, a shriek or groan told me that men were falling around me; but it was not always that the tumult of the contest suffered me to catch these sounds. A constant feeling to the centre of the line, and the gradual diminution of our front, more truly bespoke the havoc of death. As we moved, though slowly, yet ever a little in advance, our own killed and wounded lay behind us; but we arrived among those of the enemy, and those of the Spaniards who had fallen in the first onset: we trod among the dead and dying, all reckless of them.

'But how shall I picture the British soldier going into action? He is neither heated by brandy, stimulated by the hope of plunder; or inflamed by the deadly feelings of revenge; he does not even indulge in expressions of animosity against his foes; he moves forward, confident of victory, never dreams of the possibility of defeat, and braves death with all the accompanying horrors of laceration and torture, with the most cheerful intrepidity'[9]. It seems doubtful whether any man on either side would have owned to feeling cheerful on 16 May 1811.

Hardinge and Cole

The nightmare confrontation on the right had been raging for nearly an hour when relief for the British finally arrived - not from the KGL light infantry, nor from the Portuguese whom Beresford apparently ordered south, but in the shape of Cole's 4th Division.

This formation, it will be remembered, had remained impassive, though much vexed, throughout the morning's events, and now could only watch as the 2nd Division fought alone in the distance. However, the move that was to win the battle of Albuera for the Allies was not instigated by Marshal Beresford, but by two staff officers - Major Henry Hardinge, and the divisional commander Major-General Lowry Cole. Both had watched with awe the bloody spectacle unfolding before them as the brigades of Hoghton and Abercrombie stood and died in the path of Girard and Gazan; now, with no apparent prospect of decisive action from Beresford, these two officers took it upon themselves to act on their own initiative before disaster befell the whole army. Hardinge, a very promising 26-year-old staff officer commissioned in the 57th Regiment, who had already seen a good deal of action, was on detached service as Deputy Quartermaster-General to the Portuguese Army. He had

been close to the scene of the fiercest fighting throughout the day and, upon Beresford's inactivity, took himself off to General Cole and urged him to act quickly or risk seeing the battle lost. As it turned out Lowry Cole was already considering such a move, and after a hurried consultation with Lumley, commanding the cavalry, he decided to form his division and advance. In his journal Major Roverea, one of Cole's aides, wrote of his frustration at Beresford's lack of command and control:

'Our Marshal bravely exposed himself, but gave no orders, and the officers on his Staff acted as they thought best ... At the first sound of the guns I was sent to the Marshal to accompany him and to receive his orders for my General. I received none.'

And of Cole's decision to act, he wrote: ' ... he decided to attack the hill occupied by the enemy, on possession of which evidently the fate of the battle depended. In undertaking this attack without having received an order from the Marshal, and on taking on himself the responsibility of a decisive movement, he acted with a moral courage of which few English generals have given an example'[10].

It was indeed a brave decision, but it must have been fairly obvious that it was the only one to take if the day were to be saved. The urbane and aristocratic Lowry Cole was a more secure personality than Beresford, much liked for his good nature and kindliness and on easy social terms with Wellington. Appreciating the situation and decision himself, Roverea went on:

'All of this happened just at the moment when the Marshal, frightened by his losses and with no further hope of victory, had begun to evacuate the village of Albuera and to give the first orders for the retreat. This retreat, with an enemy fortress (Badajoz) and a river (Guadiana) without a bridge in our rear, and considering the superiority of their cavalry, would have been very difficult to carry out'[11].

Sir Charles Broke Vere, Assistant Quartermaster-General of the 4th Division, was another who deplored Beresford's lack of decisive action and who applauded Cole's decision:

'General Cole continued anxiously to watch the progress of the contest, and he sent his A.D.C. to Sir W. Beresford to request authority to carry his Division to the support of the troops engaged. Colonel Rooke, D.A.G., and also Major Hardinge, Deputy Quartermaster-General, had suggested, and the latter strongly urged on the General, the necessity of his advancing to reinforce the 2nd Division, but they brought no order from Sir W. Beresford, neither did his A.D.C. return with any answer. General Cole was impatient with being compelled to withhold support under an evident demand for succour, and at length the critical state of the conflict seemed to be so great that he took upon himself the responsibility of moving his Division to reinforce the battle without receiving any order from his superior to do so'[12].

The scene was thus set for the final phase of the battle of Albuera.

Cole's division on the field, as we have seen, consisted only of Myers's brigade - the 1/7th (Royal Fusiliers), 2/7th and 1/23rd (Royal Welsh Fusiliers) - and Kemmis's one company each from the 2/27th (Enniskilling), 1/40th (2nd Somersetshire) and 97th (Queen's Own) Foot. In all the divisional strength was just 104 officers and 2,076 men - not even half that of Werlé's French brigade, which lay in wait for them. Fortunately, they were ably assisted by William Munday Harvey's Portuguese brigade, which consisted of the strong 11th and 23rd Infantry, and the green-clad light infantry of the 1st Battalion, Loyal Lusitanian Legion, making a brigade strength of 2,927 officers and men[13]. To support the infantry Lumley mustered the entire Allied cavalry force and Lefebure's battery of horse artillery.

There was about a mile of open country to cross before Cole could link up with the British infantry fighting on the slopes away to the south, and the movement was fraught with danger – Latour-Maubourg's cavalry were still manoeuvring not far off. After a hurried consultation with Lumley and other senior officers, Cole ordered his division to be formed in the following order: on the left flank, the Loyal Lusitanian Legion was to advance in open column, ready to form square, with the 23rd Fusiliers in line on the Legion's right. Next to the 23rd were the two battalions of the 7th Fusiliers, again in line, with Harvey's Portuguese battalions on their right, also in line. The right flank was made up of a second open column, comprising all of the light companies of these battalions, along with the three orphaned companies from Kemmis's brigade. Cole therefore had five battalions in line, with a column on each of his flanks, ready to form square if attacked by French cavalry.

It was at about 12.15pm when the 4th Division finally began its advance to engage the enemy. Away to the south, French cavalry picked up the movement of the mile-long line of Allied infantry, giving Soult time to order forward his reserves to bar Cole's path. First of all, Werlé was ordered to advance and put his 5,500 infantry between Cole and the two British brigades still fighting Soult's 5th Corps. In the meantime, Latour-Maubourg was to send four regiments of dragoons to attack Cole as his long line rolled on across the meadowland and vineyards. Marching with the 2/7th Fusiliers was Private John Spencer Cooper:

'At this crisis, the words, "Fall in Fusiliers" roused us; and we formed line. Six nine-pounders, supported by two or three squadrons of the 4th Dragoons took the right. The 11th and 23rd Portuguese regiments, supported by three light companies, occupied the centre. The Fusilier brigade with some small detachments of the brigade left at Badajoz, stood on the left. Just in front of the centre were some squadrons of Spanish cavalry. The line in this order

approached at quick step the steep position of the enemy; under a storm of shot, shell, and grape, which came crashing through our ranks. At the same time the French cavalry made a charge at the Spanish horse in our front. Immediately a volley from us was poured into the mixed mass of French and Spaniards. This checked the French; but the Spanish heroes galloped round our left flank and we saw them no more'[14].

The four regiments of French dragoons swept down upon Cole's line, only to be met by a withering fire that rolled out from the Allied infantry. The musketry of Harvey's Portuguese line battalions was particularly destructive as the French attack was aimed largely at their section of the line. The French dragoons did not get within a sabre's length of the Allies before they turned and fled, leaving the Portuguese in particular to cheer their success and jeer the enemy as they rode off. And this brief action was an important success, too, for this was their blooding – the 11th and 23rd Portuguese had yet to see any real action in the war. Sir William Myers of the 7th, commanding the Fusilier Brigade, watched with satisfaction and, no doubt, some relief, secure in the knowledge that he could continue his advance without worrying about interference from enemy cavalry, and that the strong but previously untried Portuguese battalions were up to the job.

Cole's line picked up the pace and continued south towards the scene of the main fight. This was no outflanking move but a direct attack upon Soult's 5th Corps, and in order to confront it Cole's line had to advance obliquely, more or less in a south-south-easterly direction to hit the French left flank. As they picked their way towards the slopes they saw in the distance three large dark columns approaching them. It was Werlé's brigade.

Soult had finally realised that if he did not act now the battle would be lost. He had thrown absolutely everything at the British and Spanish infantry, but had gained not an inch of ground; they simply could not be moved. In fact, Soult is reputed to have said later of the British, 'The day was mine, but they did not know it and would not run.' He had refused to commit Werlé's strong brigade against them when an attack against the flank of the weakening British

A view from the Valverde road, looking south towards the main fighting area at Albuera, which lies amid the trees on the skyline. This photograph was taken close to the starting point of the Fusilier Brigade's march, and shows the distance which it had to cover to engage the French, while Latour-Maubourg's strong cavalry hovered menacingly behind the rolling ground in the right background.

'That astonishing infantry': released from their ordeal on the lower slopes of the hill at Albuera, the Fusilier Brigade steps forward out of the maelstrom and advances against Werlé's brigade to turn the battle for the Allies. Wollen's wonderful painting mistakenly shows the Fusiliers wearing their bearskin caps, which were not taken into the field.

infantry would certainly have won the day for him; but now it was too late. With Cole's line advancing rapidly towards him Soult was forced to use Werlé not in an offensive role but in a defensive one, to prevent the 4th Division linking up with the 2nd Division.

'The iron tempest'

Werlé's brigade was formed into three large regimental columns, with three battalions of the 12th Light in one column, three of the 55th Line in another and three more of the 58th Line in the last. All three regiments were veterans of Austerlitz, the 12th and 58th of Friedland, the 55th of Jena and Eylau, the 58th of Vimeiro and Talavera. Each of the three columns had a frontage of two companies and a depth of nine. The question must thus be asked, had Werlé learned nothing from the fight between Girard and Gazan and the 2nd Division? There, on the bloodstained slopes in front of him, Werlé had seen for himself the ineffectiveness of the column against the line, in a fight that had been in progress for almost an hour. Yet here he was, leading his own brigade against a line of Allied infantry, having formed his men into columns each of which had a frontage of no more than 120 men. It was the old story, and Werlé was about to pay for his unyielding belief in the column.

The Allied line finally arrived with its left flank close to the low hill upon which were strewn the bodies of Colborne's men. Down to meet them came Werlé's brigade. The French columns were drawn in against the three British battalions, each of which selected a column as its target and made ready for action. Commanding the 2/7th Fusiliers was Colonel Edward Blakeney, who later recalled the moment

when, after having closed to within 40 yards of the French, his men opened fire:

'From the quantity of smoke, I could perceive very little of what went on in my own front. The 1st battalion of the 7th closed with the right column of the French: I moved on and closed with the second; the 23rd took the third. The men behaved most gloriously, never losing their rank, and closing to the centre as casualties occurred. The French faced us at a distance of about thirty or forty paces. During the closest part of the action I saw their officers endeavouring to deploy their columns, but all to no purpose. For as soon as a third of a company got out, they would immediately run back, to be covered by the front of their column'[15].

Apart from the numerical superiority of firepower of the line over the column, Blakeney's letter also identifies the psychological advantage of fighting in line. In a column the 'herd instinct' was a strong factor, with the many – those within the column - made secure by the few - those at the front. To move out from the protection of a column and deploy into line when already within range was to expose oneself to the fire of the enemy, and the French simply could not do it. They would attempt to deploy, but the British volleys kept them in their compact formation – their firepower restricted, their position static and their prospects dire. Private Cooper again:

'Having arrived at the foot of the hill, we began to climb its slope with panting breath, while the roll and thunder of furious battle increased. Under the tremendous fire of the enemy our thin line staggers, men are knocked about like skittles; but not a step backward is taken. Here our Colonel and all the field officers of the brigade fell killed or wounded, but no confusion ensued. The orders were "Close up;" "Close in;" "Fire away"; "Forward"'[16].

The advance of the Fusilier brigade at Albuera is another of the great episodes of the Peninsular War, in a battle full of such moments. The duel against Werlé's columns was shorter than that fought by Hoghton and Abercrombie against Girard and Gazan, but it was no less ferocious. The French columns may not have possessed the firepower of the British line but, again, they did have plenty of guns to support them, and it was these that made the confrontation murderous. Canister shot from the French cannons tore huge gaps in the British line, but the Fusiliers simply stepped over their dead and wounded and closed to the centre. Their fire rolled from one end of their line to the other, volley after volley crashing out and bringing scores of French soldiers to the ground with every discharge. To their great credit the French stood, giving as good as they got, trading volleys with the British amidst the thick banks of dirty smoke which hung in the heavy air.

Somehow - over the deafening, bewildering racket of massed musketry, artillery, and the screams and shouts of the combatants - the Fusiliers managed to hear the beating of their drums as the orders were given to advance. It had become clear to Myers that to simply stand and fight was to invite disaster, and that the only way to achieve victory was to advance in the teeth of the enemy's fire. To the astonishment of the French, the three British battalions charged their bayonets and advanced through the smoke to carry the fight to the enemy, who slowly began to give ground. The advance inspired the greatest soldier/historian of the war, William Napier, to write one of his most memorable passages:

'Such a gallant line, issuing from the midst of the smoke, and rapidly separating itself from the confused and broken multitude, startled the enemy's heavy masses, which were increasing and pressing onwards to an assured victory: they wavered, hesitated, and then vomiting forth a storm of fire, hastily endeavoured to enlarge their front, while a fearful discharge of grape from all their artillery whistled through the British ranks. Myers was killed, Cole, the three colonels, Ellis, Blakeney, and Hawkshawe, fell wounded, and the fuzileer battalions, struck by the iron tempest, reeled, and staggered like sinking ships. But suddenly and sternly recovering, they closed on their terrible enemies, and then was seen with what a strength and majesty the British soldier fights. In vain did Soult, by voice and gesture, animate his Frenchmen; in vain did the hardest veterans, extricating themselves from the crowded columns, sacrifice their lives to gain time for the mass to open out on such a fair field; in vain did the mass itself bear up, and fiercely striving, fire indiscriminately upon friends and foes while the horsemen hovering on the flank threatened to charge the advancing line. Nothing could stop that astonishing infantry'[17].

The Fusilier brigade began to move slowly but steadily up the hill, driving Werlé's men back and stopping every now and then to unload another volley into the packed ranks of the enemy. There was, as Napier wrote, no stopping them, until eventually the French could take no more. The rear ranks of the blue columns began to turn and slip away - first a dribble, then a steady stream, and finally a torrent, as they broke and fled up and over the hill behind them in chaos, with the grim-faced British Fusiliers rolling on up the slope behind them.

'No sudden burst of undisciplined valour, no nervous enthusiasm, weakened the stability of their order, their flashing eyes were bent on the dark columns in their front, their measured tread shook the ground, their dreadful volleys swept away the head of every formation, their deafening shouts overpowered the dissonant cries that broke from all parts of the tumultuous crowd, as slowly and with a hor-

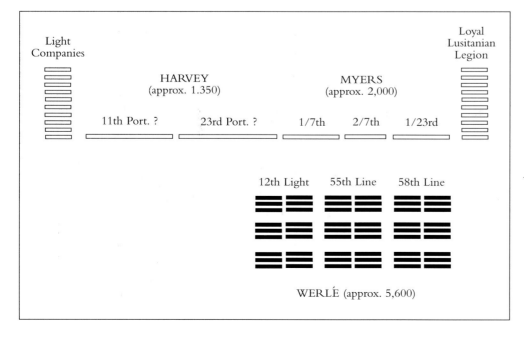

Representational sketch of the 4th Division attack against Werlé. The exact order of Harvey's brigade is not known. Frontages are approximate, based on formations and numbers of men present. The British and Portuguese regiments were without their light companies, which were combined on the right flank together with the three companies from Kemmis's brigade. An account dated 24 May by Lieutenant John Harrison, an acting company commander in the 1/23rd who was wounded in the action, states that the regiment went up the slope in company columns until 'within musket shot of the French when we closed and deployed [into line] on our first battalion company'.

rid carnage, it was pushed by the incessant vigour of the attack to the farthest edge of the height. There, the French reserve, mixing with the struggling multitude, endeavoured to sustain the fight, but the effort only increased the irremediable confusion, the mighty mass gave way and like a loosened cliff went headlong down the steep'[18].

Werlé's brigade streamed over the hill, back in the direction they had come when they had advanced that morning brimming with zeal and confident of victory. Meanwhile, the fight between the 5th Corps and the brigades of the 2nd Division reached its climax. Like Werlé's troops on their left, Gazan's and Girard's men were beginning to wilt under the incessant fire of the much reduced but still battling British infantry in front of them. The remains of Hoghton's brigade had not yielded an inch, and nor had Abercrombie's battered battalions. With French troops beginning to make for the rear, Abercrombie wheeled his left flank forward to pour volley after devastating volley into the right flank of the French. Thus caught between two fires, the French could take no more; they broke and fell back, leaving the bodies of the dead and wounded laying piled high in heaps. While those at the rear of the French mass simply ran, the front rank men struggled to turn and break off the action amid the crush and confusion. The great formation was finally driven back over the hill from where it had come, leaving the dazed, exhausted British infantry to advance and take the hill from which Soult's artillery had earlier wrought such havoc in their ranks. 'The rain flowed after in streams discoloured with blood,' wrote Napier, 'and fifteen hundred unwounded men, the remnant of six thousand unconquerable British soldiers, stood triumphant on that fatal hill!'[19].

The butcher's bill
With the bulk of the 5th Corps in full flight, Beresford's infantry advanced to take possession of the enemy's ground. Although the 57th had taken fearful casualties, the survivors still moved forward in pursuit of the French until Beresford himself ordered them to halt, crying, 'Stop! Stop the Fifty-seventh, it would be a sin to let them go on.' The men of Abercrombie's brigade, having suffered fewer casualties, did push forward, however, to ensure that the French were driven back across the Chicapierna stream. The fields to the south of the hills on which the main fighting had taken place were covered with retreating French infantry, most of them in anxious but not panic-stricken flight, covered by their artillery and by Latour-Maubourg's faithful cavalry, which was still too strong for Lumley and the Allied horse. By now Lefebure's guns were up and firing into the French, while Ballasteros and De España finally saw fit to move their men forward in support of Abercrombie. Harvey's Portuguese infantry passed by the victorious Fusiliers, who were too exhausted and reduced in number to pursue the French much farther than 'the fatal hill.'

The Allied troops, and in particular the British, could hardly believe they had achieved a victory. The dazed survivors looked around themselves with a mixture of awe, bewilderment and horror at the blood-soaked field of battle. Moyle Sherer recalled the scene in his memoirs:

'The roar of the battle is hushed; the hurry of action is over; let us walk over the corpse-encumbered field. Look around, behold thousands of slain, thousands of wounded, writhing in anguish, and groaning with agony and despair. Move a little this way, here lie four officers of the French

hundredth, all corpses. Why, that boy cannot have numbered eighteen years? How beautiful, how serene a countenance! Perhaps on the banks of the murmuring and peaceful Loire, some mother thinks anxiously of this her darling child. Here fought the third brigade; here the fusiliers; how thick these heroes lie! Most of the bodies are already stripped; rank is no longer distinguished. Yes: this must have been an officer; look at the delicate whiteness of his hands, and observe on his finger the mark of his ring. What manly beauty; what a smile still plays upon his lip! He fell, perhaps, beneath his colours; died easily; he is to be envied. Here charged the Polish lancers; not long ago, the trampling of horses, the shout, the cry, the prayer, the death-stroke, all mingled their wild sounds on this spot; it is now, but for a few fitful and stifled groans, as silent as the grave. What is this? A battered trumpet; the breath which filled, this morning, its haughty tone, has fled, perhaps, for ever. And here again, a broken lance. Is this the muscular arm that wielded it? 'Twas vigorous, and slew, perhaps, a victim on this field; it is now unnerved by death. Look at the contraction of the body, and the anguish of these features; eight times has some lance pierced this frame. Here again lie headless trunks, and bodies torn and struck down by cannon shot; such death is sudden, horrid, but 'tis merciful. Who are these, that catch every moment at our coats, and cling to our feet, in such a humble attitude? The wounded soldiers of the enemy, who are imploring protection from the exasperated and revengeful Spaniards. What a proud compliment to our country!'[20].

The battlefield afterwards was a shocking sight. The worst area was that where the brigades of Colborne, Hoghton and Abercrombie had fought and died, a relatively small area which was literally covered with dead and wounded redcoats. In front of them lay an equally shocking scene, with French soldiers piled three high in places, covering an even smaller area owing to their tighter formation. No sooner had the battle ended than the cold rain, which had so affected Colborne's brigade earlier in the day, returned to wash away the blood, which now ran in streams down towards the Chicapierna.

The battle of Albuera had begun at around 8am, and by about 2pm it had ended. During those six hours no fewer than 5,916 Allied soldiers became casualties, of which 4,159 were British. (It is also worth remarking that apart from the 23rd Royal Welsh Fusiliers all the British regiments were English ones, there being not a single Scottish or Irish regiment present - which was unusual. Even so, of course, the ranks of these English regiments were as always filled out with many Irish, Scots and Welshmen in addition to Englishmen.) Portuguese casualties were 389 and Spanish casualties 1,368, over half of which were from Zayas's division.

It is only when one breaks down the battalion casualties, however, that the full horror and heroism of Albuera really strike home. We have already mentioned the horrific losses to Colborne's brigade, which left the 1/3rd with just seven officers and 85 men standing out of a battalion strength of 755 all ranks. Of 452 officers and men, the 2/48th was left with 109, while the 2/66th lost 272 out of a strength of 441 men. The 1/31st, meanwhile, shielded to some extent by the accident of its deployment, suffered a much lower figure of 155 out of 418 all ranks, yet even that is 37 per cent - an unremarkable figure for, say, an attacking British infantry

The scene of the great fight between Myers's Fusiliers and Werlé's brigade on the slopes beneath 'the fatal hill' of Albuera. The Fusiliers advanced diagonally across this ground from left to right.

battalion of the Second World War, but one which would be regarded today as a disaster. As we have seen, together these losses left the brigade with a strength of just 653 all ranks out of an original figure of 2,066, or casualties of over 68 per cent.

The casualties amongst Hoghton's and Abercrombie's brigades were equally appalling. Hoghton's brigade went into action with a total strength of 1,651, and emerged with just 607 - losses of 64 per cent. Worst hit was the 1/57th, which began the day with 31 officers and 616 men but emerged with just 219 all ranks - 67 per cent casualties. Robert Abercrombie led 1,597 men into action and brought off 1,207, which perhaps reflects his brigade's position during the fight, being slightly to one side of the French mass. Myers's Fusilier brigade, meanwhile, advanced to contact with a strength of 2,015 and finished on the fatal hill with just 970 men - a loss of 52 per cent. Such was the casualty rate amongst officers that Hoghton's brigade was brought off the field by a captain of the 48th (ironically, an emigré Frenchman named Cimetière), the 29th by a junior captain, and the 48th and 57th by lieutenants. Junior officers who had been well down the ladder of seniority found themselves leading their battalions from the field, or suddenly leaping several steps on the list in a single day.

Official French figures put Soult's losses at 5,936 although this is almost certainly too low. In his despatch to Napoleon, Soult actually returned just 2,800 killed and wounded, which is simply incredible. Both Oman and Fortescue, working from French returns, established the fact that the official figure of just under 6,000 was incomplete or probably falsified. They calculated - as did many French observers - that the real figure was closer to 8,000. Whatever the true figure, Soult's army, which had about 10,000 fewer than Beresford's before the battle, was severely weakened. Three generals of the 5th Corps - Pepin, Maransin and Brayer - were killed, the colonel and all the senior officers of the leading French regiment became casualties, and even Gazan himself was wounded - as was Werlé, mortally.

For relentless intensity of killing over a small area of ground, there would be no other Peninsula battlefield that looked as shocking as the field of Albuera. Nor would there be any face-to-face infantry duels that came anywhere near matching the ferocity of that endured by Hoghton's, Abercrombie's and Myers's brigades – not in the Peninsula, nor even at Waterloo. Only the sight of the corpse-choked breaches of Badajoz could stand comparison with Albuera for sheer horror; but though many of those who had fought on 16 May 1811 would indeed take part in the assault on Badajoz the following year, the storming of a fortress was always an experience apart. In terms of a regular, pitched, open-field battle Albuera has no equal; losses at Talavera in July 1809 were greater, but were spread over two days and a much wider area.

There would be greater battles to come, at Salamanca, Vittoria and the Nivelle; but for sheer bloody slaughter none could compare with the nightmare of Albuera. Little wonder that Oman called it 'the most honourable of all Peninsular blazons on a regimental flag'[21].

CHAPTER TEN

'Oh Glorious Field of Grief!'

The grim task of searching the battlefield for wounded began on the evening of 16 May 1811, but it would be days before the final survivors were brought in and the dead buried. Most of the latter were simply interred where they fell, in huge pits, most of which were concentrated on the slopes where the 2nd Division had fought and on the plain where the Fusilier Brigade had made its decisive attack. Arriving at Albuera on the day after the battle, a soldier of the 27th was horrified by what he saw:

'Before us lay the appalling sight of upwards of 6,000 men, dead, and mostly stark-naked, having, as we were informed, been stripped by the Spaniards during the night; their bodies disfigured with dirt and clotted blood, and torn with the deadly gashes inflicted by the bullet, bayonet, sword or lance, that had terminated their mortal existence. Those who had been killed outright, appeared merely in the pallid sleep of death, while others, whose wounds had been less suddenly fatal, from the agonies of their last struggle, exhibited a fearful distortion of features.

'Near our arms was a small stream almost choked with bodies of the dead, and from the deep traces of blood on its miry margin, it was evident that many of them had crawled thither to allay their last thirst. The waters of this oozing stream were so deeply tinged, that it seemed actually to run blood. A few pirches distant was a draw-well, about which were collected several hundreds of those severely wounded, who had crept or been carried thither. They were sitting, or lying in the puddle, and each time the bucket reached the surface with its scanty supply, there was a clamorous and heart-rending confusion; the cries for water resounding in at least ten languages, while a kindness of feeling was visible in the manner this beverage was passed to each other.

'Turning from this painful scene of tumultuous misery, we again strolled amongst the mangled dead. The bodies were seldom scattered about, as witnessed after former battles, but lying in rows and heaps; in several places whole subdivisions or sections appeared to have been prostrated by one tremendous charge or volley'[1].

The evidence of the carnage was still plain to see days after the battle. Moyle Sherer, who had been in the thick of the action with the 2/34th, returned to the battlefield four days afterwards:

'Our wounded were removed with as much expedition as possible to Valverde; but the field hospitals, for two or three days after the engagement, presented scenes, at the recollection of which humanity shudders. I can never forget seeing, on the twentieth, the small chapel at Albuera filled with French wounded, very great numbers of whom had suffered amputation, and who lay on the hard stones, without even straw, in a dirty, comfortless state; all of which was unavoidably the case, for we had nothing to give them on the spot, and, owing to the want of conveyances, they were forced to wait till our people had been carried to the rear. This same day I again went down to that part of the field, which was covered with the slain; they lay ghastly and unburied: here and there, indeed, you might remark a loose-made grave, where some officers or soldiers had been to perform an act of private friendship.

'I was much struck with one affecting, though simple proof of the attachment of our peninsular allies: the hands, of vast numbers of the British corpses, had been clasped together in the attitude of prayer, and placed by the Spaniards in the manner they superstitiously imagine to lay out their dead'[2]. Sherer's story is not unusual, for many others who either took part in the battle or who passed over the field during the following days committed to paper similar observations.

Albuera is not a large village even today, and in 1811 was, of course, even smaller. Much of it was destroyed during the fighting, while those buildings that remained standing were quickly filled with the dying and wounded. Surgeons worked furiously to save lives, to amputate limbs and to do whatever they could under the most trying circumstances to alleviate the pain and suffering of the thousands of wounded. These, naturally, included hundreds of French soldiers who remained on the battlefield after Soult's retreat. Thousands more filled carts and wagons and followed the French Army to Seville. Countless villages along the way, such as Villagarcia and Llerena, quickly filled with wounded as vehicles deposited their wretched loads. The more seriously wounded of Beresford's men likewise remained at Albuera, while hundreds more made their painful way to Elvas to be treated by their regimental surgeons. It was here that Daniel Hoghton was laid to rest; he was one of the lucky ones, for the vast majority were simply tipped into the mass graves on the battlefield.

★   ★   ★

Having failed to relieve Badajoz, and having been sorely tried at Albuera, Soult dallied before the village throughout 17 May, gathering his wounded, and on the 18th began his retreat to Seville. British troops followed him as far as Usagre, whereupon Latour-Maubourg turned his cavalry about and brought the pursuit to a halt. Soult then had the task of writing his despatch to Napoleon, explaining away the loss of thousands of the Emperor's troops. As usual, it was largely a work of fiction, with a much-reduced casualty figure. Deep down, however, Soult knew the extent of his defeat. He had fought with far fewer troops than Beresford, and by not employing Werlé sooner had fumbled the opportunity of inflicting a potentially catastrophic defeat on the Allies. With Badajoz behind him, and with just a single bridge over the Guadiana, a retreat for Beresford would have been attended with almost certain disaster. For the

'The King, Mr President'- the only two unwounded officers of the 2/28th Regiment (North Gloucestershire) drink the loyal toast after the battle of Albuera (the 'president' refers to the president of the Mess).

Allies the only possible saving grace might have been the fact that Soult's army had been so severely mauled itself that it would not have been able to press home his advantage to its full extent – though Latour-Mauburg's cavalry would probably have been more or less intact. But all such speculation is meaningless; Soult 'had shot his bolt and failed'[3].

Beresford, meanwhile, was not convinced that the threat from Soult was over, and throughout 17 May his army remained on the alert. In fact there was little cause for alarm, owing to the huge losses that Soult had sustained. Beresford, on the other hand, still had a fairly sizeable force, the great majority of the Portuguese and Spanish units – save for Zayas's division – having been hardly involved in the battle; while Alten's Germans, although committed, had suffered few casualties – 106 out of 1,098 present. Beresford also continued to receive reinforcements, with the remainder of Kemmis's brigade joining him on the 17th. There was therefore little cause for Beresford to worry about enemy activity during the coming days. What he did have to worry about, however, was the reaction of his chief to the losses sustained by his precious infantry.

Albuera was an Allied victory, simply because Soult had failed in his objective to relieve Badajoz and had left the field to Beresford; but there was little cause for celebration. Indeed, such was the reaction to the battle that it was as though Beresford had been defeated. No sooner had the dead been laid in their shallow graves than voices began to be raised, demanding to know why so many British troops had been lost. Twenty years after the event William Napier published the third volume of his great work on the Peninsular War, and his account stirred up a pamphlet war almost as fierce as the campaign itself. A stern critic of Beresford, Napier roundly condemned the Allied commander for his conduct at Albuera and for his general conduct of his detached command during the 1811 campaign in Estremadura. It was an argument that involved many of the

participants, each of whom had his own version of events – and this controversy therefore had the fortunate result of leaving us a wealth of material upon which to draw when studying the battle.

Wellington himself first received news of the battle from Beresford during his ride south from Sabugal on 17 May. The mere tone of Beresford's letter was enough for Wellington to expect the worst, for this brief account informed him that the battle had been fought with heavy loss of life. Wellington was still fuming at the failure of his men to prevent the escape from Almeida of Brennier and the French garrison on 11 May, and this further unwelcome news was hardly likely to lighten his mood. It was certainly this sequence of events, and his consciousness of the need to 'manage' political opinion at home, that brought his first gruff reaction when reading Beresford's account of Albuera dated 18 May: 'This won't do. Write me down a victory'[4]. He also wrote to Charles Stuart, British minister in Lisbon, requesting him to stop any reports of Albuera being sent home:

'I think it is very desirable that, if possible, no flying details of the battle of Albuera should go home till Sir William Beresford's report shall be sent. I conclude that the account that there had been a battle went by the mail yesterday, which is of no importance; but where there are many killed and wounded the first reports are not favourable; and it is not doing justice to the Marshal to allow them to circulate without his'[5].

Such was the despondency in the Allied camp following the battle that Wellington, with the Almeida episode still fresh in his mind, was seriously worried about the adverse effect the news of Albuera might have on the British public. It should not be forgotten that in early 1811 the war in Spain was still relatively unpopular. The summer and autumn of 1810 had been the most anxious period of the war for Wellington, with loud calls for the army to be recalled to Britain, while the success of his campaign against Masséna had been insufficient to win over popular opinion. News of the losses at Albuera, coming so soon after Brennier's escape, would do little to increase enthusiasm for a war which was costing Britain many millions of pounds in financial and material aid to Spain and Portugal. Wellington therefore had Beresford re-write his account of the battle; the new version, although it did nothing to lessen the loss of life, had a rather more positive tone. The army was amazed when it read Beresford's revised account. Newspapers such as *The Times*, the *London Gazette* and the *Morning Chronicle* – great favourites with Wellington's officers – all carried the despatch, which was greeted with sarcasm and derision. John Mills, of the Coldstream Guards, was severely critical of Beresford, for both his handling of the battle and his subsequent despatch. Writing to his mother on 27 June 1811, Mills wrote:

'We are all here much surprised at the Vote of Thanks to Genrl.Beresford. Good John Bull, how easily art thou duped. Genrl.Beresford is the most noted bungler that ever played at the game of soldiers, and at Albuera he out-bungled himself. Lord Wellington riding over the ground a few days after with Beresford observed that there was one small oversight; that his right was where his left should have been. I have learned one thing since I have been in this country, and that is to know how easily England is duped; how completely ignorant she is of the truth of what is going on here, and how perfectly content she is, so long as there is a long list of killed and wounded'[6].

John Mills's anger was further inflamed when he crossed the battlefield in March 1812, when his division formed part of Graham's force covering the third siege of Badajoz. This time his stinging condemnation of Beresford was contained in a letter to his sister:

'On our march to Santa Martha we passed over the field of Albuera. The numerous bones and remnants of jackets still tell the tale and I cannot help wondering that so nefarious a military delinquent should still wear his head, and regretting that it should be in the power of a fool to throw away the lives of 6,000 men. The ground he chose convicts him. He had the choice of two positions 200 yards distant from each other, chose the worst and lost his men in taking up the other after he had perceived his error'[7].

These were strong words indeed; and while Wellington never committed to paper quite such a brutal condemnation, he must surely have harboured strong opinions which he thought best kept to himself. In fact, rather than attaching any blame or holding any kind of inquest, his broader responsibility as commander-in-chief obliged him to take an outwardly optimistic tone in order to encourage some of his more despondent senior officers. Beresford himself received encouragement in a letter from Wellington, since much quoted, written three days after the battle. 'Your loss, by all accounts, has been very large,' he wrote; 'but I hope that it will not prove so large as was at first supposed. You could not be successful in such an action without a large loss; and we must make up our minds to affairs of this kind sometimes, or give up the game'[8].

Sadly, one suspects that while Wellington hoped the casualty figure would not be as large as at first thought, it was possibly even higher, for the following day he wrote to General Marmaduke Peacocke, governor of Lisbon, and Dr Frank, the Inspector General of Hospitals, asking for 2,000 sets of bedding for the wounded. He added that whilst it was impossible to place an accurate figure on the number of wounded, he thought it likely to be that number[9].

Meanwhile, Wellington visited the battlefield and the wounded himself and made his own pertinent observations. 'We had a very good position,' he wrote to Brent Spencer, 'and I think should have gained a complete victory in it, without any material loss if the Spaniards could have manoeuvred; but unfortunately they cannot'[10]. This is an obvious reference to the performance of Blake and España, whose men had simply refused to move. The reference to

A detail from St Clair's drawing of Fuentes de Oñoro shows soldiers carrying a stretcher, and surgeons working on wounded men, one of them sitting on a chest. In the background is another of the interesting images so characteristic of this soldier/painter: a company of infantry sitting on the ground in ranks. We often read of Wellington's infantry being ordered to lie down in ranks, to avoid artillery fire.

the battlefield and its 'good position', however, is slightly odd, considering other comments made on the position by Wellington. We read in John Mills's letter quoted above that he is supposed to have said to Charles Stewart, whilst riding over the battlefield, that Beresford had positioned his troops with one oversight – that his right was where his left should have been[11]. In his own memorandum for operations in 1811 he wrote, 'all the loss sustained by those troops [the British] was incurred in regaining a height which ought never for a moment to have been in possession of the enemy'[12].

Wellington's frustration at Beresford's handling of the battle surfaced further in a private letter, which again criticised his deployments: 'The battle of Albuera was a strange concern. They were never determined to fight it; they did not occupy the ground as they ought; they were ready to run away at every moment from the time it commenced till the French retired; and if it had not been for me, who am now suffering from the loss and disorganisation occasioned by that battle, they would have written a whining report about it which would have driven the people in England mad'[13].

When we consider that 'they' meant Beresford, we may well gauge Wellington's feelings. After returning from visiting the battlefield Wellington called in on one of the hospitals in Elvas to see the wounded. The men knew full well that they had come through a nightmare, and knew also that had Wellington been there they would have been spared the ordeal, for he would not have exposed them to such punishment. Lying in one corner of the hospital was a group of men from the 29th, one of Hoghton's regiments. 'Oh, old 29th, I am sorry to see so many of you here!' said Wellington, to which they replied, 'Oh, my lord, if you had only been with us, there would not have been so many of us here!'[14].

Beresford certainly knew himself that he had not been at his best, and that it was only the staying power of his infantry that had saved the day – if not his own reputation. He paid full tribute to them in his report to Wellington:

'It is impossible by any description to do justice to the distinguished gallantry of the troops; but every individual most nobly did his duty, which will be well proved by the loss we have suffered, through repulsing the enemy; and it was observed that our dead, particularly the 57th regiment, were lying as they had fought in ranks, and every wound was in front'[15].

Post mortem

The arguments that raged between Beresford, Napier, Long, D'Urban and their respective supporters and denigrators following the publication of Napier's *History* were fought out in the pages of the *Strictures, Further Strictures, Letters, Justifications*, and other pamphlets. Napier's case rested on several 'errors' committed by Beresford, including the positioning of his troops. The problem was that Napier – like many of today's historians – put forward his arguments without having seen the ground. Indeed, his description of the battlefield is more than merely flawed; it bares little relation to the actual ground. The correspondence between the various disputants threw up all sorts of arguments and information relating to Beresford's campaign, and to Albuera and Campo Mayor in particular. While the present writer has no intention of engaging in any revival of these disputes – which would be both long and tedious – it nevertheless seems legitimate to examine a few aspects of the controversy. Like the original pamphleteers, we have the luxury of hindsight; but that seems no good reason to ignore these contrary opinions altogether.

The first question is often considered to be Beresford's choice of position. This is certainly true to an extent; but is it really the most important factor? Beresford took up a position astride the Seville-Badajoz road. It is important to remember that in 1811 the road ran through Albuera, west to Valverde and north to Badajoz. Today, the road runs directly north from Albuera to Badajoz. So, in fairness to Beresford, he was in the right place.

The question remains whether it was really sensible to place the village of Albuera at the centre of the Allied position. It would appear that by doing so Beresford left little to prevent the French from adopting the outflanking move to the south. After all, there was no really dominating feature upon which to anchor his right flank. The best that could be achieved was to occupy the hill upon which the battle finally ended, that is to say, the hill over which Girard and Gazan appeared. The solution to the problem almost certainly lay in the erection of a field work, situated upon that hill, which would have given the French considerable diffi-

The French logistic system may have been inferior to the British, but they were - theoretically - more advanced in their care for the wounded. Baron Larrey, the famous Surgeon-General of the Grand Army, was renowned for his humanitarian reforms, including the invention of the first purpose-built ambulances with sprung suspension. How far this affected the practical care of a wounded French soldier far away in Spain is questionable, however. Many of the British casualties who survived long enough to be evacuated to the rear areas suffered agonies as they lurched and banged along the endless, primitive roads in these unsprung ox-carts with solid wooden wheels; the maddening squealing of the axles is mentioned in several memoirs.

Both entrances to the village of Albuera are marked today by a memorial plaque bearing a verse from Byron's Childe Harolde's Pilgrimage.

culty had it been occupied with artillery and a strong force of infantry. Many participants in the battle advocated this course of action. Beresford certainly had the time to erect a fieldwork and the manpower to do it. He did not need engineers to dig such a position, as most diligent field officers were familiar with the business of constructing such simple works. When Wellington said after the battle that Beresford's right was where his left should have been, he seems simply to have been pouring more fuel on the fire: this would have taken the Allied line clear of both the village of Albuera and the road to Badajoz.

But once again, it seems to the present writer that instead of debating the choice of Beresford's position we ought really to be considering his control of the battle, which appears to be the main cause of the high casualties sustained at Albuera. Despite the threat to his right flank, Beresford showed a marked lack of decisive action in getting sufficient troops into position to confront Girard and Gazan. True, he was badly let down by Blake; but it is difficult to see a commander such as Wellington allowing Blake to get away with such a blatant disregard for orders. When Wellington is criticised for not devolving enough authority to his subordinates we can well understand why he was so reluctant to do so. Imagine what might have happened at Salamanca, for example, if Pakenham, upon receipt of Wellington's order to attack Thomieres's division, had taken it upon himself to ignore it, perhaps thinking that the real action would occur at the village of Los Arapiles. Wellington chose to deliver his order himself; and at Albuera Beresford should have been there in person to supervise the movement of his troops, rather than simply relying upon written orders. The consequence was that by failing to get Blake to realign his troops, Beresford condemned Zayas to face the initial French onslaught alone. The isolated incident of his manhandling the officer from Carlos de España's brigade does not count as exercising control, and it was anyway too late by that stage. Once the massive French attack began the Spaniards simply lost heart, and who can blame them?

Once the main fighting had begun, Beresford is also guilty of issuing no orders whatsoever, despite claiming later that he had done so. Virtually all the senior participants in the battle accuse him of doing nothing to assist Hoghton or Abercrombie, which is why Lowry Cole emerges as both the saviour of these two brigades and as the real victor of Albuera. It was his decision alone, even before Hardinge had consulted him, to bring the 4th Division into action; and, given the military culture of the day, such a decision

took real strength of character. It is also worth pointing out Stewart's part in the destruction of Colborne's brigade, for it was he who ordered them to deploy against the advice of Colborne.

Ultimately, we must judge Beresford to have been fortunate to escape public censure for his actions, since - judging from his private correspondence - Wellington's loyalty to him must surely have been stretched to the limit. He had backed Craufurd following the debacle on the Coa in July 1810 which had exposed Almeida to Ney's advance; and now he was backing Beresford. When the Speaker of the House of Commons rose to thank Beresford on behalf of the nation for delivering them victory at Albuera, he really ought to have been thanking Lowry Cole, Abercrombie, Hoghton and - most important of all - 'that astonishing infantry.'

A gruesome reminder of the realities of Napoleonic warfare, from John Hennen's Principles of Military Surgery, *1818. All these skulls show the sort of damage sabres could inflict. Fig.1 has a portion cleft clean off; 2 to 4 show similar fatal cuts; 5 – the skull of a cuirassier from Waterloo – has several visible sabre cuts, though it was noted that he in fact died from the effects of a wound to the elbow. Figs. 6 and 7 show musket balls distorted and fragmented by contact with the cranium.*

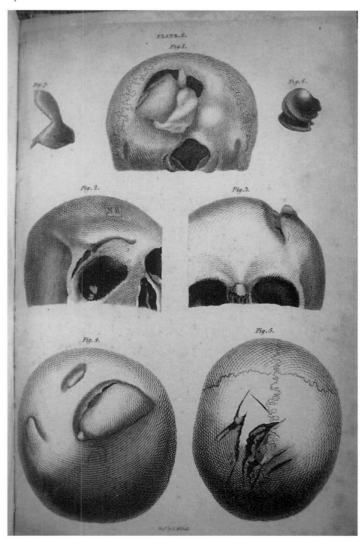

CHAPTER ELEVEN

Badajoz: 'Down We All Came Together'

With Soult's relieving army repulsed at Albuera, Beresford and Wellington could turn their attention once again to the business of laying siege to Badajoz – the reason they had come south in the first place. The withdrawal of Beresford's troops from around the city on 12 May had allowed Phillipon, the French governor of the fortress, to begin filling in the parallels dug by the besiegers and destroying any works which had been begun. Armand Phillipon was to prove the most active and resourceful of all the French garrison commanders whom Wellington encountered in the Peninsula. Never content to simply wait for the appearance of a relieving force, Phillipon conducted a vigorous defence with the personnel and resources at hand. He had a town blessed with extremely strong walls that would be difficult to breach at the best of times, as the French had discovered themselves. For an army such as Wellington's, possessing few heavy guns, an inadequate supply of even such basics as entrenching tools, and a woeful shortage of officers skilled in the art of siege warfare, the challenge was daunting.

As already described briefly in Chapter Eight, the castle at the north-eastern corner of Badajoz stood about 130 feet above the Rivellas stream. The northern wall was protected by the Guadiana river; facing it on the northern bank was the strong outwork of Fort San Cristobal, protected by the river cliffs, a ditch and a glacis. Fort Pardaleras protected the southern wall of the town, opposite the San Juan and San Roque bastions. On the east bank of the Rivellas were two more outworks, Fort Picurina and the San Roque lunette.

The blockade of Badajoz resumed on 18 May when Hamilton's Portuguese division took up positions on the south bank of the Guadiana. It was not for another week,

however, that the real siege operations got underway, on 25 May. Just as during the first brief siege at the beginning of the month, Wellington's army faced an uncertain time limit: could they take the place before another French relief force intervened? Wellington's favoured plan involved an attack against the southern front, but it was estimated that to achieve this even with the requisite number of heavy guns and equipment would take about 22 days of 'open trenches'. Since he did not have such resources he was looking at a siege of much longer duration. This, of course, meant that a relieving force would almost certainly arrive on the scene well before the city could be assaulted.

Wellington was therefore forced to consider a second plan. This involved attacks on Fort San Cristobal and the castle; these two positions were integral parts of the defence system, and their capture – particularly that of the castle – should lead to an immediate surrender by the French. This plan relied heavily upon the ability of his men to storm Fort San Cristobal, following which he would be able to erect batteries inside the fort to fire across the Guadiana at the castle. The defences on the south bank were designed to frustrate attacks against the town's southern front, and would be rendered ineffective if they came under fire from the direction of Fort San Cristobal. It was reckoned that, if the fort could be taken, it would take about four further days to breach the castle walls, the lowest sector of which faced San Cristobal. While the majority of the town's defences had been modernised, it was always assumed that an attack from the river side was virtually impossible, so the walls along the northern perimeter were in the same state as the day they were erected by the Moors.

Fort San Cristobal stands on top of a steep cliff above the

Jerumenha, as seen from the right bank of the Guadiana river. It was close to here that the pontoon bridge was constructed in April-May 1811, and in March 1812. The area also saw several cavalry skirmishes, most notably the infamous capture by the French of Captain Lutyens' piquet of the 11th Light Dragoons in June 1811 - an incident that occurred very close to this spot.

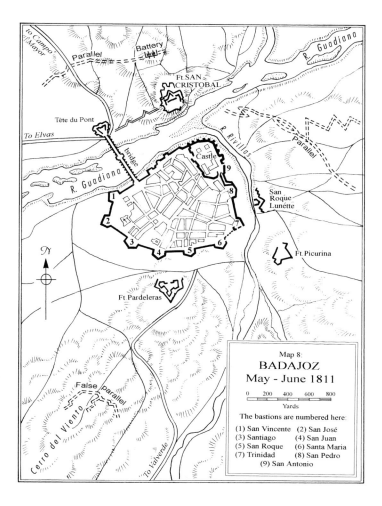

Map 8:
BADAJOZ
May - June 1811

0   200   400   600   800
Yards

The bastions are numbered here:
(1) San Vincente (2) San José
(3) Santiago   (4) San Juan
(5) San Roque   (6) Santa Maria
(7) Trinidad   (8) San Pedro
(9) San Antonio

ions and some cavalry of the 9th corps, are on their march to join Soult, and I think will join him the second week in June'[1].

Breaking ground

The supplies, tools, ammunition and other siege matériel having been brought forward from Elvas, Wellington's men broke ground on the night of 30 May. One parallel was dug on the south bank of the Guadiana, facing the castle at a distance of about 800 yards, and once it had been extended north-westwards towards the river batteries would be constructed for the guns. The business of 'breaking ground' was not simply a matter of handing hundreds of men a pick or shovel and setting them to dig, but was a precisely calculated business - after all, if a trench was dug at the wrong angle this could have dire consequences for its occupants later on. All of the digging took place in darkness. First, engineers and other staff officers led the men to the designated ground, which had already been marked out by white tapes. The working parties consisted of 1,600 men, covered against the possibility of sorties by the defenders by a further 1,200 light infantry and other troops. Their progress was impressive: by dawn on 31 May they had dug a 1,000-yard zig-zag approach to the parallel, in addition to the parallel itself, which was a further 1,100 yards long.

Wellington's chief of artillery, Major Alexander Dickson, did a fine job in procuring sufficient guns for the operation, but their quality was not particularly high, most being antiquated pieces from Elvas. For the attack on Fort San Cristobal he had collected twelve 24-pounders, four 16-pounders, two 8-inch howitzers and two 10-inch howitzers, the howitzers to fire at an angle of 30 degrees elevation like mortars[2]. For the attack on the castle Dickson had gathered 14 more 24-pounders, two 10-inch howitzers and four 8-inch howitzers, the latter again to be used as mortars. There were 3,500 entrenching tools, 60,000 sandbags, 600 gabions, a few fascines and a supply of splinterproof timber. As to personnel, 169 infantrymen were seconded to the department of engineers to be used as overseers; there were 48 carpenters and 48 miners, and 25 rank and file from the Royal Military Artificers - a forerunner of the Corps of Sappers and Miners. In addition to these was the besieging force on the south bank, which consisted of the 3rd Division and Hamilton's Portuguese division, altogether numbering 12,000 men. On the north bank, besieging Fort San Cristobal, were about 5,000 men from the 7th Division, the 17th Portuguese Regiment and the Tavira and Lagos Militia[3].

The French garrison in Badajoz awoke on the morning of 31 May to discover the huge eastern parallel that had been dug during the night, and immediately opened fire on it. Phillipon now knew the true direction from which Wellington's attack would be coming; two nights earlier 300 workmen had reopened the parallels begun during the brief and abortive first siege on the Cerro del Viento opposite Fort Pardaleras to the south-west of the city, in an attempt to draw the defenders' attention away from the real point of attack.

On the north bank of the Guadiana, meanwhile, Wellington's men had begun work on the parallels about 450 yards from Fort San Cristobal. Here the besiegers ran into problems almost immediately. The ground was composed largely of rock and there was very little soil for the

Guadiana, at a distance of about 500 yards from the walls of Badajoz itself. In many ways it was the key to the city, for once a besieger took possession of it he would be able to overlook completely all of the city's northern defences, which were much lower than the fort. Apart from possessing a very effective glacis which shielded the walls from view, the fort benefited from having no obvious weak point, that is to say there was no place from which enemy guns could easily dominate it. The only practical place for a battery was on the hilltop immediately to the north, and this is where Wellington proceeded to site his guns. (The significance of this was not lost upon the French; when Wellington returned in 1812 he found a sizeable outwork built upon this previously open ground, named after Werlé, who had fallen at Albuera.) The fort's commander was Captain Chauvin of the I/88th Line, and while it has been difficult to establish the exact number of the garrison it is known that there was certainly a battalion inside it at one point.

Wellington had around 14,000 troops at his disposal for the siege, being the 3rd and 7th Divisions and Hamilton's and Collins's Portuguese divisions. With around 19 battalions of infantry and some cavalry of the French 9th Corps on their way to join Soult, Wellington knew that this was precious few troops with which to prosecute the siege and simultaneously fend off a relief force; and on 29 May he wrote to his brother Henry expressing his concerns: 'We break ground at Badajoz to-morrow, and we hope to get the place in a few days. If we do not succeed in a few days, we shall not succeed at all, as the seventeen or nineteen battal-

workmen to dig. When Beresford had abandoned the first siege the ever-active Phillipon had marched his men out of the fort to scrape away all of the soil to the north where Allied parallels were certain to be dug in future if Beresford returned. In places gunpowder charges now had to be used in order to blast away the rock for the batteries. With his men unable to dig protective parallels, Wellington was forced to employ gabions, fascines and woolpacks in order to protect the working parties (gabions were tubular baskets filled with earth, and fascines bundles of brushwood). It was not a satisfactory situation but it was the best he could do.

At 9.30am on 3 June the besiegers' guns opened fire on their targets. The 24-pounders were immense weapons, capable of hurling a solid iron ball weighing 24lbs about 20 times in each hour. These were the kings of siege warfare; although there would seem to be little difference between 18- and 24-pounder guns, Colonel J.T.Jones, Royal Engineers, the historian of the Peninsula sieges, said that no self-respecting engineer should settle for 18-pounders when 24-pounders were available, adding that the power of the larger guns had to be seen to be appreciated. Night firing was considered a waste of ammunition; and firing during a calm day also had its problems, since it took longer for the smoke to clear before the next shot could be laid and fired. Aiming was by line of sight, and while gunnery with muzzle-loading smoothbore cannon may seem to us a fairly crude 'hit or miss' affair it was, in fact, a fairly advanced science developed over more than two centuries. A trained gunner was capable of hitting a relatively small target, such as the area of wall singled out for a breach, at considerable range. Indeed, a breach looked very small indeed from a distance of 800 yards, which was the range at which the guns on the south bank of the Guadiana were firing.

Dickson's guns had been firing for no more than a day, however, when their defects - and those of the ammunition assembled for them - began to reveal themselves in often spectacular ways. By the time darkness brought a close to the first day's bombardment two guns on the north bank and two on the south had blown themselves up. Five more guns were put out of action the following day, again by their own

discharges. Indeed, by the end of the siege 15 out of the total of 26 24-pounders, two of the four 10-inch howitzers and one of the six 8-inchers had become unserviceable, compared with just six guns which had been disabled by enemy fire. The brass museum pieces from Portuguese fortresses simply could not stand up to the rate of fire demanded of them; when a brass cannon overheats the bore becomes distorted, with dangerous consequences if firing continues. 'Windage' was also a major problem. Normally, cannon ammunition fitted snugly into the barrel; but if there was a significant space between the bore and the shot then it was almost impossible for the gunners to hit their target, as the shot would emerge only at the end of a process of 'rattling around' on its way up the barrel. Another consequence was that the priming and firing vent at the breech end of the barrel simply exploded. Dickson wrote of the problems faced by his artillery at Badajoz:

'The brass guns could not stand the necessary fire, and their destruction I am of the opinion was considerably occasioned by the lowness of the shot which generally had so much windage that you could put your fingers between the shot and the bore. I think 17 or 18 24-pounders were put hors de combat, two of which only were by the enemy's fire, and the remainder by drooping at the muzzle and unbushing'[4].

Scorched, cursing, and no doubt watching these unloved guns with intense suspicion, the gunners stuck to their task, blasting away at the walls of the castle and of Fort San Cristobal, which became increasingly damaged at each successive shot. However, they proved much tougher than had first been thought, particularly those of Fort San Cristobal - where if the ground was hard, the walls were even harder. The gradient of the glacis was so effective that it was (and still is) virtually impossible to see the walls from where the guns were sited. That the Royal Artillery gunners were able to hit their target and make a breach at all is a fine testament to their skills, although one wonders just how practicable the breach was when it was eventually attacked. Even the walls of the old Moorish castle were proving a headache for Dickson, who thought the parallels were con-

Fort San Cristobal, Badajoz, showing the ravelin which protected the curtain wall. The British attacks in June 1811 went in to the left of the fort as seen here.

The effectiveness of the glacis at Fort San Cristobal can easily be judged from this photograph. It is almost impossible to see the actual walls of the fort owing to this terraced slope raised on the northern side of the fort, protecting it from the British gunners in the battery on the hill to the north. It is little wonder that Wellington considered the walls to have remained largely intact, despite optimistic reports to the contrary.

structed too far away from the walls and hence the range slightly too great for his guns. This was the first true siege that Wellington's army had undertaken, and the first step on a very steep learning curve that was never really negotiated satisfactorily. (Even the siege of San Sebastian, in July and August 1813, was a matter of sheer bludgeon-work on the part of the artillery, engineers and infantry.) In spite of all these problems Dickson's artillery continued to pound the walls, until by 6 June a practicable breach was reported in the flank of Fort San Cristobal. Wellington decided to assault the place that night.

The first assault on San Cristobal
The key to the successful storming of a breach lay in the ability of the artillery to blast away at the foot of the walls in order to bring a section crashing down into the ditch. This, in theory, would provide a convenient ramp of rubble for the storming parties to clamber up. Naturally, the defenders would do their best to prevent this by blocking the breach with all manner of obstacles: not only woolpacks and gabions, but also the dreaded chevaux-de-frise - large beams of wood with spikes and old sword blades sticking out at all angles, and often chained together. These proved to be a very effective and deadly means of defending a breach, particularly when backed up by determined infantry with plentiful loaded weapons, perhaps even supported by cannon dragged up inside or delivering enfilade fire from neighbouring bastions. Mines were also used, buried in the rubble of the ramp; and grenades and firepots could be hurled down on the stormers. But the most effective way of preventing an enemy from entering a breach was simply to remove the spoil from the ditch and deny them their access ramp - a task normally performed under cover of darkness.

Despite these measures, there was little a garrison could do if enough stormers were hell-bent on getting inside whatever the cost. If they succeeded, they were entitled to put the garrison to the sword if they so wished. By the unwritten but universally accepted 'rules of war', dating back to medieval times, when a garrison fought on after a practicable breach had been made in their walls, and thus condemned the attackers to pay the usually bloody price of

storming it, they forfeited all claims to mercy. This knowledge would inspire the French defenders to fight like tigers for their very lives.

The attack on Fort San Cristobal involved a 'Forlorn Hope' of 25 men and a main storming party of 180 drawn from the British 51st and 85th and 17th Portuguese regiments. The Forlorn Hope would enter the ditch ahead of the main storming party, find the breach and be the first to attempt to mount it, whereupon the main party would follow after them. The Forlorn Hope was what we would probably call today a suicide squad, for they had little hope of survival and every chance of being the first to die. And yet there was never any shortage of volunteers: it might mean instant promotion for any officer who was lucky enough to return with his head still on his shoulders, and the soldiers too could expect appropriate rewards. The stormers waited in silence for the appointed hour to arrive. One of them was Private William Wheeler, of the 51st:

'In the evening we advanced towards the fort, but lay hid until the shades of night had cast her mantle over us, then moved on towards the breach observing the strictest silence. To divert the attention of the enemy all our guns were opened on the Fort, but the French Commandant was not to be duped, the sly old fox had anticipated our visit and had prepared every thing to give us a warm reception. Each man in the fort was provided with six loaded firelocks. Live shells were placed so as to be rolled into the trench. In short, nothing that would annoy us was forgotten'[5].

At midnight on 6 June the stormers moved forward in the darkness guided by Lieutenant Forster of the Royal Engineers, while the Forlorn Hope was led by Ensign Dyas of the 51st. The men moved in silence across the open ground until they reached the edge of the glacis, whereupon ladders were lowered and the men entered the ditch. Forster then groped his way forward and led Dyas and the Forlorn Hope to the breach. The two officers must have been praying for an easy, uncomplicated ascent, but when they arrived at the foot of the breach their worst fears were confirmed. The French had removed the rubble; in front of them was an ascent of seven feet, above which yawned the breach, which was blocked by carts and chevaux-de-frise.

Watching and waiting on the ramparts above were the defenders, their muskets primed, and armed with scores of grenades and other combustibles ready to be dropped into the ditch below. William Wheeler again:

'We advanced up the glacis close to the walls. Not a head was to be seen above the walls, and we began to think the enemy had retired into the town. We entered the trench and fixed our ladders, when sudden as a flash of lightning the whole place was ablaze. It will be impossible for me to describe to you what followed. You can better conceive it by figuring to your mind's eye a deep trench filled with men who are endeavouring to mount the wall by means of ladders. The top of this wall crowded with men hurling down shells and hand grenades on the heads of them below, and when all these are expended they have each six or seven loaded firelocks which they discharge into the trench as quick as possible. Add to this some half dozen cannon scouring the trench with grape. This will immediately present to your imagination the following frightful picture. Heaps of brave fellows killed and wounded, ladders shot to pieces, and falling together with the men down upon the living and dead. Then ever and anon would fall upon us the body of some brave Frenchman whose zeal had led him to the edge of the wall in its defence, and had been killed by their own missiles or by the fire of our covering party'[6].

Amid the shouts, the deafening gunfire and the chaos of struggling bodies Ensign Dyas tried in vain to force his way up to the breach. With the debris removed there was no other choice but to mount the ladders. These, however,

'A View of Badajoz, from the North Bank of the Guadiana.' This print from a drawing by one Captain Elliot, published in August 1812, shows the river, the Roman bridge which crossed it, and (left skyline) the Alcazar or castle which dominated the north-eastern defences. At the extreme left edge of the print Fort San Cristobal can be seen on the north bank. The river made it impossible for Wellington to attack from this side; hence, in June 1811 and again in March and April 1812, most of his army took up positionss away to the south-east of the town.

were found to be too short; and the men groping at the lip of the breach were simply bayoneted or shot, while those below were mangled by the hand grenades that were dropped over the wall into the crowded ditch. The darkness was illuminated by the glare of these explosions, revealing nothing to the stormers but the silhouettes of the defenders above them. Dyas and Forster attempted to retire, only to be met by the oncoming main storming column jumping into the ditch. These troops brought forward more ladders, 15 feet tall, with which they attempted to scale the walls, but they too proved hopelessly short. Several men ran along the foot of the walls searching in vain for a lower point at which to try to escalade them, all the time under fire from the French. There was simply no way in. At length, Dyas gave the order to withdraw, whereupon the survivors scrambled up the ladders and out of the ditch, carrying as many of the wounded as they could manage, while the last few French muskets blasted at their backs. The cheers from the ramparts of Fort San Cristobal were enough to tell the besiegers the outcome of the fight even before the battered and dazed survivors came streaming back to their lines. They had suffered twelve killed and 80 wounded; the French lost just one man killed and five wounded. Amongst the British dead was Lieutenant Forster, who was shot down as he withdrew.

It was Forster who had pronounced the breach practicable, although one wonders whether this was really the case. It was impossible to see the breach from any great distance; only by creeping close under cover of darkness would it have been possible to tell. In later sieges the breaches were visible in daylight, and from a great distance; at Fort San Cristobal, however, the glacis hid all but the top of the walls from view. Did Forster pay with his life for his own error of judgement?

The gallant defence of Fort San Cristobal bought precious time for Phillipon at Badajoz, and Wellington soon began to despair of taking the town. He received news that both D'Erlon and Marmont were advancing towards Badajoz, and estimated that if the place did not fall by 10

June he would have to raise the siege and retire west.

The second assault

The guns continued to fire upon the walls of the fort and the castle, although it appears that no real attempt to attack the breach in the castle walls was planned. Instead, another assault on Fort San Cristobal was prepared, this time for the evening of 9 June. By timing the attack for shortly after sundown it was hoped that the French would not have time to emerge and clear away the debris at the foot of the breach. The attempt on the 6th was also deemed to have failed partly because the storming party was too small, although it has to be said that no matter how many men were committed to the attack it would still have been extremely difficult to find a way in - the likelihood is that there would simply have been even greater casualties. Nevertheless, it was decided to increase the number of assaulting troops for the second attempt.

The Forlorn Hope again consisted of 25 volunteers, while the main storming column numbered 200 men, again from the 51st, 85th and the 17th Portuguese, to which were added men from the Brunswick-Oels Jägers and Chasseurs Brittanniques. In addition to these 200 stormers, a further 100 men were to be deployed to open fire on the defenders, while still others would ensure that no reinforcements reached the fort from the direction of the bridge over the Guadiana[7]. Thus the actual storming column was not increased significantly, but the addition of the covering parties would be very useful.

At 9pm on 9 June Major McGeechy of the 17th Portuguese led the storming column forward towards Fort San Cristobal. Once again the troops were guided to the breach by an officer of the Royal Engineers, Lieutenant Hunt, and once again the courageous Ensign Dyas led the Forlorn Hope, for the second time in four days. The second attempt to storm the fort met with the same tenacious defence as the first. Once again, French defenders lined the ramparts and simply rolled their grenades into the ditch to explode amid the crowded stormers. William Wheeler found himself in the same predicament as on 6 June:

'This second attempt was attended with the same ill success as the first. It is true we had profited by the discovery of the ladders being too short, but the old fox inside was too deep for us. He had caused all the rubbish to be cleared out of the trench. This again placed us in the same predicament, our ladders were again too short and if possible we received a warmer reception than before. The ladder I was on was broken and down we all came together, men, firelocks, bayonets, in one confused mass, and with us a portion of the wall. After some time the fire slackened, as if the enemy were tired of slaughter, when an officer Lieutenant Westropp came running from the western angle of the fort calling out to retire - the enemy were entering the trench by the sally port. We then began to leave the trench. Poor Mr Westropp was assisting a wounded man in getting out, when he was shot dead just as he had effected his purpose'[8].

Major McGeechy was shot several times as soon as he entered the ditch, while Dyas was slightly wounded by a 'slug', a charge containing four small pellets. Others were not so lucky; many were blown up by enemy grenades or shot down by the defenders. At one point several men made for the front angle of the fort, which had been damaged by artillery fire, thinking it was the breach; these were shot down before the error was realised. Not a single Allied soldier entered the fort, for no sooner did a man reach the top of his ladder than he was either shot or bayoneted. With little prospect of success and with men falling fast, the bugles sounded the retreat and once again the would-be stormers fell back - but this time having lost 139 killed and wounded out of the 225 who had originally advanced to the ditch. Remarkably, Ensign Dyas survived his second Forlorn Hope, while Private Wheeler could count himself fortunate that he was not taken prisoner:

Another view of Badajoz, again from the north bank, with in the foreground the tête du pont, a fortified work at the head of the bridge.

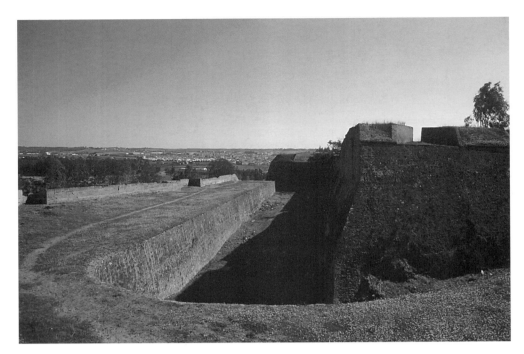

The ditch of Fort San Cristobal. It was at this spot that Ensign Dyas of the 51st Regiment twice entered the ditch at the head of the 'Forlorn Hope'. The attacks failed due to the exertions of the garrison in clearing away the rubble from the breach made by the Allied artillery, and to their tenacious resistance to the night assaults. They rolled grenades and barrels of gunpowder from the ramparts into the ditch below, burning and deafening the stormers - who included one of the finest of all memoirists from the ranks of Wellington's Peninsula army, Private William Wheeler.

'As we were retreating down the glacis, a misfortune befell me and I had a very narrow escape of being made prisoner, being cut off from my comrades by the party who sallied. There were eight or nine in the same mess. These the enemy obliged to go into the Fort. However, I hit upon an expedient that answered well. I threw myself down by a man who was shot through the head and daubed my white haversack with his blood. I showed this to the enemy when they ordered me to get up and go into the Fort. From the appearance of the blood they must have thought I had a very bad wound in the hip, so they all left me - except one who searched my pockets, took off my shirt, boots and stockings'[9]. (That last sentence reminds us of the astonishing greed for petty plunder of the Napoleonic soldier.)

At 10am the following day a truce was arranged and the dead and wounded were brought back either for treatment or burial. The inquests into the disastrous failure of the assault began soon afterwards. Dyas claimed that the ditch was much deeper than had at first been thought, and also said that on a reconnaissance prior to the second assault he had noticed the debris had been cleared away. Wellington himself said in a despatch written on 10 June that no practicable breach had been made in either the fort or the castle, suggesting that an assault should never have been made at all[10]. It was probably the time factor represented by the approaching relief force which prompted him to take the risk just before his self-imposed deadline of 10 June.

With the repulse of the second assault on Fort San Cristobal, Wellington decided to abandon the siege. The heavy guns continued to fail, spirits were low, and with the approach of Marmont there was little prospect of taking Badajoz or, for that matter, even the fort. Those stores which could not be moved were destroyed, and everything else was gathered up and taken back to Elvas. The siege had cost Wellington nine officers and 109 men killed, and 25 officers and 342 men wounded.

With hindsight we may feel that perhaps the most tragic aspect of this failure was that the battle of Albuera might have been fought for nothing. True, Beresford would still have had to fight to prevent himself being caught between Soult and the garrison of Badajoz and with the Guadiana at his back. However, the fact remains that the whole point of fighting at Albuera was to prevent Soult coming to the relief of Phillipon and his garrison; but it turned out that Soult's intervention was unnecessary, given Phillipon's gallant defence and Wellington's failure to take the place. This may seem a harsh conclusion; but the reality is that the heroic efforts of the British infantry at Albuera had ultimately come to nothing.

CHAPTER TWELVE

Manoeuvre, Consolidation and Raid

On 18 June 1811 the two French armies of Soult and Marmont, between them numbering around 60,000 men, finally concentrated at Merida, about 40 miles east of Badajoz. Wellington remained on the south bank of the Guadiana river, having sent all of his supplies, stores and what remained of his siege train back to Elvas, eleven miles west of Badajoz. His failure to take the town irritated him, although one suspects that he must have known that his chances of accomplishing the task with the means at his disposal had always been slim. Furthermore, his field army was still dispersed, with part of it at Badajoz and the bulk of it still to the north around Almeida. One wonders whether he would have been able to hold on to the fortress even if his efforts had proved successful; 60,000 French troops represented a very formidable force.

Upon the approach of Soult and Marmont towards Badajoz, Wellington withdrew his troops to the north bank of the Guadiana to await the remaining divisions of his army that had been ordered south to join him. Meanwhile, on 20 June, a relieved Phillipon swung open the gates of Badajoz to welcome Soult and Marmont, and to begin distribution of the provisions the two had brought with them. They had arrived not a moment too soon, for the garrison's provisions had run out that very same day. The Allied trenches were filled in and their works destroyed, while Phillipon's engineers set to work repairing the breaches at the castle and Fort San Cristobal. An outwork was then constructed on the site of the Allied battery north of San Cristobal. Everything practicable was done to strengthen the works, to shore up the defences and to make Badajoz an even stronger fortress - measures that would cost Wellington's army dear

when he returned the following year to make his third attempt on the place.

The summer of 1811 was not a particularly happy time for Wellington. His men had suffered hugely at Albuera; he had failed to take the fortress which controlled the southern corridor for any possible advance into Spain; and now he faced the threat posed by Marmont and Soult leading a considerably larger army. His temper had not been improved by the news that he had received on 10 June from Sir Brent Spencer, who had remained in the north to command Wellington's troops there, informing him that Spencer had blown up the remaining works at Almeida and had begun to march south in the face of the threat from Marmont. Almeida had been badly damaged by the great explosion in August 1810, and again in May 1811 when Brennier's garrison had escaped. Nevertheless, its availability for use as a base for the future siege of Ciudad Rodrigo would have been extremely useful. Wellington considered the destruction of the works to have been premature and ill-judged, and was proved correct when Marmont moved away without the slightest suggestion of an offensive move against Spencer, marching instead to join Soult at Merida.

It was at such times that Wellington despaired of the conduct of some of his senior subordinates. Beresford, Graham and Craufurd, all of whom had enjoyed independent commands, had all caused him anxious moments, while others - including Cole, the hero of Albuera - would do so in future. Only Rowland Hill appears to have been capable of waging war on the French without the guiding hand of his chief constantly on his shoulder – as his later conduct at Almaraz, Arroyo dos Molinos and St Pierre was to prove.

The Quinta da Sao Joao, north of Elvas. This fine building became Wellington's headquarters after the failed siege of Badajoz in June 1811, until he moved north that August.

An impression of Henry Ridge and the 2/5th Regiment (Northumberland) in action against French dragoons at El Bodon, 25 September 1811. As usual Richard Simkin has got the shakos wrong; he has, however, shown the regiment's white plume, a distinction gained after an action against the French on St Lucia in 1798. At El Bodon the 2/5th achieved the notable feat of successfully attacking French cavalry whilst in line.

The only comfort to Wellington, as he withdrew to the north bank of the Guadiana, was the news that the rest of his army was due to arrive very soon. Indeed, even as Phillipon was welcoming Soult and Marmont at Badajoz on 20 June, the last of Wellington's troops were arriving after their march south. His force numbered 44,000, of which some 37,000 were British, and was thus outnumbered by the enemy to the tune of around 16,000 men. This was more than compensated for by his choice of position, which extended for 15 miles along a ridge from Oguella, a small fortified town, south to Campo Mayor and on to Elvas, upon which his right flank rested. This was a position of some strength, though divided at its mid-point by the Caya, an unhealthy river which 'abounded in leeches and devils' and caused a great deal of sickness in Wellington's army.

There was little activity during the coming days, save for a French reconnaissance in force on 23 June that led to the capture of a piquet of the 11th Light Dragoons under Captain Benjamin Lutyens – an incident that caused Wellington more irritation, involving as it did a regiment that had arrived in the Peninsula only weeks before. By the end of June it was clear that the French were not about to make any offensive manoeuvres against Wellington. Indeed, affairs in Andalusia caused Soult to depart on 28 June, leaving Marmont to ponder his next move. Provisions were beginning to run low and, as was the French way, the army had to move in order to find more. And so, on 15 July, Marmont and his army marched away to the north-east leaving Badajoz well stocked with provisions and in a much healthier state than it had been two months earlier. Wellington himself, tired of waiting on the unhealthy Caya, marched north three days later and took up headquarters at Portalegre, whilst his troops went into cantonments over a wide area between Estremoz and Castello Branco.

The following month Wellington moved again, this time shifting his headquarters to Fuenteguinaldo, which he reached on 12 August. He moved north in the comfort of knowing that the southern corridor between Portugal and Spain was being ably guarded by Rowland Hill with a force which included the 2nd Division; with them he would fight several small skirmishes and actions, but theirs is another story. For now, Wellington contented himself with the knowledge that his most capable lieutenant was active in the south, and he had no qualms about leaving him there for the time being.

In the north, meanwhile, Wellington began to position his troops for the blockade of Ciudad Rodrigo, which commanded the northern corridor between Portugal and Spain. He was still unable to prosecute a regular siege as his siege train was still being unloaded at Oporto. Therefore he was forced to maintain his infantry and cavalry in positions around the place, with the Light and 3rd Divisions to the south and Julian Sanchez's irregulars to the north, while other divisions lay in close proximity. The blockade itself never really threatened Ciudad Rodrigo, for on 23 September Marmont's Army of Portugal joined forces with the Army of the North under Dorsenne. With a combined strength once more of 60,000 troops the two French commanders were more than a match for Wellington, who with his 46,000 men was unable to prevent Ciudad Rodrigo from being revictualled on 24 September. The Allied army lay to the west and south of Ciudad Rodrigo, holding a line about 70 miles long from Barba del Puerco in the north to Pedrogao in the south – a wide front, given the number of French troops close at hand.

The cavalry fight at Carpio

Wellington, meanwhile, continued to maintain his own position at Fuenteguinaldo. His headquarters had been here since August, during which time field works and retrenchments had been thrown up along the ridge that ran both east and west of the place. The position on the ridge was three miles in length, with the right flank resting upon the Agueda river and the left falling away into an extensive plain[1]; the terrain here afforded him a classic reverse slope position to conceal his true strength and dispositions from an enemy. It was not long before the inquisitive Marmont decided to make a foray from Ciudad Rodrigo in order to ascertain the true strength of Wellington's forces, and on the morning of 25 September 1,300 of Dorsenne's cavalry began to push westwards against the Allied outposts.

The cavalry force consisted of 14 squadrons from Wathier's and Lepic's brigades, mainly the Lanciers de Berg and the 26th Chasseurs. These German and French light horse quickly ran into the outlying piquets of the British 14th Light Dragoons, who were easily driven back across the Azava river. Six French squadrons were left at Carpio a few miles west of Ciudad Rodrigo, the remaining eight squadrons pushing on in the direction of Espeja, which lay to the south-west. Just in front of Espeja the single squadron of the British 14th Light Dragoons was joined by two squadrons from the 16th Light Dragoons as well as the light infantry companies of the 11th, 61st and 53rd, from Hulse's brigade of the 6th Division, all of which were concealed in a wood on some heights.

Wathier advanced with great caution, sending forward four of his eight squadrons into the wood. They had barely entered it when two squadrons of blue-jacketed light dragoons, one each from the 14th and 16th, burst forth and charged full pelt at them. The surprised French were driven back towards the Azava, where they rallied on the remaining four squadrons. It was then the turn of the British light dragoons to turn and run, with the white-clad lancers and green-clad chasseurs hot on their heels. The fleeing British cavalry got clear of their pursuers and reached a clearing in the wood, there to await the French, who were not long in arriving on the scene.

Wathier's cavalry now received a most unwelcome surprise, for no sooner had they reached the clearing than Hulse's light companies emerged from their cover and opened up a galling flanking fire into the startled French ranks. At the same time the British cavalry turned and charged, driving the panic-stricken French back to the bridge over the Azava and across to the other side – a distance of about two miles – before they halted. The French suffered around 50 casualties to a dozen British. This was a very minor action, which has long since been forgotten, but it was significant in one respect: it was the first time that British cavalry had met enemy lancers in a stand-up fight, and they had emerged as the victors. It is true that British

heavy and light dragoons had briefly engaged the Vistula Lancers during the early stages of Albuera, but on that occasion they had been used more or less in a covering role for the infantry and had only really been employed in seeing off the lancers who had crossed the Albuera river. The engagement at Carpio, however, saw light dragoons engaging lancers in a head-on fight and, as at Campo Mayor, the British troopers proved more than a match for their much-vaunted adversaries[2].

El Bodon

The fighting of 25 September was not over yet, however, for while Wathier was being rebuffed at Carpio, Montbrun was making a much stronger move further south on the road to Fuenteguinaldo. Here 2,500 French cavalry, having moved south from Ciudad Rodrigo, made a thrust at the area between Pastores, El Bodon and Campillo de Azava, which was occupied by Picton's 3rd Division scattered over a front of around seven miles. The road from Ciudad Rodrigo runs south through the first of these villages before continuing on to Fuenteguinaldo, as did the road from Campillo de Azava. In 1811 a further road, also from Ciudad Rodrigo, ran between these roads before again reaching Fuenteguinaldo. With two roads running south from Ciudad Rodrigo, it became a problem of deciding which of the two Montbrun would take. The units of the 3rd Division were therefore divided to cover both. In the event, Montbrun chose to move along the road in the centre, which ran over a steep ridge to the west of El Bodon, before continuing south-west to Fuenteguinaldo.

The road to the west of El Bodon runs south-west from Ciudad Rodrigo across a plain covered with oak and olive trees until it reaches the ridge about two miles west of the village itself. As the sandy road reaches the crest it turns from sand into rock, and is bordered on either side by rocky outcrops. There is very little soil here and it must have been particularly difficult going for the horses. The rocks provided good cover for infantry, while the crest afforded a commanding view of the plain before it.

Covering the road was Major Henry Ridge with the

The battlefield of El Bodon. This is the view that the French had as they charged up the road, time and again, only to be driven back by the successive charges of the 11th Light Dragoons and the King's German Legion 1st Hussars. When they did get up and in among the Portuguese guns, the 2/5th Foot met them at the top of the rise and drove them back down again.

Major, later Lieutenant-Colonel Henry Ridge of the 2/5th Regiment (Northumberland). This hero of El Bodon is traditionally supposed to have been the first man to enter Badajoz in the storming of 6 April 1812, having scaled the walls of the castle; sadly, he was killed shortly afterwards.

2/5th (Northumberland) from Colville's brigade, whom Wellington quickly reinforced with the 77th (East Middlesex) and the 21st Portuguese regiments. To Ridge and his battalion would fall one of the more unusual achievements of the war. The importance of the position which they held cannot be overemphasised. Should they be driven from it, the enemy would cut off, with serious consequences, one half of Wallace's brigade from the 3rd Division - the 74th (Highland) and three companies of the 5/60th Rifles - which occupied Pastores, covering the more easterly road. Meanwhile, Wallace was at El Bodon itself with the other half of his brigade - the 1/45th (Nottinghamshire) and 1/88th (Connaught Rangers). He must have been apprehensive indeed as he looked up at the ridge away to his left, where huge clouds of dust signalled the advance of the French cavalry. Nevertheless, he quickly formed his men and began to make off along the road to Fuenteguinaldo, while up on the ridge to the west Henry Ridge and his men prepared to meet the oncoming hordes of French horsemen – no less than seven regiments of them.

Wellington himself was on the scene very quickly, bringing forward not only the 77th and the 21st Portuguese but also two batteries of Portuguese artillery and five squadrons of Alten's cavalry - the 11th Light Dragoons and the 1st Hussars of the King's German Legion. The Portuguese guns completely commanded the road leading up to the crest, and swept it with canister shot. It was at this point that the five squadrons of Allied cavalry took centre stage, with a succession of bold charges against a much stronger enemy. The KGL hussars and British light dragoons swept forward over the crest of the ridge and drove the French back time after time, halting, reforming and returning to their original positions before repeating the exercise. Despite their efforts, however, Montbrun's cavalry finally surged forward up the road to the summit of the ridge, where they managed to get in amongst the Portuguese guns. Although the French captured one battery their success was short-lived, for behind the crest lay Henry Ridge and his battalion.

The 2/5th had watched the French cavalry as they darted in among the gunners, cutting at them and driving them off. Wellington had yet to lose a gun in battle, and Major Ridge was not going to allow it to happen now. The normal tactic for infantry when facing cavalry was to form square, but Ridge threw away the manual, formed his men into line, and advanced. The attack was strictly against the principles of war; but the 2/5th caught the French cavalry in a disordered state while they were still swarming around the Portuguese guns. Taken unawares by the sheer audacity of the attack, the French horsemen were thrown off the crest and pursued down the slope until Ridge halted his men and led them back to the summit. It was an astonishing feat of arms, and one that steadied the Allied position at a time of great peril. Captain Michael Childers was in the thick of the action, leading his squadron of the 11th Light Dragoons:

'We waited on a height where there was a fine plain, in fact the whole of the country from Ciudad to Fuenteguinaldo is open but hilly and rocky in some places. We waited there a considerable time with the infantry and some Portuguese guns, having detached some skirmishers who were employed the whole time, and we were informed that a strong column of cavalry was advancing, which they shortly did, charging the guns that were on the edge of the high ground to our right. They also charged the 5th and 77th who drove them down the hill like a flock of sheep and retook the guns.

'They then came to our front and rather to our left, and the Brigade... was ordered to charge them as soon as they made their appearance upon a part of the hill that was more accessible to the rest. [Here Childers's punctuation becomes confusing, as he explains that the 1st Hussars KGL had three squadrons present, of between 26 and 30 files each; and that the two squadrons of the 11th L D had 32 and 24 files.]The Hussars were ordered to charge and the 11th to support, as we got the order some time before it was put in execution we were complaining that we were not first sent, but we soon found that there was game enough for both parties and we both instantly charged and drove them down the hill where there was an immense column. We of course did not follow them down the hill but retired about 100 yards, they immediately followed us and we charged and drove them down again, this continued for a long time, I should think an hour at least, in which it was reckoned we charged 8 times, each time 5 or 6 [times] our number'[3].

Watching the fight from El Bodon were Wallace and the 88th, amongst whom was Ensign William Grattan: 'We had a clear and painful view of all that was passing,' he wrote, 'and we shuddered for our companions; the glittering of the countless sabres that were about to assail them, and the blaze of light which the reflection of the sun threw across the brazen helmets of the French horsemen, might be likened to the flash of lightning that preceded the thunder of Arentschildt's artillery - but we could do nothing. A few seconds passed away; we saw the smoke of the musketry - it did not recede, and we were assured that the attack had failed; in a moment or two more we could discern the brave 5th and 77th following their beaten adversaries, and a spontaneous shout of joy burst from the brigade'[4].

Three miles up the road at Pastores the other half of Wallace's brigade was effectively cut off, although Colonel Trench of the 74th brought the unit safely home by crossing the Agueda, which ran to the east of Pastores, and marching upon Fuenteguinaldo via Robleda. Wallace, meanwhile, continued to bring his own men south along the road from

El Bodon to Fuenteguinaldo. As they retreated Wellington brought back the troops who had fought so bravely up on the ridge above El Bodon. It was an episode reminiscent of Craufurd's retreat from Poço Velho during the battle of Fuentes de Oñoro, when he had shepherded home the 7th Division while surrounded by French cavalry. Here at El Bodon the same scene was being re-enacted as the men of the 3rd Division fell back in moving squares, gallantly supported by some 500 cavalry, while Montbrun's seven regiments of horsemen pressed in on them. It was a desperate task for the Allied squadrons to keep Montbrun's much more numerous cavalry at bay. Captain Childers again recalls the fight:

'The last charge we made with not more than 20 men. We got so mixed with them as they stood firm and advanced on both flanks at the same time that we were obliged to retreat at a good gallop with them at our heels - in fact I saw them stab one of our men, who like a fool was not looking behind him. We galloped I should think about 3/4 of a mile when we came up with a solid square of infantry of the above named regiments [5th and 77th], and as we passed within 16 yards of them they opened their fire on our pursuers and knocked a good many over who we turned back and sabred. We were so mixed with the French that when the infantry fired they killed one of ours and a hussar. The conduct of the infantry was admirable' [5].

Gradually the Allied infantry and cavalry converged upon Fuenteguinaldo, where Wellington's force was drawn up, and in spite of a few French artillery rounds thrown in amongst them the men made good their retreat. Considering the dangerous nature of this fighting withdrawal - across no less than six miles of open country - the Allied casualties of 140 were remarkably light; of these, almost half occurred amongst the cavalry, while the remainder, amongst the infantry, were caused by French artillery fire. French losses were put at 200 or so.

Fuenteguinaldo

At nightfall on 25 September Wellington's situation at Fuenteguinaldo was not particularly good; in fact, it was perilous. He had with him only two British infantry divisions, one Portuguese brigade, and three brigades of cavalry, in all around 16,000 men. Marmont, on the other hand, could call upon almost 40,000 French troops. Graham and Craufurd were in close proximity, but would not join Wellington until late the following afternoon. Marmont found himself in a most advantageous position; but ironically, he did not know it. The position at Fuenteguinaldo afforded Wellington that most vital defensive feature - a good reverse slope behind which he could hide his troops. It was at Fuenteguinaldo that the psychological hold which Wellington had already established over his French adversaries was clearly demonstrated. Although he himself knew that Marmont had a numerical superiority over him of about two and a half to one, the French commander did not attack: he could not be sure what lay in wait for him on the reverse slope. Marmont spurned his opportunity, and the arrival of Craufurd's Light Division on the afternoon of 26 September put an end to hours of anxious waiting by Wellington.

Craufurd had in fact received orders from Wellington to march on the evening of the 25th, but after only a few hours' march he halted his division, reluctant to continue in the dark. By refusing to press on by night Craufurd endangered Wellington, and his arrival at the latter's headquarters prompted one of the most memorable exchanges between the commander-in-chief and his often wayward lieutenant. 'Oh, I am glad to see you are safe, Craufurd,' said Wellington, to which Craufurd replied, 'Oh, I was in no danger, I assure you.' Wellington then snapped, 'But I was, from your conduct.' Turning away from that blazing blue glare, which had before now reduced strong men to stammering tears, 'Black Bob' made the heroically off-hand remark, 'He's damned crusty today!' [6].

Wellington withdrew his force west into Portugal and took up a strong position behind the Coa river. When Marmont realised the Allies had gone he too marched west in pursuit, but turned back as soon as he saw the strength of Wellington's new position. The French commander marched back to Ciudad Rodrigo and, after revictualling the place, he continued his march back to Salamanca. The frontier fortress was thus left isolated, and can never have

A 'British' view of the battlefield of El Bodon, looking back down the sandy slope along the old road to Fuenteguinaldo. Wellington's cavalry charged down this road several times to drive back the far more numerous French cavalry. Such was the part played by the King's German Legion 1st Hussars that it was awarded to them as a battle honour; indeed, some Imperial German units still carried the honour 'El Bodon' on their Picklehaube helmets when they went to war against the British Army in 1914.

been far from Wellington's thoughts. He knew that it must be his next objective, but the timing of the attack would depend on the first favourable opportunity. His siege train was at last ashore, and – occupying 160 river boats and no less than 1,000 vehicles – had lumbered up to Almeida. The next time he settled down before a fortress he would have the proper tools to hand.

Meanwhile, with the approach of winter, operations in the Peninsula began to close down as all the armies sought well-protected quarters in which to sit out the months when cold and hunger gripped the devastated land. Before winter came, however, there were still one or two episodes worthy of mention, and none more so than Rowland Hill's audacious raid on Girard at Arroyo dos Molinos on 28 October.

Hill at Arroyo dos Molinos

During the middle of October the infantry division led by General Girard, veterans of Albuera, crossed the Guadiana near Merida and began to make a nuisance of themselves in the northern districts of Estremadura. 'Daddy' Hill decided to put a stop to Girard's operations by making a direct attack upon him, and after a brief reconnaissance discovered that the French, some 5,500 strong, were billeted in and around the village of Arroyo dos Molinos to the west of Trujillo. The village is tucked away beneath the rugged Sierra de Montanches with just three roads leading out; if these were blocked it would effectively prevent any troops in the village from escaping, other than by climbing the mountains themselves.

Crossing into Spain south of the Tagus and making forced marches, by the evening of 27 October Hill had his 10,000-strong combined force of British, Portuguese and Spanish within four miles of the French when a storm got up, forcing him to halt during the hours of darkness. To ensure total surprise Hill had seen to it that the villages nearby were surrounded to prevent any warning being given to the enemy, while his own troops spent the stormy night in the open. Early on the morning of 28 October Hill covered the last few miles to Arroyo dos Molinos under cover of the atrocious weather, encountering not a single French piquet until he was just half a mile away. When they did stumble into the small French outpost it was quickly overcome, although some of them escaped and dashed off into the darkness to warn the French force.

Fortunately for the French, two of Girard's regiments – the 64th and 88th Line – had marched an hour earlier escorted by one dragoon regiment, and thus avoided capture. Warned, the remaining 4,000 French troops hastily prepared to make good their escape; all was hustle and bustle when Hill's leading troops – the 71st (Highland Light Infantry) and 92nd (Gordon Highlanders) – burst into the village with a crash of musketry, their pipes skirling above the din. The charging, cheering Scots swept aside the French battalion trying to hold the village, capturing scores of prisoners and taking Girard's baggage. The startled General Bron, commanding the divisional cavalry, emerged from his house only to be pulled rudely from his horse by a happy, exuberant Scot who then paraded his 'trophy' before his comrades.

After clearing the village of French troops the 71st came upon the rear of a French brigade still trying to form up for the march. The French were quickly thrown into disarray

Rowland Hill (1772-1842), the victor of Arroyo dos Molinos. Even this adulatory print by Jenkins, showing him in his full glory as lieutenant-general, viscount and Knight of the Bath cannot make 'Daddy' Hill's homely face look like a stern god of war, but his military talents were beyond question. The legends of his kindliness to all ranks abounded; in an age of hard swearing he was a notably mild-spoken man; and Wellington prized his calm competence as a divisional commander - 'The best of Hill is that I always know where to find him'. His finest hour was probably on 13 December 1813 at St Pierre near Bayonne, when his 14,000-man command was cut off by a rising river and washed-away bridges, faced by Soult with 30,000 men. He personally led his dwindling reserves into action, and spent a long day moving from point to threatened point in the front line of battle until reinforcements at last came up.

when the Highland Light Infantry opened fire on the rear of their column, as did three Allied guns which had come forward. The column hurried on along the road leading to Merida, but soon found its way barred by Hill's cavalry, forcing Girard to launch his own chasseurs and dragoons against them in order to buy time for the escaping infantry. The French cavalry fought gallantly against the 9th Light Dragoons and the 2nd Hussars KGL, but they were outnumbered and forced to retire, leaving many of their number to be taken prisoner.

The rest of Girard's infantry, meanwhile, set off eastwards along the Trujillo road at the foot of the mountains with the Allied infantry of Howard's brigade hot on their heels. As the French peered through the early morning mist they saw to their horror the light companies of the 28th (North Gloucestershire), 34th (Cumberland) and 39th (Dorsetshire) rushing to cut them off. Despite having a vastly superior number of troops at his disposal, Girard ordered his men to avoid the three British companies and instead try to escape by heading into the mountains on their left. This decision precipitated a remarkable scene, with officers hastily abandoning their horses and infantry scrambling up the steep slopes to escape. Girard was one of the lucky ones: he, along with about 500 others, managed to reach the top of the mountain and evaded the clutches of Hill's men. Even here, however, they were not entirely safe, for the merciless Spaniards of Morillo's brigade came clambering after them, bayoneting all those they came up with.

No less than 1,300 French troops were taken prisoner, most of whom surrendered at the foot of the mountains. As well as General Bron the prisoners included the colonel of the 27th Chasseurs, the Prince of Aremberg, and 30 other officers. Hill's force suffered just seven men killed and seven officers and 57 men wounded; the Spaniards recorded just 30 casualties. It was a most satisfactory end to the year's campaigning; and although Hill failed in another surprise attack – at Membrillo on the last day of the year – his success at Arroyo dos Molinos confirmed his status as Wellington's most able lieutenant. This reputation would be enhanced by his subsequent actions at Almaraz in May 1812, and at St Pierre in December 1813; despite his Pickwickian appearance, and the mild and kindly manner for which he was loved throughout the army, Rowland Hill was a formidable fighting general.

Further north, meanwhile, Wellington continued to watch and wait for developments. They would bring him the opportunity he sought much sooner than anyone expected, and he was ready when the chance offered. In January 1812 the balance would shift, with the recall of all Imperial Guard and Polish troops to France in early preparation for Napoleon's Russian adventure - an order which cost the marshals in Spain some 22,000 high quality troops. The removal from the Portuguese frontier region of 12,000 of Marmont's men, despatched to the east to assist Suchet in his fight against Spanish guerrillas, would give Wellington the window of opportunity he was waiting for, and he leapt for it. On 19 January 1812 the fortress of Ciudad Rodrigo would at last fall into his hands.

★   ★   ★

The year 1811 offers us examples of many of the governing factors at work during the Peninsular War. It began with Wellington emerging from the Lines of Torres Vedras - a masterpiece of forethought and patient preparation - to inflict a great deal of damage on Masséna's larger army and drive it from Portugal. This in turn led to Masséna's dismissal by his arbitrary and unforgiving emperor, and his replacement by the less dangerous Marmont.

Most of the year's campaigning demonstrated the essential contradictions of the 'Spanish dance'. When Wellington advanced towards the strategic frontier fortresses upon which any future offensive operations depended, the dispersed but much stronger French armies gathered to threaten him - thus neglecting the subjugation of other regions of chronically rebellious Spain, and ensuring that trouble in their rear would soon distract them. Lacking a siege train, and too weak in numbers to fend off the relief forces until mere blockades could succeed, Wellington was unable to seize the fortresses before the marshals' approach forced him to abandon these attempts.

When he chose to meet these stronger adversaries in open battle he avoided defeat over and over again, outfighting them by deploying his own small but excellent army with a brilliant eye for ground, and employing superior infantry tactics. But the disparity in numbers and lack of control of the frontier fortresses meant that his victories could only be local and temporary, and when the marshals concentrated against him he was obliged to retreat once more within the safe haven of Portugal, where Torres Vedras still offered him the ultimate insurance against disaster.

All the time, however, Wellington was growing gradually stronger, and - thanks to British gold and massive material aid - so were his Portuguese and Spanish allies, although the contrast in the quality of co-operation he could expect from the two Iberian nations was still striking. Meanwhile, the dispersed armies of the French marshals had begun to die the death of a thousand cuts.

In the year to come Napoleon would weaken them further by taking tens of thousands of their best men for his Russian campaign - men who would never return; and the Spanish irregulars would grow stronger and more audacious. Simultaneously Wellington's sudden seizure of Ciudad Rodrigo and Badajoz, and his stunning victory at Salamanca – a victory of manoeuvre, not defence – would transform the face of this war. It would take two further years to win it, but the end was not in doubt after 1812.

In the meantime, however, the manoeuvres and countermanoeuvres of his several adversaries obliged Wellington to rely now and then upon subordinates in independent command of detached forces. Sometimes - like Graham at Barrosa, and Hill at Arroyo dos Molinos - they justified his trust; but more often they demonstrated the army's need for his own guiding hand at all times. And the most notorious of these occasions provided, among the many remarkable feats of arms recorded in the Peninsula, the awesome spectacle of the ultimate face-to-face fight between Frenchman and British redcoat: the battle that took place on 16 May 1811 on Byron's 'Glorious Field of Grief'- the bloody slopes of Albuera.

Wellington's headquarters at Freneida, where he saw out the winter of 1811-12. Wellington's officers, who found few home comforts in that bleak winter, loathed this small village, and it came as a relief when they packed up and moved south to Badajoz after the capture of Ciudad Rodrigo in January 1812. It remains today one of the most evocative places in the Peninsula.

NOTES AND SOURCES

Chapter One: The Spanish Ulcer

(1) J.Gurwood (Ed), *The Despatches of Field Marshal the Duke of Wellington during his various Campaigns*, (London, 1832), IV, 1.

(2) Captain John Patterson, *Adventures of Captain Patterson*, (London, 1837), 45-46.

(3) Jac Weller, *Wellington in the Peninsula*, (London, 1962), 71.

(4) By far the best work on the Lines is Col.J.T.Jones's *Journal of the Sieges in Portugal and Spain*, the best edition of which is the three-volume third edition, published in London in 1847.

(5) Wellington to Admiral Keats, Celorico, 2 August 1810. MSS, in the collection of Mr Richard Old.

(6) These papers, in particular those by Captain Goldfinch, can be found amongst the archives of the Royal Engineers Museum, Brompton.

Chapter Two: Wellington's Army – 'The Moral Power of Steadiness'

(1) *Despatches*, XI, 306.

(2) Ian Fletcher (Ed), *For King and Country; The Letters and Diaries of John Mills, Coldstream Guards, 1811-14*, (Staplehurst, 1995), 41-42.

(3) Captain John Kincaid, *Random Shots from a Rifleman*, (London, 1835), 310-311.

(4) These quotations are invariably misinterpreted. It is often forgotten that Wellington used the phrase 'the scum of the earth' on two separate occasions. The first use came on 2 July 1813, in a despatch to Earl Bathurst, *Despatches*, X, 495-496. The second use came in 1831 in conversation with Earl Stanhope, see *Notes of Conversations with the Duke of Wellington*, (London, 1888), 14. It was only on this second occasion that Wellington added, 'it is only wonderful that we should be able to make so much out of them afterwards.'

(5) Captain H.H.Woolwright, *History of the Fifty-Seventh (West Middlesex) Regiment of Foot, 1755-1881*, (London, 1893), 400.

(6) Fletcher, *For King and Country*, 77.

(7) See the Adjutant General's comment on page vii of *Regulations for the Formations and Movements of the Cavalry*, (London, 1796).

(8) The best study of the administration of Wellington's army is S.G.P. Ward's *Wellington's Headquarters; A Study of the Administrative Problems in the Peninsula, 1809-1814*, (Oxford, 1957).

Chapter Three: The French Armies – 'Coming On in the Old Style'

(1) See Philip Haythornthwaite's *Weapons and Equipment of the Napoleonic Wars*, (London, 1996), 4.

(2) This figure is based upon the French returns, published in Oman's *History of the Peninsular War*, (London, 1902), IV, 634.

(3) Marshal Thomas Robert Bugeaud, quoted in John Naylor's *Waterloo*, (London, 1960), 38; and in *Napoleon's Army*, Col.H.C.B.Rogers, (London, 1974), 70-71.

Chapter Four: Wellington Clears Portugal – 'Handsome Men Biting the Dust'

(1) The returns in the *Archives Nationales*, Paris, are quoted in Oman's *Peninsular War*, IV, 638-642. They give the strength of the French Army in Spain, as of July 1811, as being 354,461.

(2) George Simmons, *A British Rifleman; The Journals and Correspondence of Major George Simmons, Rifle Brigade, During the Peninsular War and the Campaign of Waterloo*, (London, 1899), 176-178.

(3) Oman, *Peninsular War*, IV, 614-616.

(4) Ibid, IV, 617.

(5) Ibid, IV, 203.

(6) A.H.Norris & R.W.Bremner, *The Lines of Torres Vedras: The First Three Lines and Fortifications south of the Tagus*, Lisbon, 1986), 5.

(7) Ciudad Rodrigo had fallen to the French in July 1810 after a protracted defence by the governor, Herrasti. Badajoz, on the other hand, had been delivered up to the French, under Soult, by the inept and treacherous José Imaz. He had succeeded to the governorship of the town upon the death of General Menacho, who had led a gallant defence of the place.

Chapter Five: Fuentes de Oñoro – 'A Dance of Life'

(1) *Despatches*, VII, 514-515.

(2) C.Hibbert (Ed), *A Soldier of the Seventy-First*, (London, 1975), 60-61.

(3) Ibid, 61.

(4) Ibid, 62.

(5) John Stepney Cowell, *Leaves from the Diary of an Officer of the Guards*, (London, 1854), 84. British memoirists are sometimes too ready to identify French troops as belonging to the Imperial Guard, perhaps deceived by grenadier bearskins and the plumes and other finery of Line infantry regimental *têtes de colonnes*; but on this occasion Bessières did have Lepic's Guard Cavalry Brigade with him - the Polish Lancers, Chasseurs à cheval, Grenadiers à cheval, and Mamelukes.

(6) William Napier, *History of the Peninsular War*, (London, 1833), III: 519.

(7) Lt.Col.J.Leach, *Rough Sketches of the Life of an Old Soldier*, (London, 1831), 134.

(8) Napier, *History*, III: 520.

(9) Elizabeth Longford, *Wellington: The Years of the Sword*, (London, 1969), 252.

(10) J.W.Fortescue, *A History of the British Army*, (London, 1917), VIII: 165-166.

(11) Hibbert, *A Soldier ...* , 62-63.

(12) Charles Oman (Ed), *William Grattan: Adventures in the Connaught Rangers, 1809-1814*, (London, 1902), 67.

(13) Ibid, 69.

(14) Fletcher, For *King and Country*, 35.

(15) *Despatches*, VII, 547.

(16) Ibid, VII, 565.

Chapter Six: Barrosa – The First Eagle

(1) Oman, *Peninsular War*, III, 92-93.

(2) Delavoye, *Life of Lord Lynedoch*, (London, 1880), 466-467.

(3) The map in Wyld's Atlas actually refers to the battle as taking place at the Vigia de la Barrosa.

(4) Delavoye, *Lord Lynedoch*, 467.

(5) Not for the first time, Oman confuses his directions. He claims that Graham retreated westwards, which is nonsense – a retreat in this direction would have taken him into the Atlantic. Much of this confusion lies in the fact that Oman never visited the battle-field. His map of the battle of Barrosa, in Volume IV of his *Peninsular War*, has no compass, and thus one might assume that north is at the top of the map, which it is not; in fact the top of his map lies in an east-north-east direction. Claiming that Ruffin ascended the hill by its northern slope compounds the error; this would have cut off Browne and his flankers. Ruffin in fact ascended the hill by its north-eastern slopes, which allowed Browne time to get off and march after Graham. Oman's account of the battle sparked a lively criticism from Willoughby Verner, the historian of the Rifle Brigade, who lived close to the battlefield during the early part of the 20th century. Verner's account of the battle is one of the more accurate. (See Verner, *History and Campaigns of the Rifle Brigade*, II, 183-215.)

(6) Accounts vary as to the sequence of events at this point. Some claim that the Spaniards abandoned Browne, whereas others claim Browne himself retreated in the face of a hopeless situation. Whatever the truth, the Allies had little hope of maintaining the hill in the face of the determined attack by Victor's 7,000 infantry, with cavalry and artillery support.

(7) Accounts of the exchange between Graham and Browne vary, but perhaps the most entertaining is to be found in the autobiography of Robert Blakeney, *A Boy in the Peninsular War*, (London, 1899), 187-188.

(8) According to Brett-James's biography, Graham, riding along the line, waved his cocked hat in the air and shouted 'Now my lads, there they are. Spare your powder, but give them steel enough.' Ibid, 211. However, he then goes on to describe how Graham had his horse shot beneath him whilst advancing with Wheatley's brigade. Surely he could not have been in two places at the same time?

(9) Ruffin died in captivity, and is buried in the grounds of the old garrison church in Portsmouth.

(10) Fortescue, *British Army*, VIII, 58.

(11) Gough is mistaken here, for it was the 45ᵉ and not the 47ᵉ Ligne that was present at Barrosa.

(12) Robert S.Rait, *The Life and Campaigns of Hugh, First Viscount Gough, Field Marshal*, (London, 1903), II, 53.

(13) A descendant of Masterson won a Victoria Cross at Ladysmith in 1900 during the Boer War.

(14) Charles Cadell, *Narrative of the Campaigns of the Twenty-Eighth Regiment*, (London, 1835), 96.

(15) Ibid, 97-98.

(16) Fortescue, *British Army*, VIII, 62.

Chapter Seven: Campo Mayor – 'Undisciplined Ardour'?

(1) *Despatches*, VII, 374-375.

(2) C.R.B.Barratt, *History of the 13th Hussars*, (Edinburgh, 1911), 130.

(3) 'The Courier', 20th April 1811, supplied by Philip Haythornthwaite.

(4) Ibid.

(5) Long, *Peninsular Cavalry General*, edited by T.H.McGuffie (London, 1951), 76.

(6) Ibid, 78. In the row that followed the fight Beresford alleged that it was Long himself who told Tripp that the 13th Light Dragoons had been taken. Although Long had taken up a poor position during the action he was hardly likely to be the source of the report. The issue of who actually spread the false rumour has no real bearing on the business. According to Lieutenant Madden, 4th Dragoons, the heavy brigade was halted just 200 yards from the French column - see 'The Diary of Lieutenant Charles Dudley Madden', *Royal United Services Institute Journal*, April 1914, LVIII, 511.

(7) Colborne's infantry are put at various distances from the scene of the action. Oman, for example, claims that Colborne was still two miles away (see *Peninsular War*, IV, 259), although Colborne himself saw the whole action and must, therefore, have been very close. It certainly appears that the 66th Regiment, in addition to some light troops, was with Colborne.

(8) Some suggestions have been made that the 13th sustained casualties from the guns in Badajoz itself. This seems very unlikely, however. Badajoz was never threatened from the north owing to the Guadiana river preventing any attacking force from approaching from this direction; therefore few guns, if any, were ever placed facing north. Furthermore, there are no ramparts on the northern side of Badajoz; it is simply a wall. The fire which caused casualties in the ranks of the 13th Light Dragoons almost certainly came from Fort San Cristobal, which they would have had to pass in order to approach the bridge to the town.

(9) These figures are from Barratt, *13th Hussars*, 138.

(10) Ibid, 135.

(11) *Despatches*, VII, 412.

(12) Barratt, *13th Hussars*, 136.

(13) McGuffie, *Peninsular Cavalry General*, 89.

(14) Barratt, 13th *Hussars*, 136, and Fortescue, *British Army*, VIII, 133.

(15) For a full treatment of the action at Campo Mayor and, indeed, the British cavalry in the Peninsula, see Ian Fletcher, *Galloping at Everything; The British Cavalry in the Peninsula and at Waterloo, 1808-1815 - A Re-appraisal*, (Staplehurst, 1999).

Chapter Eight: Albuera – A Storm of Lancers

(1) *Despatches*, 23 April 1811. All of this is from a return of 1 May 1811 in the *Archives Nationales*, printed in Oman, Peninsular War, IV, 634-635. See also page 367 for details of Soult's artillery.

(3) Lumley was appointed, in Long's own words, 'rather indelicately.' See McGuffie, *Peninsular Cavalry General*, 106.

(4) Fletcher, *For King and Country*, 126.

(5) *Further Strictures on those parts of Col. Napier's History of the Peninsular War which relate to the Military Opinions and Conduct of General Lord Viscount Beresford*, (London, 1832), 118.

(6) Roverea, quoted in *Memoirs of Lowry Cole*, (London, 1934), 71, edited by M.L.Cole and S.Gwynn.

(7) Although Albuera was the first time British cavalry had met enemy lancers in the Peninsula, it was a very brief encounter. The first real fight between the two came at Carpio on 25 September 1811 - see Chapter Twelve.

(8) Both Fortescue and Oman maintain that Blake's line was incomplete when the French attack hit. However, according to the author of *Further Strictures*, 142, it was complete, although somewhat hurried.

(9) Weller, *Wellington in the Peninsula*, 175.

(10) Oman, *Peninsular War*, IV, 380.

(11) N.Ludlow Beamish, *History of the King's German Legion*, (London, 1832), I, 338.

(12) Major William Brooke, 'A Prisoner of Albuera,' printed in Charles Oman's *Studies in the Napoleonic Wars*, (London, 1929), 177-178. The French 28th Light Infantry, which Brooke claimed to identify, were in Gazan's division.
(13) Capt.C.R.B.Knight, *Historical Record of the Buffs, East Kent Regiment, 3rd Foot*, (London, 1935), III, 349.
(14) Ibid, 351.
(15) Brooke, quoted in Oman's *Studies*, 178-179.
(16) Acknowledged to Col.F.R.T.T.Gascoigne, DSO; variously anthologised, most recently in *The Mammoth Book of War Diaries & Letters*, Jon E.Lewis (Ed), (London, 1998), 28-29.

Chapter Nine: Albuera – 'That Astonishing Infantry'
(1) Weller, *Wellington in the Peninsula*, 177. There is no reliable source to give credence to Weller's theory, although by the same token there is no specific reason to doubt it.
(2) See Moyle Sherer, *Recollections of the Peninsula*, (London, 1827), 159.
(3) Oman erroneously gives Sherer's regiment as the 1/48th.
(4) Sherer, *Recollections*, 159-161.
(5) Fortescue, *British Army*, VIII, 200.
(6) W.H.Maxwell, *Peninsular Sketches*, (London, 1845), II, 330.
(7) Ensign Benjamin Hobhouse to his father, 17 May 1811, *The Times*, 25 February 1925; kindly supplied by Phoebe Turpin.
(8) Major Francis Duncan, *History of the Royal Regiment of Artillery*, (London, 1879), II, 296.
(9) Sherer, Recollections, 161.
(10) Cole & Gwynn, *Lowry Cole*, 72-73.
(11) Ibid, 73.
(12) Ibid, 76-77.
(13) Oman and Fortescue give the 11th and 23rd Regiments with two battalions each. Portuguese regimental organisation was ordered changed in July 1808, from two five-company battalions to one ten-company battalion, with an establishment of 1,552 all ranks. Previously unblooded in any major action, the two units had notably higher strengths than British battalions – see Appendix I - which may have contributed to this confusion. See Chartrand, R., *The Portuguese Army of the Napoleonic Wars (1)*, (Oxford, 2000), 37-39.
(14) John Spencer Cooper, *Rough Notes of Seven Campaigns*, (Carlisle, 1869), 60.
(15) Blakeney, quoted in Oman, *Peninsular War*, IV, 392.
(16) Cooper, *Rough Notes*, 60-61.
(17) Napier, *History*, III, 546-547.
(18) Ibid, 547.
(19) Napier, *History*, III, 547.
(20) Sherer, *Recollections*, 161-163.
(21) Oman, *Peninsular War*, IV, 394.

Chapter Ten: Albuera – 'Oh, Glorious Field of Grief!'
(1) 'Two Months Recollections of the Late War, by a private soldier', *Colborn's United Services Journal*, n.d. 420
(2) Sherer, *Recollections*, 165.
(3) Oman, *Peninsular War*, IV, 397.
(4) Longford, *Years of the Sword*, 257.
(5) *Despatches*, VII, 579.
(6) Fletcher, *For King and Country*, 46.
(7) Ibid, 126.
(8) *Despatches*, VII, 573.
(9) Ibid, VII, 574.
(10) Ibid, VII, 579-580.
(11) Charles Stewart, quoted in Fortescue, *British Army*, VII, 190.
(12) *Despatches*, VIII, 508.
(13) The letter is quoted in Fortescue's *British Army*, VII, 210, but he does not give the source.
(14) Maxwell, *Peninsular Sketches*, II, 331.
(15) *Despatches*, VII, 591.

Chapter Eleven: Badajoz – 'Down We All Came Together'
(1) *Despatches*, VII, 622.
(2) Jones, *Sieges in Spain*, I, 33.
(3) Ibid, I, 34.
(4) Major John H.Leslie (Ed), *The Dickson Manuscripts*, (Woolwich, 1905), 405.
(5) B.H.Liddell Hart (Ed), *The Letters of Private Wheeler*, (London, 1951), 60-61.
(6) Ibid, 61.
(7) It is curious that Oman got his maths wrong here, and quoted the storming party as being 400 strong. Houston's orders for the attack (quoted in Jones's *Sieges*, I, 60-61) clearly state that the storming party consisted of 200 men, divided into two detachments, while the other 200 were either to cover the stormers or prevent enemy interference.
(8) Liddell Hart, *Private Wheeler*, 62.
(9) Ibid, 62.
(10) *Despatches*, VII, 653.

Chapter Twelve: Manoeuvre, Consolidation and Raid
(1) The description of the position can be found in the 1814 edition of Jones's *Sieges*, 79. Curiously, the description was omitted from the 1846 edition, which is considered to be the best.
(2) For more on the fight at Carpio see this author's *Galloping at Everything*.
(3) Capt.Michael Childers, quoted in Capt.Trevelyan Williams, *The Historical Records of the Eleventh Hussars Prince Albert's Own*, (London, 1908), 127.
(4) Grattan, *Connaught Rangers*, 112-113.
(5) Childers, quoted in Williams, *Eleventh Hussars*, 127-128.
(6) Sir George Larpent (Ed), *The Private Journal of F.Seymour Larpent*, (London, 1853), I, 107.

SELECT BIBLIOGRAPHY

Barratt, C.R.B., *History of the 13th Hussars*, (Edinburgh, 1911)

Beamish, N.Ludlow, *History of the King's German Legion*, (London, 1832)

Blakeney, Robert, *A Boy in the Peninsular War*, (London, 1899)

Cadell, Charles, *Narrative of the Campaigns of the Twenty-Eighth Regiment*, (London, 1835)

'Two Months Recollections of the Late War, by a private soldier', *Colborn's United Services Journal*, n.d.

Cole, M.L. & Gwynn, S, (Eds), *Memoirs of Lowry Cole*, (London, 1934)

Cooper, John Spencer, *Rough Notes of Seven Campaigns*, (Carlisle, 1869)

Delavoye, A., *Life of Lord Lynedoch*, (London, 1880)

Duncan, Major Francis, *History of the Royal Regiment of Artillery*, (London, 1879)

Fletcher, Ian (Ed), *For King and Country; The Letters and Diaries of John Mills, Coldstream Guards*, 1811-14, (Staplehurst, 1995)

Fletcher, Ian, *Galloping at Everything; The British Cavalry in the Peninsula and at Waterloo, 1808-1815. A Re-appraisal*, (Staplehurst, 1999)

Fortescue, The Hon.J.W., *A History of the British Army*, (13 Vols, London, 1899)

'Further Strictures on those parts of Col.Napier's *History of the Peninsular War* which relate to the Military Opinions and Conduct of General Lord Viscount Beresford', (London, 1832)

Gurwood, J. (Ed), *The Despatches of Field Marshal the Duke of Wellington during his various Campaigns*, (London, 1832)

Haythornthwaite, Philip, *Weapons and Equipment of the Napoleonic Wars*, (London, 1996)

Hibbert, C. (Ed), *A Soldier of the Seventy-First*, (London, 1975)

Jones, Colonel J.T., *Journal of the Sieges in Portugal and Spain*, (London, 1847)

Kincaid, Captain John, *Random Shots from a Rifleman*, (London, 1835)

Knight, Captain C.R.B., *Historical Record of the Buffs, East Kent Regiment, 3rd Foot*, (London, 1935)

Larpent, Sir George (Ed), *The Private Journal of F. Seymour Larpent*, (London, 1853)

Leach, Lieutenant Colonel J., *Rough Sketches of the Life of an Old Soldier*, (London, 1831)

Leslie, Major John H. (Ed), *The Dickson Manuscripts*, (Woolwich, 1905)

Liddell Hart, B.H. (Ed), *The Letters of Private Wheeler*, (London, 1951)

Longford, Elizabeth, *Wellington: The Years of the Sword*, (London, 1969)

McGuffie, T.H. (Ed), *Peninsular Cavalry General*, (London, 1951)

Madden, Charles, 'The Diary of Lieutenant Charles Dudley Madden', *RUSI Journal*, April 1914, LVIII

Maxwell, W.H. (Ed), *Peninsular Sketches*, (London, 1845)

Napier, William, *History of the Peninsular War*, (6 Vols, London, 1828)

Naylor, John, *Waterloo*, (London, 1960)

Norris, A.H., & Bremner, R.W., *The Lines of Torres Vedras: The First Three Lines and Fortifications south of the Tagus*, (Lisbon, 1986)

Oman, Charles, *History of the Peninsular War*, (7 Vols, London, 1902)

Oman, Charles, *Studies in the Napoleonic Wars*, (London, 1929)

Oman, Charles (Ed), *William Grattan: Adventures in the Connaught Rangers, 1809-1814*, (London, 1902)

Patterson, Captain John, *Adventures of Captain Patterson*, (London, 1837)

Rait, Robert S., *The Life and Campaigns of Hugh, First Viscount Gough, Field Marshal*, (London, 1903)

Regulations for the Formations and Movements of the Cavalry, (London, 1796)

Sherer, Moyle, *Recollections of the Peninsula*, (London, 1827)

Simmons, George, *A British Rifleman; The Journals and Correspondence of Major George Simmons, Rifle Brigade, During the Peninsular War and the Campaign of Waterloo*, (London, 1899)

Stanhope, Earl, *Notes of Conversations with the Duke of Wellington*, (London, 1888)

Stepney Cowell, John, *Leaves from the Diary of an Officer of the Guards*, (London, 1854)

Verner, Willoughby, *History and Campaigns of the Rifle Brigade*, (London, 1913)

Ward, S.G.P., *Wellington's Headquarters; A Study of the Administrative Problems in the Peninsula, 1809-1814*, (Oxford, 1957)

Weller, Jac, *Wellington in the Peninsula*, (London, 1962)

Williams, Captain Trevelyan, *The Historical Records of the Eleventh Hussars Prince Albert's Own*, (London, 1908)

Woolwright, Captain H.H., *History of the Fifty-Seventh (West Middlesex) Regiment of Foot, 1755-1881*, (London, 1893)

The Allied Army at Albuera, 16 May 1811

This and Appendix II are from figures compiled in Oman's *History of the Peninsular War*, IV, 631-635.

	Present Offs.	Present Men	Killed Offs.	Killed Men	Wounded Offs.	Wounded Men	Missing Offs.	Missing Men	Total loss
BRITISH									
2nd Division									
(William Stewart)									
Colborne's Brigade:									
1/3rd	27	728	4	212	14	234	2	177	643
2/31st	20	398	–	29	7	119	–	–	155
2/48th	29	423	4	44	10	86	9	190	343
2/66th	22	417	3	52	12	104	–	101	272
Brigade totals:	100	1,966	11	337	43	543	11	468	1,413
Hoghton's Brigade:									
29th	31	476	5	75	12	233	–	11	336
1/48th	33	464	3	64	13	194	–	–	280
1/57th	31	616	2	87	21	318	–	6	428
Brigade totals:	95	1,556	10	226	46	745	–	17	1,044
Abercrombie's Brigade:									
2/28th	28	491	–	27	6	131	–	–	164
2/34th	28	568	3	30	4	91	–	–	128
2/39th	33	449	1	14	4	77	–	2	98
Brigade totals:	89	1,508	4	71	14	299	–	2	390
Div. light troops – 3 coys., 5/60th:									
	4	142	–	2	1	18	–	–	21
2nd Division totals:									
	288	5,172	25	636	104	1,605	11	487	2,868
4th Division (Lowry Cole)									
Myers's Brigade:									
1/7th	27	687	–	65	15	277	–	–	357
2/7th	28	540	2	47	13	287	–	–	349
1/23rd	41	692	2	74	11	246	–	6	339
Brigade totals:	96	1,919	4	186	39	810	–	6	1,045
Kemmis's Brigade – 3 detached coys., 2/27th, 1/40th, 97th:									
	8	157	1	5	–	14	–	–	20
4th Division totals:									
	104	2,076	5	191	39	824	–	6	1,065
Alten's Independent Brigade, King's German Legion:									
1st Light Bn.									
	23	565	–	4	4	59	–	2	69
2nd Light Bn.									
	19	491	1	3	1	31	–	1	37
Brigade totals:									
	42	1,056	1	7	5	90	–	3	106
Cavalry (Lumley)									
De Grey's Brigade:									
3rd Dragoon Guards									
	23	351	1	9	–	9	–	1	20
4th Dragoons									
	30	357	–	3	2	18	2	2	27
13th Light Dragoons									
	23	380	–	–	–	1	–	–	1
Brigade totals:									
	76	1,088	1	12	2	28	2	3	48
Artillery									
British (Lefebure's & Hawker's coys.)									
	9	246	–	3	1	10	–	1	15
KGL (Cleeve's & Sympher's coys.)									
	10	282	–	–	1	17	1	30	49
Staff	?	?	1	–	7	–	–	–	8
Grand totals of British:									
	529	9,920	33	849	159	2,574	14	530	4,159
PORTUGUESE									
(Note that Present figures include all ranks.)									
Hamilton's Division:									
Fonseca's Brigade									
2nd Line	1,225		–	3	–	5	–	–	8
14th Line	1,204		–	–	–	2	–	–	2
Campbell's Brigade									
4th Line	1,271		–	9	1	50	–	–	60
10th Line	1,119		–	–	–	11	–	–	11
Harvey's Brigade:									
11th Line	1,154		–	2	2	4	–	5	13
23rd Line	1,201		1	3	1	14	–	–	19
1st Bn.LLL	572		–	66	6	89	–	10	171
Collins's Brigade:									
5th Line	985		–	10	4	36	–	10	60
5th Cazadores	400		–	5	–	25	–	1	31
Cavalry (Otway)									
1st Regt.	327		–	–	–	–	–	–	–
7th Regt.	314		–	–	–	2	–	–	2
5th Regt.	104		–	–	–	–	–	–	–
8th Regt.	104		–	–	–	–	–	–	–
Artillery (Arriaga & Braun)									
	221		–	2	–	8	–	–	10
Staff	?		1	–	1	–	–	–	2
Grand totals of Portuguese:									
	10,201		2	100	15	246	–	26	389

	Present		Killed		Wounded		Total
	Offs.	Men	Offs.	Men	Offs.	Men	loss

SPANISH

(Note that no figures are available for Missing, so the total Spanish losses – marked ★ – cannot be calculated.)

Blake's Army:

Vanguard Division
(Lardizabal)
Regts.Murcia (2 Bns.), Canarias, 2nd Leon & Campo Mayor:

Offs.	Men	Offs.	Men	Offs.	Men	Total loss
107	2,291	4	59	13	215	291

3rd Division
(Ballasteros)
Regts.1st Catalonia, Barbastro, Pravia, Lena, Castropol, Cangas de Tineo & Infiesto:

154	3,371	3	64	15	193	275

4th Division
(Zayas)
Regts.2nd & 4th Spanish Guards, Irlanda, Patria, Toledo, Ciudad Real, Walloon Guards & Legion Estranjera:

197	4,685	–	106	26	549	681

Cavalry (Loy)
Regts.Santiago, Husares de Castilla, Granaderos, & Escuadron de Instrucion:

93	1,072	–	7	2	31	40

Artillery (1 battery)

7	96	–	2	–	7	9

Staff

?	?	2	–	9	–	11

Totals of Blake's troops:

558	11,515	9	238	65	995	1,307

Castaños's Army:

Infantry
(Carlos de España)
Regts.Rey (3 bns.), Zamora, Voluntarios de Navarra, 1 coy. sappers:

57	1,721	–	–	4	29	33

Cavalry (Penne Villemur)
Detachments of seven regts., none over squadron strength:

87	634	–	11	3	14	28

Artillery (1 battery)

4	58	–	–	–	–	–

Totals of Castaños's troops:

148	2,413	–	11	7	43	61

Grand totals of Spanish:

706	13,928	9	249	72	1,038	1,368

Grand totals of the Allied army:

British	present, all arms:	10,449		total losses:	4,159
Portuguese		10,201			389
Spanish		14,634			1,368★

Totals

	35,284		5,916★

(★ = plus Spanish missing)

APPENDIX II

Soult's Army at Albuera

	Present		Killed		Wounded		Missing		Total
	Offs.	Men	Offs.	Men	Offs.	Men	Offs	Men	loss

5th Corps Infantry:
1st Division (Girard)
II & III/34th Line

Offs.	Men	Offs.	Men	Offs.	Men	Offs	Men	Total loss
23	930	4	104	13	298	–	–	419

I & II/10th Line

35	778	4	35	9	226	1	73	348

I, II & III/64th Line

50	1,539	5	99	18	361	–	168	651

II & III/88th Line

21	878	–	–	5	253	6	141	405

2nd Division (Gazan)
II & III/21st Light

43	745	3	61	11	154	2	24	255

I & II/100th Line

33	705	4	50	8	152	2	51	267

I, II & III/28th Light

62	1,305	7	53	10	313	1	112	496

I, II & III/103rd Line

38	1,252	4	48	10	148	3	74	287

5th Corps totals:

305	8,132	31	450	84	1,905	15	643	3,128

Werlé's Brigade
I, II & III/12th Light

62	2,102	3	108	14	511	1	132	769

I, II & III/55th Line

58	1,757	4	68	6	235	–	38	351

I, II & III/58th Line

55	1,587	6	23	15	258	2	24	328

Brigade totals:

175	5,446	13	199	35	1,004	3	194	1,448

Godinot's Brigade
I, II & III/16th Light

49	1,624	2	39	7	321	–	12	381

I, II & III/51st Line

65	2,186	–	2	–	1	–	–	3

Brigade totals:

114	3,810	2	41	7	322	–	12	384

Grenadiers of 45th, 63rd, 95th Line, 4th Poles (11 coys.)

33	1,000	(only gross total of losses given★)						372

Totals of infantry:

627	18,388	46	690	126	3,230	18	849	5,332★

(continued overleaf)

	Present		Killed		Wounded		Missing		Total
	Offs.	Men	Offs.	Men	Offs	Men	Offs.	Men	loss

Cavalry (Latour–Maubourg):

Briche's Brigade

	Present		Killed		Wounded		Missing		Total
2nd Hussars	23	282	1	4	3	57	–	8	73
10th Hussars	24	238	1	3	4	21	–	3	32
21st Chasseurs	21	235	–	3	3	19	–	–	25

Bron's Brigade

	Present		Killed		Wounded		Missing		Total
4th Dragoons	21	385	3	27	1	38	–	1	70
20th Dragoons	22	244	1	6	3	10	1	4	25
26th Dragoons	27	394	1	5	2	12	–	1	21

Bouvier des Eclat's Brigade

	Present		Killed		Wounded		Missing		Total
14th Dragoons	17	299	–	6	1	17	–	–	24
17th Dragoons	17	297	–	12	3	29	–	1	45
27th Dragoons	14	235	–	2	3	11	–	3	1 9

Unattached cavalry

	Present		Killed		Wounded		Missing		Total
1st Lancers of the Vistula Legion	28	563	1	41	9	78	1	–	130
27th Chasseurs	22	409	–	7	2	11	1	5	26
4th Spanish Chasseurs	14	181	–	2	–	4	–	–	6

Totals of cavalry:

	Present		Killed		Wounded		Missing		Total
	250	**3,762**	**8**	**118**	**34**	**307**	**3**	**26**	**496**

Artillery (48 guns), Engineers, Transport:

	Present		Killed		Wounded		Missing		Total
Of 5th Corps	18	590	1	19	3	72	–	–	95
Of other units	25	600	(no returns whatsoever)						
Etat Major	?	?	5	–	8	–	–	–	13

Totals for army:

	Present		Killed		Wounded		Missing		Total
	920	**23,340**	**60**	**827**	**171**	**3,610**	**21**	**875**	**5,936**

Total present: 24,260   Total losses: 5,936

ACKNOWLEDGEMENTS

My thanks go to a number of friends who were kind enough to loan me items from their collections or send me useful pieces of information. In particular, though in no particular order, I have to thank Mrs Phoebe Turpin, Philip Haythornthwaite, John Strecker, and Michael Tänzer of Hanover, Germany. Michael was extremely helpful with information about the King's German Legion, and sent me a number of photos of a few of the Legion's officers. I also have to thank my usual travelling companions, John Seabrook, David Chantler, Richard Old and John Strecker, who walked the battlefields of Barrosa, Campo Mayor and Albuera with me in the spring of 2000. As usual, we had extremely useful discussions about the events and positions of the various actions. I also have to thank Martin Windrow, for inviting me to write the book in the first place, and Gerry Embleton, for bearing with my shortcomings as regards uniform details, and for producing such realistic paintings of the men of both armies who waged war on each other in 1811.

Finally, it was my privilege to attend the annual commemoration ceremonies at Albuera on 16 May 2000, after which I escorted a group across the battlefield itself. Standing upon the 'Glorious Field of Grief' I read from the manuscript of this book the chapter on the battle, which was a truly memorable moment. It inspired my good friend Harry Turner to compose the poem 'The Slopes of Albuera'. Thanks, Harry.

THE SLOPES OF ALBUERA
by Harry Turner
1st Bn. Middlesex Regiment (57th 'Diehards'), 1953-55.

Those rolling slopes lie peaceful now
Under the noonday sun,
And only the sound of birdsong
Has replaced the crack of the gun.
And the rich red soil on which wildflowers bloom
Is the colour of soldiers' blood,
As they died and fell,
In that smoky hell,
Covered in sweat and mud.

Shoulder to shoulder they stood there,
Fusiliers, Diehards and Buffs,
Mere lads from the counties of England,
To the French, just a gaggle of scruffs.

But the red line stood steady
With guns at the ready,
And no power on earth was to break it,
Not a drum-beating Frenchman,
nor his fierce Polish henchman
Could penetrate, scatter or shake it.

Yes, those rolling slopes are peaceful now,
Under the noonday sun,
And beneath our feet lies buried
Many a mother's son.

Let's remember them with heavy hearts,
Tinged with a surge of pride,
For they were English soldiers,
And it was for all of us that they died.

The men of Albuera are not forgotten. Each year on the anniversary of the battle, representatives from all of the combatant nations gather to remember the battle with a series of ceremonies including the laying of wreaths, speeches, and demonstrations of traditional Estremaduran dance and folk songs.

INDEX